LITERACY INTERVENTION IN THE MIDDLE GRADES

Also from the Authors

Assessment for Reading Instruction, Fourth Edition
Katherine A. Dougherty Stahl, Kevin Flanigan, and Michael C. McKenna

Developing Word Recognition
Latisha Hayes and Kevin Flanigan

Literacy Intervention in the Middle Grades

Word Learning, Comprehension, and Strategy Instruction, Grades 4–8

Kevin Flanigan
Latisha Hayes

Foreword by Katherine A. Dougherty Stahl

THE GUILFORD PRESS
New York London

A Division of Guilford Publications, Inc.
370 Seventh Avenue, Suite 1200, New York, NY 10001
www.guilford.com

Printed in the United States of America

This book is printed on acid-free paper.

Last digit is print number: 9 8 7 6 5 4 3 2 1

Library of Congress Cataloging-in-Publication Data is available from the publisher.

ISBN 978-1-4625-5101-9 (paperback)
ISBN 978-1-4625-5102-6 (hardcover)

About the Authors

Kevin Flanigan, PhD, is Professor in the Literacy Department at West Chester University (WCU) in Pennsylvania. He works in the WCU Reading Center along with master's students to assess and teach children and young adults who struggle to read and write. A former middle-grades classroom teacher and reading specialist/coach, Dr. Flanigan researches and writes about developmental word knowledge and interventions for students with reading difficulties and challenges. He is coauthor of several books, including *Assessment for Reading Instruction, Fourth Edition*; and *Developing Word Recognition*.

Latisha Hayes, PhD, is Associate Professor in the Department of Curriculum, Instruction, and Special Education at the University of Virginia (UVA), where she teaches courses focused on the language structures of English and data-based decisions to inform interventions for students with reading difficulties. She is also Director of UVA's McGuffey Reading Clinical Services, where she works with preservice and inservice teachers to provide students across the grades with diagnostic and tutoring services. As a special educator and reading specialist, Dr. Hayes has taught students with reading difficulties across the elementary and middle grades. She is coauthor of several books, including *Developing Word Recognition*.

Foreword

We have passed through a time period unlike any other. The COVID-19 pandemic has impacted the educational system and students' lives in unprecedented ways. As I write, the American Rescue Plan Act is distributing $125 billion to K–12 school districts to provide supplementary support to address the student learning that was hindered during the pandemic. However, ambitious goals will not come to fruition if our educational systems do not strategically implement research-validated instruction that meets students where they are developmentally and academically. The timing of this book by Kevin Flanigan and Tisha Hayes could not be more perfect. This guidebook provides a North Star to help educators in the middle grades navigate the diagnostic process, select appropriate interventions, and implement progress monitoring tools to ensure maximum literacy growth for their students who need help.

In addition to their academic positions, both Kevin and Tisha spend a great deal of time in schools interacting with teachers and their students. These experiences have influenced the tone and content of this book. The authors provide clear, explicit explanations of a diagnostic process and intervention protocols that are sustainable within the constraints of real schools. They do not recommend rigid, scripted procedures. Unlike commercial intervention programs that require extensive blocks of time, leave students alone on a computer, and follow a cookie-cutter sequence, the interventions in this book make allowances for the diverse needs of students who require support beyond the general curriculum.

Kevin and Tisha are also sensitive to other challenges that teachers encounter in the middle grades. With each progressive grade level, the types of possible reading challenges increase, and the range of the performance gap within the cohort expands. Often schools do not have the resources, hours in a day, or know-how to schedule skill-based differentiation groups. As a result, administrators may formulate grade-level intervention groups randomly. Other well-intentioned administrators may use standardized test score ranges to group students. When schools use these models to formulate intervention groups, the diverse needs of students can make it difficult for teachers to provide specialized instruction to any of their students. Teachers often feel that the only solution is to cover some general skills that will appear on the next standardized test and hope that something sticks—or what I call the Pin the Tail on the Donkey approach. This guidebook will not provide a Band-Aid or a quick fix. Following the recommendations in this book will help teachers improve the effectiveness of each student's reading performance by building on the student's strengths and eliminating any hurdles that are blocking fluency, understanding, and motivation.

Teachers can use the suggestions in this book regardless of what program or intervention model their school might have adopted. This book will benefit literacy specialists, special education teachers, and classroom teachers who wish to accommodate students whose literacy abilities are compromising their academic performance. The consistent chapter structure and helpful graphics contribute to the book's friendliness. The recommendations are viable in many contexts. Although Kevin and Tisha do not simplify the complexity of teaching reading at this developmental stage, the presentation is friendly, conversational, and often entertaining. Such was the case with their description of the value of helping students use "insider information" and teaching them to avoid "rookie mistakes." Teachers who read these sections will immediately recall students who made common "rookie mistakes" and will kick themselves as they recall lessons that could have been more explicit.

Kevin and Tisha have vast experience working with struggling readers in clinical settings, including the highly regarded University of Virginia McGuffey Reading Services. In addition to providing a clinical protocol (screening, identifying practical diagnostic assessments, and matching interventions with students' needs), they also emphasize the importance of having a clinical mindset and theoretical framework. While by no means prescriptive, they share a straightforward heuristic for identifying the points at which a student's reading performance is getting off track. Chapters 4–8 provide descriptions of research-based interventions appropriate for middle-grades students, even those who are performing well below grade level. Sample lesson plans for three case study students enhance clarity.

Readers who are familiar with *Assessment for Reading Instruction, Fourth Edition* (Stahl, Flanigan, & McKenna, 2019), will recognize the cognitive model as the foundation for the diagnostic process. Just as that book emphasizes diagnosis while providing some ideas for intervention, this new book describes the essential diagnostic process but focuses primarily on how to remediate reading difficulties. Professors, preservice teachers, and classroom teachers will find that the two books make good companions.

Whether middle-grades students are in a self-contained classroom in an elementary school or changing classes for each disciplinary content area in a middle school, the reading intervention setting is only one period a day. Most of the students' days are spent reading and writing in other contexts with other teachers who are unlikely to be literacy experts. Additionally, in the middle grades learning new disciplinary content and communicating that learning is dependent on the students' ability to read and write well. Kevin and Tisha provide helpful information for all classroom teachers on ways to support a classroom of students with a range of reading abilities. Like other practices described in the book, these recommendations are based on research. The practices are generic enough to be adapted to the English language arts, social studies, science, and math. None of the techniques are discipline-specific, but all are ways for classroom teachers to accommodate students who find reading and writing challenging.

Kevin and Tisha wrote this book to support teachers who work with students in a "critical window" of their lives, grades 4 through 8. Certainly, the impact of the COVID-19 pandemic has made the needs of these students and their instructors more urgent. Whether schools are redefining their preexisting multi-tiered systems of support or building a new intervention system to work with students who are encountering literacy challenges during this critical window, this book will be a gift and a useful guide as they navigate the pathway to ensure literacy success for all students.

KATHERINE A. DOUGHERTY STAHL, EdD
literacy consultant and retired Clinical Professor of Literacy, New York University

REFERENCE

Stahl, K. A. D., Flanigan, K., & McKenna, M. C. (2019). *Assessment for reading instruction* (4th ed.). New York: Guilford Press.

Acknowledgments

Our deep gratitude to Sara Mohler, our remarkable graduate student and graduate assistant, for her brilliant, painstaking, and creative efforts in helping us craft the figures in this book.

At the core of this book lies the cognitive model originally developed by Mike McKenna and Steve Stahl. We thank Mike, Steve, and Kay Stahl for providing us this foundational and powerful lens to view the reading process.

Thanks also to Craig Thomas, Elizabeth Geller, Jeannie Tang, and the rest of the Guilford team, for all of their expert guidance, feedback, and support throughout this project.

Finally, thanks to our undergraduate and graduate students and the K–12 children and young adults we work with in schools and in our Reading Centers. They are the inspiration for this book.

Contents

CHAPTER 1

Middle-Grades Readers

Introducing Three Case Studies and Debunking Common Myths

As former middle-grades teachers who have worked with students who experience literacy challenges for over 25 years, we (Kevin and Tisha) are all too aware that reading problems don't magically disappear when a student enters grade 4 or starts middle school. Some students' literacy difficulties persist even after robust instruction in the primary grades. Other students—adequate readers throughout the primary grades—suddenly find it difficult to tackle the very different literacy challenges posed by the middle-grades curriculum.

In this book, we define "the middle" as grades 4–8. Why 4–8? We believe this period of time represents a "critical window" in these young people's lives. First, *the general demands* of reading and learning change dramatically from the primary grades, with an increased focus on learning content, making sense of sophisticated academic language, and grasping more difficult conceptual knowledge. The *texts* also change, with more emphasis on informational texts that come with less familiar text structures. Finally, the *specific reading tasks* change, with students increasingly required to use more advanced ways of thinking, including summarizing, analyzing, and sourcing. To make matters even more difficult for students with literacy challenges, they are expected to do much of this reading and writing independently, often outside of class, and at a higher volume than ever before to keep up with the curriculum.

Our goal in this book is to provide you with research-based assessment guidance and instructional practices for teaching middle-grades students with these continued literacy challenges. We believe that if we can "catch them before they fall" in the middle grades, we have a good chance of setting them on firm footing as they enter high school, and beyond. While we acknowledge writing is an essential component of literacy instruction, the focus of this book is reading.

THREE MIDDLE-GRADES READERS WITH LITERACY CHALLENGES

Let's meet Aliyah, Zach, and Andres, the three middle-grades students we will be following throughout this book.

Aliyah: An Eighth Grader with Decoding and Fluency Challenges

Aliyah is an outgoing, high-energy eighth grader with a lot of friends at Great Neck Middle School. She is involved in a number of school clubs and activities, including student government and soccer. Until last year, she had consistently received A's and B's across her subjects. However, with the stepped-up academic demands in middle school, she is having trouble keeping up with the increased volume of reading she's expected to do each night and meeting expectations on assignments requiring a written response, particularly in English/language arts, social studies, and science.

Despite the literacy interventions Aliyah had been receiving since fifth grade, she did not meet grade-level benchmarks on the beginning of eighth-grade screeners, and, as a result, her educational team met to discuss ways to support her. As her team of content teachers meet with the school reading specialist, Mr. Jackson, they discuss Aliyah's literacy strengths and challenges:

Literacy Strengths

- When *orally* presented information—such as during class discussions, via video, and through audio-enhanced texts such as are available on Audible—Aliyah's comprehension is quite strong, and her ideas are insightful.
- Aliyah has a rich vocabulary, peppering her conversation with sophisticated words and phrases such as *evidence, rebel, on-point,* and *perishable foods.*
- Aliyah brings a wealth of background knowledge and a wide range of experiences to group discussions and collaborative activities.

Literacy Challenges

- When Aliyah is required to *independently read* a text or novel, her comprehension is spotty. She often has trouble following class lessons and lectures based solely on assigned readings.
- She struggles to decode multisyllabic words (words such as *isotope, furthermore, spontaneous*) and reads very slowly, often word by word, with little phrasing or expression in grade-level texts.
- Aliyah's lack of automatic word recognition and fluency not only (1) prevents her from keeping up with her core class readings every night, but also (2) likely makes it more difficult for her to comprehend what she reads by herself.

Mr. Jackson explained how Aliyah's word recognition and fluency issues are affecting her comprehension: "Aliyah's reading brain is working overtime—much harder than the average eighth grader—to decode those bigger words. She's working so hard to decode each word, that by the time she reaches the end of a sentence, she may forget what the beginning of the sentence was about."

Zach: A Sixth Grader with Oral Language Comprehension, Vocabulary, and Reading Strategy Challenges

Zach is a quiet, thoughtful sixth grader who has two main passions: skateboarding and art. When not skateboarding at the local skate park with his friends, he can be found sketching scenes that wow his classmates at Great Neck Middle School. Zach told his teachers that he "loves anything to do with anime." Back in elementary school, Zach was able to keep up with the content when he had only one classroom teacher all day. However, now that he's entered middle school, with four different core content teachers—each with their own different set of expectations—he's struggling to keep organized and stay on top of his work.

Like Aliyah, Zach did not meet grade-level benchmarks on the beginning-of-year sixth-grade screener. As Zach's team of content teachers meet with the school reading specialist, Mr. Jackson, they discuss Zach's literacy strengths and challenges:

Literacy Strengths

- Zach is an excellent decoder. In contrast to Aliyah, he can quickly and effortlessly recognize most multisyllabic words that he encounters while reading (words such as *remarkable* and *generation,* unless they are *not* in his oral vocabulary, such as *simultaneous*).
- Zach not only reads most individual words accurately and automatically, he also reads at a good reading rate and with generally solid fluency in context, including reading his textbooks and class novels smoothly, and with, for the most part, phrasal reading.
- Zach is highly motivated to improve. He is willing to work hard, he said, "As long as I see some results!"

Literacy Challenges

- Zach's reading is often passive and disengaged. He thinks of reading as simply "calling out words," rarely reading with a purpose or actively try to make sense of what he is reading.
- Zach has experienced difficulty comprehending a number of the key concepts introduced in the sixth-grade curriculum, such as comparing and contrasting: (1) *potential energy* vs. *kinetic energy* in science and (2) different

forms of government such as *democracy* vs. *dictatorship* vs. *monarchy* in social studies.

- While Zach can automatically decode many "big words," such as *deforestation,* and *generation,* he often does not know a word's meaning.
- As the texts become more complex and his comprehension breaks down, his generally solid fluency also starts to break down.
- In contrast to Aliyah, Zach's comprehension struggles seem to occur both when the information is presented *orally* and when he has to *independently read* to learn new information.
- When asked to identify main ideas or summarize information in a text, Zach seems to simply repeat everything he can remember, which is often a series of disconnected details.

Mr. Jackson explained Zach's literacy challenges to his team of content teachers this way: "Zach can read most texts accurately and at a good pace. Decoding and fluency aren't his issues. What gets in the way of Zach's comprehension is his lack of *vocabulary knowledge* and *reading strategies.* He often doesn't know the meaning of key vocabulary words and concepts in the sixth-grade curriculum. And when Zach's reading comprehension breaks down, he doesn't appear to have any 'go-to' reading comprehension strategies—like inferring, questioning, or summarizing—to fix the problem."

Andres: A Disengaged Fifth-Grade Reader

Andres is a fifth grader with an incredibly supportive extended family, which includes his parents, three younger siblings, grandparents, and many cousins. He spends most of his time outside of school with his extended family, helping to take care of his three younger siblings and constantly attending family gatherings, sporting events, and celebrations. While not talkative, he will open up and relate family stories with enthusiasm.

In terms of his academic work, Andres has struggled with a number of literacy issues since he first entered kindergarten at Roberto Clemente Elementary School. As his fifth-grade classroom teacher, Ms. Carter, meets with the school's intervention team, including one of the school's reading specialists, Ms. Hauser, they discuss Andres's literacy strengths and challenges:

Literacy Strengths

- Andres has a wide range of rich and interesting family stories and anecdotes that he is willing to share, once he feels comfortable with his teacher and classmates.
- Andres is bilingual, speaking both English and Spanish fluently. He often translates for his parents and for classmates.

- When given the opportunity and scaffolding, Andres can make strong connections between the curriculum and his personal experiences.
- Andres is highly engaged in activities and subjects where his interests are piqued and that don't require much reading or writing. For example, he has always been a strong, talented math student and enjoys science, particularly hands-on experiments.

Literacy Challenges

- Andres struggles to read fluently in fifth-grade level materials, often reading difficult texts in a word-by-word fashion, with a monotone expression.
- Andres does not always have the background knowledge needed to make sense of new information presented in class, significantly impacting his comprehension of grade-level concepts.
- Most troubling for Ms. Carter, she sees Andres starting to "mentally drop out" of reading-related tasks. Andres has shared that he doesn't like school reading and doesn't see much use for reading in his own life.

Andres's intervention team has decided that while he has a number of literacy challenges, the most important and pressing one to tackle is his troubling loss of motivation to read and growing disengagement with literacy and school. It's only when Andres sees the worth of literacy in his own life that he will gain the essential motivation to work on improving his literacy skills.

HOW THIS BOOK IS ORGANIZED: A CASE STUDY APPROACH

Aliyah, Zach, and Andres are composites of real cases that we have worked with across our combined 50-plus years teaching students who struggle with literacy skills in classrooms, reading centers, after-school tutoring programs, and various intervention settings. Importantly, Aliyah, Zach, and Andres all struggle to comprehend what they read.

However, they each struggle with reading comprehension for different reasons and represent three different—but common—profiles of reading difficulties that middle-grades teachers will encounter and must be prepared to teach. These different profiles of reading difficulty will necessitate different intervention approaches, different plans, and different instructional strategies.

After we introduce our instructional and assessment principles in Chapters 2 and 3, we then focus Chapters 4 through 9—our case study chapters—on different literacy interventions that directly target the different literacy components that middle-grades readers like Aliyah, Zach, and Andres find challenging (see Figure 1.1).

MIDDLE-GRADES LITERACY: DEBUNKING COMMON MYTHS

Before we dive into what *to do* with middle-grades readers like Aliyah, Zach, and Andres in the following chapters, it's important to debunk common myths that have arisen about older students, reading, and adolescent literacy in general. This "lay of the land" overview will give us a better general picture of what is, and isn't, true about middle-grades readers and writers today.

Myth #1: Students Don't Read as Well Today as They Did When I Was in School

Raise your hand if you've ever said, or heard, a variation of this myth. In fact, according to the National Assessment of Educational Progress (NAEP)—often called our "nation's report card" because it's regarded as the gold standard in national standardized tests—NAEP reading scores have remained relatively stable since 1970 (National Center for Education Statistics [NCES], 2020; Deshler, Palincsar, Biancarosa, & Nair, 2007). If you dig deeper into the data, a more nuanced picture emerges. While some subgroups' achievement scores have improved over time, concerning achievement gaps among subgroups remain (Allington, 2012; NCES, 2020).

Reader	Literacy Challenges	Chapters
Aliyah	• word recognition skills below grade-level expectations with underlying needs in decoding and spelling • listening comprehension and oral vocabulary are at least on grade level, if not exceeding • reading comprehension isn't an issue in texts she can decode well • limited reading comprehension and limited fluency are the result of word reading	• 4: Word Recognition • 5: Fluency
Zach	• word recognition skills meeting grade-level expectations • reading comprehension below grade-level expectations despite good word reading • reading comprehension difficulty due to vocabulary, background knowledge, inferencing, or other language-based difficulties • fluency issues are based in difficulties with reading comprehension rather than word reading	• 6: Vocabulary Challenges • 7: Purpose, Text Structure, and Comprehension Strategy Challenges • 8: Using Writing to Overcome Comprehension Challenges
Andres	• both word recognition and fluency below grade-level expectations • reading comprehension below grade-level expectations due to a multitude of factors, including limited practice and engagement • variable engagement in school with notable drop during reading- and writing-related tasks	• 9: Engagement Challenges

FIGURE 1.1. Case study chapters for three middle-grades readers.

So, if our nation's overall reading achievement has remained relatively stable over the last 50 years, should we be worried? Yes, we absolutely should. While the *reading achievement* of U.S. students may not have changed much, what has changed dramatically are the *literacy expectations* for today's 21st-century jobs (Deshler et al., 2007). No longer is it possible—as it might have been in 1970—for most people to find a good, stable job and earn a decent living with fourth-grade reading skills. In fact, most jobs today require much more advanced reading and writing skills to succeed. Put simply, while the overall reading achievement in the United States may have remained relatively steady over the last half century, the "reading expectations bar" has risen dramatically.

Myth #2: By the Time They Reach Middle School, Reading Isn't a Problem for Most Students

What percentage of students in fourth through eighth grade in the United States struggle to read proficiently? 20%? 40%? 50%? More? According to NAEP reading scores (NCES, 2019):

- 65% of fourth graders scored *below proficient*
- 66% of eighth graders scored *below proficient*

While we can argue over what *proficient* means, precisely, and where to draw the proficient/not proficient dividing line, the larger takeaway is that there are huge numbers of students who don't have the reading skills necessary to meet the challenging text and task demands they will encounter in the middle grades. Based on the NAEP statistics above and other information, it's not surprising that many experts believe we are in the midst of an adolescent literacy crisis in the United States (Biancarosa & Snow, 2006; Salinger, 2011). If you believe that reading is the "gateway skill" to learning in any content area, then this isn't just a literacy problem, it's a nationwide learning and achievement issue.

Myth #3: Struggling Middle-Grades Readers Are All the Same

As you can see from our discussion of Aliyah, Zach, and Andres above, middle-grades readers with literacy challenges are not a monolithic group. Some of your middle-grades students may struggle with word recognition, others with reading fluency, some with vocabulary and background knowledge, and still others with engagement. In fact, in one classic study of fifth graders who scored "below proficient" on a fourth-grade state reading assessment, the authors identified six different struggling reader profiles (Buly & Valencia, 2002; Valencia & Buly, 2004). Importantly, 58% of the fifth graders struggled with automatic word recognition and 82% of them struggled with word identification and/or fluency. This study, along with others looking at older readers (e.g., Capin, Cho, Miciak, Roberts, & Vaughn, 2021; Catts, Hogan, & Adolf, 2005; Leach, Scarborough, & Rescorla, 2003), dispels the common myth that decoding and fluency issues are only problems for kindergarten through third grade (K–3) readers.

Because middle-grades readers with literacy challenges each have different reader profiles, including different literacy strengths and challenges, they will require different interventions. It follows, then, that a "one-size-fits-all" program or approach will not work with all of your students. For precisely this reason, we decided to take a "case study approach" in this book. We want to show how (1) to use diagnostic assessments (2) to plan research-based literacy interventions (3) that will target the individual needs of your students.

Myth #4: Middle-Grades Readers with Literacy Challenges Just Need a "Second Dose" of What They Received in the Primary Grades to Catch Up

There are distinct differences between middle-grades readers and K–3 readers. For example, with our middle-grades readers who struggle with decoding, we often work on decoding *multisyllabic words*. Specifically, we teach our middle-grades readers how to decode using larger word parts such as *morphemes* (e.g., the prefix *pre-* in *preindustrial*) and *syllables* (*gov-ern-ment*) as opposed to the letter-by-letter decoding approach (*r-e-s-t* in *rest*) emphasized in the primary grades. Throughout this book, we will emphasize the distinctive characteristics of middle-grades readers, like this, and how to capitalize on them during instruction.

Myth #5: If I Can Just Find the Right Program, I Can "Fix" the Problem

Once students enter the middle grades, there is an intense sense of urgency to help them "catch up." This sometimes feels overwhelming, especially when some research has shown students who fall behind in the elementary grades rarely catch up even with intensive interventions (e.g., Juel, 1988, 1994). This situation can be discouraging, but some more recent research has shown older students can make significant gains given appropriate instruction (e.g., Archer, Gleason, & Vachon, 2003). But what is "appropriate instruction"? And how can I get my hands on some?

There are "research-based" programs seemingly everywhere. With that in mind, consider the following: If commercial literacy programs were the ultimate solution to our current adolescent literacy crisis, we wouldn't have an adolescent literacy crisis. We believe that some programs are effective, and in fact we use some in our work with middle-grades students. However, we understand that programs are tools. Tools are essential to getting a job done, but tools are only as good as the carpenter who uses them.

We follow a thoughtful, common-sense, structured adaptive approach to implementation to improve the fit as we tailor a program to our context and the needs of our students. So, if you have a program, one possibility is a "scaffolded sequence" of adaptations where the program is first implemented with fidelity and then adapted for the best fit while maintaining the program's core principles (McMaster et al., 2014; Quinn & Kim, 2017; Slavin, Madden, & Datnow, 2007). In the end, it is our teacher knowledge rather than programs that will move the needle of the adolescent literacy crisis.

That is why in this book we provide you with more than solely the tools (instructional strategies) to address your students' literacy challenges. We also discuss, in some depth, how to use these tools skillfully, including how to decide (1) which tools to use (2) with which students (3) for which instructional purposes. To this end, in our next chapter, we introduce our "North Star" instructional principles that guide our intervention approaches, plans, and day-to-day decision making. We strongly believe that this type of principle-based thinking and expertise is what separates blindly following a scripted program from providing high-quality, expert teaching that makes a real difference with students like Aliyah, Zach, and Andres. As a reminder, we do sometimes use programs, but we realize that no one program will be a best fit for all students. It is our hope that this book will serve as a guide—a guide to inform you about effective practices for middle-grades students with literacy challenges to help you move the needle for your students.

CHAPTER 2

Middle-Grades Literacy Intervention

"North Star" Principles

A group is traveling through a jungle that is so heavily forested, they can't see more than a few feet ahead of them. The group's leader, an impatient and inexperienced young man, has been pushing them to move as fast as possible because of a strict timeline to pick up much-needed supplies. After hours of grueling hiking, an experienced scout asks the young leader, "Should we stop for a minute so I can climb this tree to look ahead and make sure we're still on course?" to which the leader replies, "We don't have time for that nonsense, we've got to keep moving forward!"

This parable, recounted by Stephen Covey (1990) in his best-selling book on personal leadership, *The Seven Habits of Highly Effective People*, makes a powerful point about leadership, efficiency, and effectiveness: No matter how hard you work, how "fast" you go, or how quickly you climb your ladder, if you're doing the wrong "job," headed in the wrong direction, or climbing the wrong ladder, you'll never arrive at your destination. Worse still, you won't even know if you're on the right path. In other words, you can be very "efficient" at your job—but if you're doing *the wrong job* to begin with—you won't be very effective.

WHY "NORTH STAR" PRINCIPLES?

To arrive at your destination, you need a reference point to constantly check your bearings against—a "North Star." If you're a group hiking through the jungle, this means checking your progress against a compass and known landmarks. If you're a teacher delivering a literacy intervention to a group of sixth graders, this means establishing a strong core belief system to guide your choice of approaches,

10 Principles of Literacy Intervention

1. **What Do You Stand For?**
   Articulate Your Literacy Beliefs
2. **Don't Forget Your Map!**
   Choose and Use an Intervention Model
3. **Start with Assessments**
   Get to Know Your Students
4. **Keep the Main Thing the Main Thing**
   Design a Focused, Flexible, Doable Intervention Plan
5. **Make the Invisible Visible**
   Use the "I Do" to Be Explicit and Systematic
6. **Practice, Practice, Purposeful Practice**
   Leverage the "We Do" and "You Do" for Long-Term Transfer and Independence
7. **One Size Does Not Fit All**
   Differentiate and Scaffold When They're Not "Getting It"
8. **Time**
   Where Does It All Go and How Can I Get Some Back?
9. **Engagement**
   Get Your Students to Buy In When They've Checked Out
10. **Active, Not Passive**
    Take a Critical Stance and Read with a Purpose

FIGURE 2.1. North Star principles.

programs, resources, assessments, and strategies. In this chapter, we introduce our North Star literacy intervention principles (see Figure 2.1), which will guide our intervention practices and decisions in the rest of this book.

Principle #1. What Do You Stand For?: Articulate Your Literacy Beliefs

To paraphrase Alexander Hamilton, "If you stand for nothing, you'll fall for anything." If you don't have a set of core beliefs about literacy development and instruction, you're more likely to be swayed by the latest fad, program, or workshop. It's like trying to sail a ship without a rudder; the slightest breeze will blow you off course.

This is why it's essential that you articulate your own North Star literacy principles of instruction. When we work with teachers and schools who teach students with literacy challenges, we find that few have done this critical up-front work. They might mention a program or resource they use, but a program is a tool to help you on your journey, like a car. The car is necessary, but it will not help you make critical decisions, like deciding which road to take. For this, you need a set of research-based beliefs that is made public and that everyone not only buys into but can articulate and apply in their daily teaching.

These principles should be based on the latest science and research in literacy. They should also be written in language that is clear and straightforward. They are critical because they will guide your choice of programs, approaches, instructional strategies, and how much time you spend on the various components of literacy for different students.

For example, you might be considering a fluency program that has strong evidence of working with sixth graders; however, you want to modify it for your eighth-grade readers who struggle with their rates and prosody. Your questions include:

- Can/should you modify the program? Or, if you do so, will it lose its effectiveness?
- Can you use some parts of the intervention and supplement other parts with something else?
- What if you like the program's *instructional strategies,* but think the *reading material* that comes with the program won't engage your eighth graders? Can you use your own materials?
- Will it work in conjunction with the other approaches you're already using?
- What if you don't have the instructional time to implement the program exactly as described?

These are the types of thorny, critical "rubber meets the road" questions that have no easy answer, but that educators confront every day. If you have no belief system, you'll find yourself instructionally adrift. However, with your principles as your "instructional backbone," you can make thoughtful, informed decisions that you can justify.

For the remainder of this chapter, we lay out our foundational North Star literacy instructional principles that will guide you in your intervention work. We've based them on the latest science and research in literacy intervention coupled with our combined experience working directly with students in grades 4–8 who experience literacy challenges.

Take Action **Principle #1**

To take action on our principle #1:

- Meet with your colleagues. Discuss the most current science and research on literacy (examples of resources include the *Journal of Adolescent and Adult Literacy;* Kamil et al., 2008; National Reading Panel, 2000; and podcasts such as *Science of Reading* at amplify.com).

- Discuss what the needs of your students are and what has worked/hasn't worked in the past.

- As a group, write down your own literacy instructional literacy principles and/or beliefs about literacy. You can use our 10 principles here as a starting point and tweak them as you see fit. Try to keep the list to between 5 and 10 principles. Post them in classrooms and make sure all teachers have both hard and digital copies. If they are not written down and shared, they'll soon be forgotten.

- Keep these principles handy and refer to them during child study meetings, when planning instruction, and when making curricular decisions. Make sure they're living documents that are used, applied, and periodically revisited. If no one knows where they are and no one can talk about them, they're already dead.

Principle #2. Don't Forget Your Map!: Choose and Use an Intervention Model(s)

While having North Star principles to guide you is necessary, it's not enough. The North Star gives you a target to shoot for on your journey, but it tells you nothing about the actual terrain you're going to have to navigate to get there. For this, you need a road map. A map is not the terrain itself. Rather, it's a model of the terrain that can help you make decisions about how to cross rivers, climb mountains, and traverse forests.

In the same way, you'll need an intervention model that will serve as your "mental road map" as you try to navigate the uncertain and challenging terrain of working with students who experience literacy challenges. This intervention model will help you answer those thorny questions and cross all obstacles—the rivers, mountains, and valleys—that don't have easy answers, such as:

- I've got *no data* on a new student, so where do I start?
- I've got *too much data,* so how do I make sense of it all to design an intervention?

- Are my student's comprehension challenges due to vocabulary, background knowledge, or decoding needs? Or something else?
- Does the required state standardized test tell me what I need to design an intervention? If not, *which follow-up assessments* should I administer? With my limited time, are there some I can skip for this student?
- How should I monitor progress? My intervention time is limited so I need something efficient that will also give me data I can use.
- If the intervention plan isn't working, what should I do next?
- Which program or approach should I use? Can I modify programs, or will they lose their effectiveness?
- If I've only got 20 minutes, where, exactly, should I start at 10:14 A.M. tomorrow with this intervention group?

Over the last 25 years that we have worked with students who experience literacy struggles, the following two models—used together—have been our most useful road maps. They will guide much of our thinking in the rest of this book:

1. The cognitive model (*What to teach?*)
2. The developmental model (*When to teach the "what"*)

The Cognitive Model—What to Teach

Mike McKenna and Steve Stahl developed the cognitive model (McKenna & Stahl, 2003; Stahl, Flanigan, & McKenna, 2020), a powerful model for teachers, reading specialists, intervention specialists, and clinicians working with students who struggle to read. The cognitive model (see Figure 2.2) suggests that reading comprehension, the ultimate goal of reading, depends on three underlying pathways:

Pathway #1: Automatic recognition of the words in a text
Pathway #2: Comprehension of the language in a text
Pathway #3: The ability to use appropriate strategies (e.g., inferring, summarizing), to accomplish one's reading purpose

A reader's comprehension struggles could be due to difficulties with any one (or any combination) of these three pathways. Let's look at the literacy challenges of the three middle-grades readers we introduced in Chapter 1, Aliyah, Zach, and Andres, through the lens of the cognitive model:

- *Aliyah: Pathway #1 challenges.* Because Aliyah must spend much of her cognitive "horsepower" *decoding* difficult words, she often has little mental energy left for comprehending the important ideas in a text.

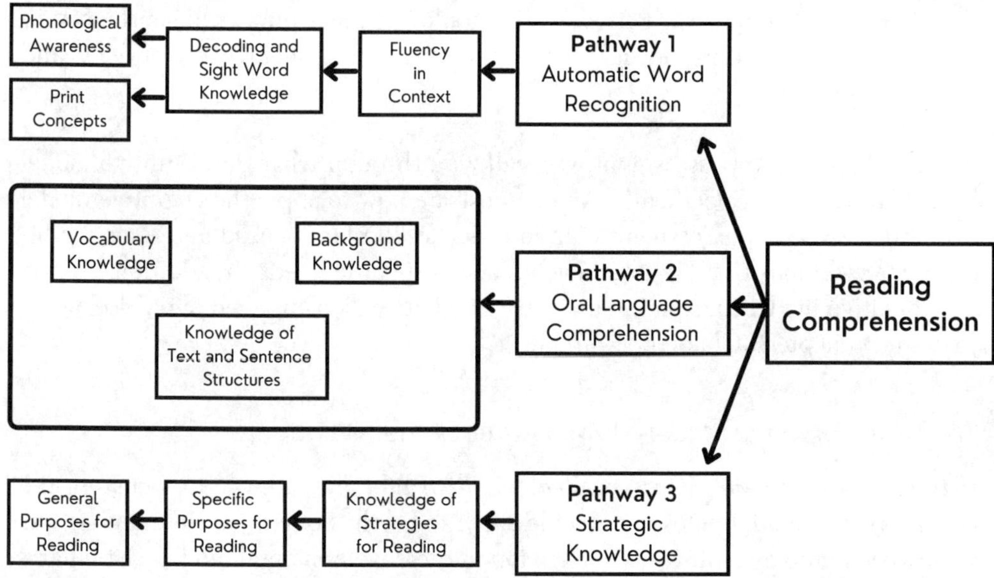

FIGURE 2.2. The cognitive model. Reprinted with permission from Stahl, Flanigan, & McKenna (2020). Copyright 2020 by The Guilford Press.

- *Zach: Pathway #2 and #3 challenges.* Zach often doesn't understand the *meanings of the words* (vocabulary) he decodes—like *redundant, however, productive,* and *isotope*—and also experiences difficulty with *comprehension strategies* (summarizing and inferring), causing his comprehension to suffer.

- *Andres: Pathway #1, #2, and #3 challenges.* Andres experiences literacy challenges in all three pathways. However, one challenge that differentiates him from Aliyah and Zach is that he struggles to see *the general purposes of reading* in his own life, which is tied to his overall *reading engagement and motivation.*

Each of these three readers has comprehension difficulties, but each for different underlying reasons. These three students will require different types of literacy interventions. So, how do you know which pathway is the issue? And what component along each pathway should you directly teach? This is where the cognitive model comes into play. It helps us answer important questions such as:

- Does the reader have a reading comprehension problem?
- If so, which pathway(s) is the root cause of this reading comprehension problem?
- Within each pathway, which component should we focus our instruction

on? For example, on Pathway #1, should we focus on a reader's fluency in context, decoding and sight word knowledge, or phonological awareness and print concepts?

In Chapter 3, on assessment, we walk you through what the cognitive model looks like in action. Specifically, we demonstrate how to apply the cognitive model to (1) analyze actual assessment data in order to (2) plan focused and effective literacy interventions that (3) target each reader's specific needs. In addition, we use the cognitive model to explain our instructional decisions in each of our following case study chapters (Chapters 4–9).

The Developmental Model—When to Teach the "What"

If the cognitive model helps you decide *which* literacy pathway to focus on, the developmental model helps you decide *when* to teach the many different concepts within each literacy pathway. We have found the developmental model particularly useful in Pathway #1: word knowledge and fluency issues. For example, suppose an initial literacy screening assessment indicates that your student's comprehension issues are mainly due to difficulties in Pathway #1, particularly a lack of phonics and decoding knowledge. That narrows it down, but there are a lot of phonics concepts and patterns to cover. Where do you start your intervention word work with this student? Beginning consonants? Short vowels? Blends and digraphs? Long vowel patterns? Multisyllabic words?

This is where the developmental model comes into play. A developmental spelling inventory or phonics assessment will help you figure out: (1) which literacy stage a reader is in, (2) which spelling or phonics features they have mastered and, importantly, (3) *which phonics features to teach next.* This is incredibly powerful because it saves you precious instructional time—helping you decide which phonics features you can skip, which to teach next, and which to save for later. See our diagnostic assessment flow chart in Chapter 3 for more information on this assessment process.

The developmental model in Table 2.1 organizes reading, writing, and spelling into five stages, each stage governed by a more sophisticated understanding of how words work. While there are many important stage models of literacy development, we have found (1) Bear, Invernizzi, Templeton, and Johnston's (2020) stage model of reading, writing, and spelling growth and (2) Ehri's (1998) phase model of word recognition growth the most useful for intervention purposes. Table 2.1 summarizes the key components of these two models, including the following: (1) Bear et al.'s reading and spelling stages; (2) the approximate reading and grade level of most students in that stage; (3) the strategy readers and spellers at that stage use to decode, process, and store words; (4) the reading and writing characteristics typical of that stage; and (5) the spelling, phonics, or word study focus of that stage (e.g., short vowels, common long-vowel patterns).

TABLE 2.1. The Development of Reading, Writing, and Spelling across Stages

Reading/spelling stage (from Bear et al., 2020)	Reading levels	Reading strategy: How readers process and store words	Reading and writing characteristics and focus	Word-study focus (spelling, decoding, and vocabulary)
Emergent readers/emergent writers	K	Prealphabetic phase (Ehri, 1998) "Reads" words by visual cues (*M* in *McDonald's*; the "tail" at the end of *monkey*)	Pretending to read Learning concepts of print Do *not* have concept of word in text	Alphabet knowledge (letter names, sounds, and formation) Beginning to build rudimentary phonological awareness (syllables, onsets, and rimes)
Beginning readers/letter name spellers	First grade	Partial to full alphabetic phase (Ehri, 1998) Partial alphabetic decoding at beginning of stage (*H* in *hat*) Full alphabetic decoding by end of stage (letter-by-letter decoding: *H-A-T* for *hat*) allows sight words to "stick"	Text-bound reading Reading aloud or mumble reading Solid concept of word (can match spoken to written words) in reading and writing, as indicated by fingerpointing Word-by-word reading and writing Fingerpoint reading	Learning sight words Developing full alphabetic decoding by end of stage Word-study features: Beginning and ending consonants Short vowels Beginning and ending blends and digraphs
Transitional readers/within word pattern spellers	Late first to late third grades	Consolidated alphabetic phase (Ehri, 1998) Processes words in letter "chunks" or patterns as single units (*-ake* in *cake*)	Approaching reading and writing fluency Beginning to read silently, with expression and in phrasal units Increased reading rates, nearing 100 WPM by end of stage	Word-study features: Common long-vowel patterns (*cake, rain*) *r*-influenced vowels (*care, store*) Less common vowel patterns (*eight*) Complex consonant patterns (*judge, patch*) Ambiguous vowels (*brown, soil*) Homographs and homophones (*bear* vs. *bare*)
Intermediate readers/syllables and affixes spellers	Late third to sixth grades	Processes multisyllabic words by syllable (*autocracy* as *au-toc-ra-cy*) Processes and stores words by across-syllable patterns (VCCV, *hopping*, vs. VCV, *hoping*)	Solid reading fluency by end of stage Reading challenges stem increasingly from conceptual load, vocabulary, and background knowledge Increased focus on strategic reading, content-area learning, and writer's craft	Word-study features: Compound words (*pancake*) Inflectional endings and doubling (*hopping* vs. *hoping*) Open and closed syllables (VCCV, *button*, vs. VCV, *bacon*) High-frequency prefixes and suffixes with base words (*reuse, redo*)

(continued)

TABLE 2.1. *(continued)*

Reading/ spelling stage (from Bear et al., 2020)	Reading levels	Reading strategy: How readers process and store words	Reading and writing characteristics and focus	Word-study focus (spelling, decoding, and vocabulary)
Advanced readers/ derivational relations spellers	Sixth grade and up	Processes words by morphemes, including Greek and Latin affixes/roots (*autocracy* as *auto-cracy*)	Exploring and developing expertise in specific topics, genres, styles, texts, and academic vocabulary Learning discipline-specific reading/writing/ thinking approaches (e.g., reading like a historian)	Word-study features: Prefixes and suffixes (*inter-*, "between"—*intercontinental*) Consonant and vowel alternations (*sign/signal/ signature*) Greek and Latin word elements (*-crat/-cracy*, "rule" —*democracy*)

Note. Reprinted with permission from Stahl, Flanigan, & McKenna (2020). Copyright 2020 by The Guilford Press.

An intervention model guides you as you navigate the intervention terrain of making sense of assessment data, planning instruction, monitoring a student's progress, and making real-time instructional tweaks along the way. Using even an excellent "off-the-shelf" program without an intervention model to guide you might take you down the wrong pathway. This is like driving a Porsche with no road map; you may put a lot of miles behind you very quickly, but you could very well be taking the wrong road.

Take Action Principle #2

To take action on principle #2:

- Meet with your assessment team and choose a literacy model(s) to guide your decision making.
- Post this model (along with your literacy intervention principles) and make sure everyone on the team has digital and hard copies.
- Use the model to analyze assessments, make instructional decisions in child study meetings, and, as appropriate, when meeting with parents and other team members.

Principle #3. Start with Assessments: Get to Know Your Students

Imagine after a weekend of arduous yardwork you wake up Monday morning with back pain. You visit the doctor, who performs a screening test and immediately tells you, "Okay, I've scheduled back surgery for you tomorrow." Hold the presses! Is the doctor certain that you need surgery? Are there less invasive options? Which part of the back is the problem? The back muscles or your spine? Or is the back really the root cause of all the pain? More tests please! (Flanigan, Solic, & Gordon, 2022).

While this scenario may seem a bit extreme, a similar problem can occur in education when we misuse universal screening assessments to make precise diagnostic and instructional decisions. This mistake can lead to choosing: (1) the wrong component of literacy to focus instruction on (focusing on comprehension when the student actually has an underlying decoding/fluency issue, like Aliyah), (2) the wrong instructional strategies, or (3) the wrong content to teach.

Screening assessments tell you if a problem exists, but don't necessarily tell you what to do tomorrow morning with your intervention group. This is where *follow-up diagnostic assessments* are critical. Follow-up diagnostic assessments can inform your instructional plan.

Take Action | **Principle #3**

To take action on principle #3:

- Identify a *literacy screening assessment.* Some schools may screen all students, while others may only screen a subset of at-risk students. Screeners should be informative and efficient.
- Identify *follow-up diagnostic assessments* to administer to students who don't pass the initial screening assessment.
- Analyze the screening and diagnostic assessment information. Importantly, rank order students' areas of literacy need. Aliyah's priority #1, for example, is decoding, with fluency her priority #2.
- Write precise instructional goals for each literacy area of instructional focus.
- Choose instructional strategies, appropriate content, and appropriate texts to best meet your students' goals.

In Chapter 3, we discuss in more depth how to implement the "take action" steps above. Specifically, we explain how to use our *assessment flow chart* (see page 38) to decide which assessments to use, when and how to use them, and which ones you can skip. We also describe how to use different assessments to target different areas of literacy, including:

- Assessments that target Pathway #1, including automatic word recognition, decoding, and fluency
- Assessments that target Pathway #2, including vocabulary and text-structure knowledge
- Assessments that target Pathway #3, including purposes for reading, strategy use, and engagement

Principle #4. Keep the Main Thing the Main Thing: Designing Focused, Flexible, Doable Intervention Plans

Sometimes when a student struggles, we try *everything* and *anything* with the hope that *something* sticks. However, this usually isn't the answer. Instead, we have found that focusing like a laser on one or two areas of need during an intervention will likely give you the biggest bang for your buck.

This is where intentional teaching comes in. Intentional teaching includes carefully analyzing your assessment data to pinpoint strengths and areas of need, prioritizing areas of literacy need (because you can't do it all at once), and relentlessly keeping the focus on the student's primary learning objective. We call continually checking ourselves to remain focused on one or two primary literacy goals "keeping the main thing the main thing."

When teachers observe effective intervention lessons in action—whether in a school setting or in our university reading centers—they are often struck by the following:

- *How relentlessly focused the lessons are on the "main thing."* The teacher keeps referring to the *instructional goal* and *purpose* throughout the lesson in their modeling, teacher talk, activities, feedback, anchor chart, and parent communication.

- *That the students know the purpose of the lesson/intervention.* Students are able to answer the questions, "What are we working on today and why?" at any point in the lesson and "What did you learn today? What will you work on for homework/classwork?" at the end of each lesson.

- *How much reading, writing, and talking the students did.* The students start reading within the first minute or two of the lesson and keep reading for the majority of the lesson. There is no lost time.

- *How doable and repeatable the lessons are.* The same basic lesson plan format is used each lesson. The only things that might change each week are the phonics features studied and the texts being read.

At the end of each of our case study chapters (Chapters 4–9), we will share sample intervention lesson plans we use for different literacy components and needs. What you'll notice in each of them is that we focus like a laser on only one or two "focus areas." One caveat here: Our focused intervention lessons do not mean that we don't also believe in a comprehensive literacy approach that includes many other important elements. We absolutely do. However, we realize that during our limited intervention times—sometimes just 20–30 minutes per day—we only have time to focus on the student's highest priority area(s) of literacy need. Because of this, we realize we also need to make sure that the student is getting high-quality literacy instruction in all important literacy components (e.g., comprehension, fluency, vocabulary, writing, rich discussions) across the rest of their day/week.

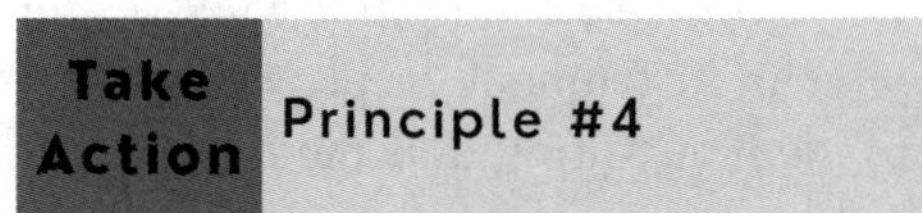

To take action on principle #4:

- Based on (1) a student's rank-ordered areas of literacy need (see principle #3 above) and (2) the time you have available for intervention, (3) identify one or two literacy components to focus on in the intervention (e.g., priority #1 is decoding and priority #2 is fluency). Discuss other ways to target the lower priority area of need across the day and week (e.g., perhaps working on writing, priority #3, during writing workshop with a small group of students once per week).

- Develop a simple, straightforward lesson that is doable and repeatable. Use the same format and routines each lesson so that when the student arrives, no time is lost figuring out the routine for that day.

- Make sure that the student is always aware of the goal and purpose of each lesson and can see concrete measures of their literacy growth.

Principle #5. Make the Invisible Visible: Use the "I Do" to Be Explicit and Systematic

One of the standout moments in my life (Kevin) that ignited my desire to become a reading specialist occurred in my second year of teaching. One of my fifth graders that year, Nate, was a truly exceptional young man—a popular athlete and natural leader who possessed magnetic charisma, genuine empathy, and strong character. He was one of those rare individuals who actively stuck up for his fellow students who found themselves on the margins of the group. More than once, I saw him intervene when he saw a fellow student being bullied, belittled, or having a hard time.

However, Nate himself had a significant challenge in his life that he tried to hide from others. Nate had been identified with dyslexia and was reading at a the late first-/early second-grade reading level. Nate's struggles with decoding and acquiring an automatic sight word vocabulary often left him near tears. In stark contrast was one of Nate's good friends, Jalen, a highly skilled and fluent reader who seemed to be able to read and understand whatever was put in his hands. One, day, incredibly frustrated and exasperated, Nate dropped his book, pointed to Jalen, and said, "Mr. Flanigan, tell me what's going on inside Jalen's head that's *not* going on inside *my* head when I read!"

I'll never forget Nate's words because he so powerfully articulated what I should have been doing all along. I should have been making *explicit* the *implicit*, "in-the-head," strategies that Jalen—and all skilled readers—naturally employ while reading. I should have been making the *invisible visible* for Nate.

So, what does explicit instruction look like? Think of a time you learned a skill from someone else, be it changing a tire, playing an instrument, or playing a sport. Most likely, your teacher or coach started by demonstrating and modeling what they wanted you to do so you could see what it looked like. I distinctly remember my soccer coach demonstrating how to perform a "give-and-go" pass. He modeled it with my teammates over and over, demonstrating what it looked like and when to do it. I can still remember his words as he dribbled and passed:

> Okay folks, today we're learning the "give-and-go" pass. This is an effective pass to use when you've got an overload—more players than the other team—in your part of the field. For many of the best teams in the world, the give-and-go pass is their bread and butter. Watch me as I walk you through it. As I'm dribbling toward the goal, I'm waiting for the exact moment Sean's defender leaves him and tries to stop me. That's one of the secrets to a great give-and-go pass—waiting for the defender to leave his man and come at you. At that moment, Sean is now open, so I pass to Sean and move. See the space I just created with my movement? Pass and move, pass and move, pass and move, waiting for Sean's return pass, just like this.

Notice what is happening here, our soccer coach (1) *publicly names* the skill (give-and-go pass), (2) explains *why and when* to use a give-and-go pass, (3) *demonstrates* the skill, and (4) *thinks aloud* what is going on inside a skilled soccer player's head to know when and how to apply a give-and-go pass on the context of a game, including (5) sharing one of the *insider "secrets"* to an effective give-and-go pass. This is what effective coaches, music teachers, and mentors all do: *They show, don't tell.* Just as importantly, notice what is *not* going on here. No worksheets, no long lectures, and little wasted time.

Over 40-plus years of research from various perspectives provides a solid base of support for using this type of explicit instruction in and out of intervention settings (see Archer & Hughes, 2011, for brief review). We recommend considering the Gradual Release Model, one of the best-known instructional models in all of education, as a framework for delivering this type of explicit teaching (Almasi & Hart, 2011; Pearson & Gallagher, 1983). Because we believe it's a particularly powerful model to use in intervention work focusing on transfer, we're going to unpack it in some detail here (see Figure 2.3).

As you can see in the first column of Figure 2.3, the Gradual Release Model is often conceptualized into the following three steps: (1) *I Do*, (2) *We Do*, and (3) *You Do*, as follows:

- *I Do*—Introduce new strategies by explicitly modeling and thinking aloud. Ensure that the students know the purpose of the strategy and the steps involved in carrying it out. Provide "insider tips" and "rookie mistakes" that will help a reader learning a strategy for the first time. Think of our soccer coach modeling and demonstrating the "give and go." Aim for around 20% of instructional time here.

- *We Do*—Follow up the "I Do" with guided practice. Think of a soccer coach watching during a scrimmage or a piano teacher sitting next to you while you practice a piece. As you try to apply the skill in context, the coach or teacher are right there, ready to step in and provide feedback, stop you if you make a mistake, and possibly have you rerun the play or replay a section until you've got it. In literacy intervention, this often happens during small-group reading or phonics and spelling instruction. To scaffold your students' practice, ask questions, provide prompts and cues, provide precise feedback, and identify the parts they got right and parts to keep working on. Aim to spend a good chunk of instructional time—perhaps 40%—here, because this is where the application of skills all start to come together for your students.

- *You Do*—Provide extensive opportunities—perhaps 40% of instructional time—for independent practice of skills. This often happens during independent reading or writing time. Importantly, students in grades 4–8 should spend *at least 30 minutes a day independently reading in context.* To those who say that they don't have 30 minutes in a school day for reading, we ask, "Would you question a minimum of 30 minutes of daily practice in anything else to become proficient, be

Gradual Release Model	Duffy's Lesson Components	Literacy Lesson Example	*Time	Sports Example	Performing Arts Example
"I Do" Model/ Demonstrate and Think Aloud	1. Make the objective public 2. Introduce the lesson 3. State the "secret" 4. Model your thinking	Mini-Lesson	20%	Skills/Drills	Practice
"We Do" Practice with Coaching and Feedback	Scaffolded Assistance	Supported (Guided) Reading	40%	Scrimmage	Dress Rehearsal/ "Tech Week"
"You Do" Independent Practice/ Performance	Continued Application to Reading	Independent Reading	40%	Game	Final Performance

*Approximate Percentage of Instructional Time in a literacy component/strategy/skill across a week

FIGURE 2.3. The Gradual Release Model unpacked. Adapted with permission from Flanigan, Solic, & Gordon (2022). Copyright 2022 by John Wiley and Sons.

it piano or soccer or learning to drive? Why would reading—one skill we *all* need to be successful—be any different?" Note that this 30 minutes could be broken up into smaller segments across a day.

One book we've found extremely helpful to support the delivery of explicit literacy teaching is Gerald Duffy's *Explaining Reading* (2014). As you can see in the second column in Figure 2.3, Duffy breaks down the initial "I Do" step of the Graduate Release Model into four smaller steps: (1) make the objective public, (2) introduce the lesson, (3) state the "secret," and (4) model your thinking. Duffy refers to the "We Do" step of the lesson as "scaffolded assistance" and the "You Do" step as "continued application to reading."

Take Action **Principle #5**

Because we use Duffy's explicit teaching steps in the sample lesson plans at the end of each of our upcoming case study chapters, we explain them in depth here. To take action on principle #5, consider including Duffy's first four steps in your "I Do" section of an explicit strategy lesson:

- *Make the objective public*—Students are better able to learn if they are clear about what they are trying to accomplish. *By the end of this lesson, you will be able to use the three-step summarization strategy to write a two- to three-sentence summary of an informational text.*

- *Introduce the lesson*—This step includes a "hook" and explanation of the "why" and often the "when" behind learning the strategy or content. We are all more likely to buy in if we know *why* we are learning something.

> Class, imagine if you asked me how my day was and I took 30 minutes to tell you, blow by blow, every single little thing I did throughout the day, including brushing my teeth. Not only would you be bored to tears, we'd never have time to focus on the important stuff that happened in my day! This is where summarizing comes in. Summarizing is one of the most important reading comprehension and communication strategies out there. It helps you identify the main ideas—the "treasure"—and place aside the unnecessary details—the "trash." Summarizing is something you'll need to be able to do your entire life, not just in this class.

- *State the "secret"*—This step includes providing expert "insider information," clues, strategy steps to follow, and tips of what to do/not to do, including "common rookie mistakes." Anchor charts can also be particularly helpful as a reference for this "secret" information. "One of the secrets to summarizing is to follow these three steps: select, reject, and then paraphrase. Let me show you what I mean. I'm going to demonstrate the steps on our summarizing anchor chart."

- *Model your thinking*—In contrast to physical activities such as playing soccer, learning piano, or changing a tire, reading is an invisible activity performed in the mind. Therefore, it's absolutely crucial that we make it visible by modeling and thinking aloud as we read. "Notice what I'm doing as I'm trying to summarize this paragraph. Hmmm. I see a bolded word here, *isotope,* telling me that the word *isotope* must be important . . . I'm going to highlight this whole phrase that includes the word, *isotope.*"

Principle #6. Practice, Practice, Purposeful Practice: Leverage the We Do and You Do for Long-Term Transfer and Independence

Raise your hand if you've ever said something like this to a colleague: "My students are spelling 100% of the words correctly on the Friday tests, but they just can't seem to transfer these spelling skills into their own writing the following week." Transferring a skill learned in isolation and applying it where it really matters, in an authentic, "real world" context—be it a game, a performance, or while reading or writing—is the ultimate goal of all learning. It's also the most evasive. Transfer can be really, really hard to accomplish. So, what can you, as a teacher, do to best support transfer for your own students?

This is where thoughtful application of the "We Do" and "You Do" steps of the Gradual Release Model can make a big difference. To get a sense of what this looks like in action, let's return to our soccer example above. In a typical 2-hour practice, our coach might spend 15 minutes demonstrating a skill (I Do). This modeling and demonstration is an excellent start, but our coach knew it was just a start. To really hone the skill, we might spend *the remaining 1 hour and 45 minutes* in drills and scrimmages, practicing the skills and ideas we learned in context (We Do) in preparation for the upcoming game on Friday night (You Do).

Now imagine if this ratio was reversed: Our coach spending 1 hour and 45 minutes demonstrating and talking about the skill (I Do) as we sat and watched him on the sideline. If there was any time left at the end of practice, we might spend a few minutes actually playing soccer with the ball. If this was our daily routine, we definitely wouldn't be ready for the game on Friday. While this scenario—spending little time actually playing soccer to get better at soccer—may seem ridiculous, this is a common intervention mistake we see in some classrooms and intervention settings: spending the bulk of time in explicit instruction—perhaps a 30- or 40-minute whole-class phonics lesson, day after day, week after week—with little time for practice applying the phonics skills in reading or writing.

Take Action Principle #6

To take action on principle #6, consider the following:

- Aim for an approximately 20/80 ratio of explicit instruction to application and practice (Allington, 2013; Seidenberg & Borkenhagen, 2020). While this 20/80 split is not set in stone, it provides a general explicit instruction/implicit practice ratio to shoot for across a week with middle-grades readers. Some days, and for some lessons and students initially learning a skill, strategy, or new concept, the "I Do" percentage might be much larger.

- Of the 80% of implicit practice, approximately 40% should be guided practice and 40% independent practice. Again, this isn't set in stone. For example, some weeks, particularly for new strategies, the "We Do" might be a larger portion of the instructional pie.

- To get a sense of how much time your students are actually reading, ask their teacher(s) to log the amount of time students read during each of their classes. Multiply this to see how much reading practice they are getting across a week, month, and year.

Principle #7. One Size Does Not Fit All: Differentiate and Scaffold When They're Not "Getting It"

Construction workers use scaffolding to provide them extra support as they build buildings. Once the scaffolding is no longer needed, they take it down. In the same way, we use instructional scaffolds to support students as they learn literacy skills, reducing the scaffolds as students become more independent.

In each of our upcoming case study chapters, we provide you with specific scaffolds you can use for each literacy component, including decoding, fluency, vocabulary, comprehension, and engagement. We also discuss how to vary the type and intensity of scaffolding to differentiate instruction for each of your student's individual needs.

Take Action Principle #7

To take action on principle #7, considering incorporating the following general types of supports for literacy intervention. You'll see these scaffolding practices included in our *sample lessons* at the end of each case study chapter:

• *Precise feedback*—Provide specific, precise, actionable feedback tied directly to your student's performance in relation to the instructional goal. "Excellent job decoding the beginning part of the word *trans-* in *transportation.* That's a real strength of yours—identifying the beginning chunks of words. I noticed that decoding the middles and ends of words is a bit more challenging for you. So that's what we're going to work on next."

• *Questions and prompts that lead to learning*—Ask questions that guide, but don't tell. Good questions and prompts remind students of important related concepts and resources and point the way to the type of thinking good readers do. Following are some example questions and prompts:

- Which parts of the word do you recognize? Which parts are tricky?
- Does this word/word part look like another word/word part you know?
- Which sentences in a paragraph usually tell us the main ideas?
- I'm thinking of a resource that we discussed yesterday that might help you here.
- What are the three steps in our summarizing strategy (teacher points to anchor chart)?

• *Breaking learning into smaller steps or chunks*—Sometimes, breaking the learning task into smaller, bite-sized chunks, and mastering each chunk before adding the next one, is extremely helpful for middle-grades readers. "Instead of just trying to summarize the whole article, let's start with the first step in summarizing: Selecting the 'treasure,' or the important ideas and key words. We'll use a highlighter for that. And let's work with the first paragraph of the article for now."

• *Starting with pictures*—Often, starting with a visual or a picture is an engaging way to give struggling readers a "toehold" into a new strategy or topic before moving to text. For example, when teaching inferencing, we often start by asking students to make inferences with *photographs* that could be interpreted many different ways, and later move to inferencing with *texts.*

• *Anchor charts*—If a concept or strategy is important enough to be taught, it's probably important enough to be referenced later. Anchor charts serve as visual reminders of the "secret" of a strategy lesson or important content (a phonics "sound board" with common spelling patterns and key words). Post these anchor charts for the "I Do" part of the lesson and constantly refer to them during the "We Do" and "You Do" parts of learning. You will see anchor charts in most of our sample lessons in the case study chapters.

• *Word banks*—Most of us probably can't spontaneously name every single fellow student from our first-grade class. However, if we were shown a class picture and a separate list of their names—a *word bank*—we could probably match many of the names and photos. This shows that the information *is* stored somewhere in our brain but is buried so deeply we need help retrieving it. In the same way, our students may have the required knowledge, but need help finding and retrieving it. This is where a word bank could prove a useful scaffold.

- *Developmental teaching*—One of the most important scaffolds is teaching students "where they are," instead of using a one-size-fits-all approach. This is particularly important in Pathway #1, which includes phonics, spelling, and fluency. Use the developmental model and spelling/phonics inventories to identify your students' reading/spelling stage. Differentiate instruction by choosing appropriate phonics features to teach and appropriately leveled texts to use. See Chapter 4 for examples of how to teach developmentally.

- *Grouping*—You can group students for different purposes, including based on *developmental level* (word work with students who are in the same within-word pattern spelling stage, all working on common long vowel patterns) and *strategy* (a small group doing extra practice summarizing texts). Because the group is small, you can provide more focused feedback and precise teaching. Because it's a group, social collaboration can be a powerful motivator.

- *Distributed practice*—One of our yoga teachers memorably said, "It's better to do *a little a lot* than *a lot a little*." This is the essence of *distributed practice,* whether it's yoga, soccer, playing the violin, or reading. We've probably all spent an all-nighter cramming for an exam—and possibly doing quite well—only to forget the information within a week or so. However, the science of learning tells us that if we took that 8 hours of cramming and, instead, distributed it across a week or two, perhaps studying for an hour per day, our learning would "stick." To cement any skill, strategy, or habit into our long-term memory, we need to practice in multiple short, "review sessions" over a longer period of time.

Principle #8. Time: Where Does It All Go, and How Can I Get Some Back?

Time may be your most precious commodity as a teacher. How do you make every minute count? How can you get any spare time back? First, it's important to realize that becoming skilled at anything is going to take lots of purposeful, meaningful practice. Expert studies on the violin, piano, skating, and wrestling all found that *adult experts spend 500% more time practicing* than adult novices (Ericsson, 1996). We don't all have to be skilled violinists, pianists, or wrestlers to make it in today's world, but we do all have to be adequately skilled readers to thrive in the 21st century. And for those of us working with readers who struggle, consider the following:

- High-achieving fourth-grade readers *spend 600% more time reading* than low-achieving fourth graders (Guthrie, 2004).
- *Every 2 months,* a child whose scores are in the top 10% on standardized tests will read as much as a child whose scores are in the bottom 10% *has read his/her entire life* (Anderson, Wilson, & Fielding, 1988).
- Interventions with word-level reading difficulties that produced the largest gains all contained the following component: *Students had ample opportunities to apply word-level skills to reading connected text* (Kilpatrick, 2015).

Take Action **Principle #8**

The amount of *purposeful practice* matters. The clock is ticking for our middle-grades readers with literacy challenges. This means that they should spend the bulk of intervention time practicing their skills—actually reading and writing. To take action on principle #8, here are steps to consider for making every minute count in your intervention lessons:

- *Cut out the extraneous!* Be ruthless about cutting out anything extraneous, particularly anything that doesn't serve the lesson objective. Watch out for too much teacher talk, transitions that take too long, and time spent gathering supplies.

- *Be wary of worksheets.* There is no research to show that worksheets improve reading achievement. Be wary of worksheet work. We've seen too many worksheets that: (1) are ill-conceived, (2) don't match the learning objective, and/or (3) don't require much practice actually reading or writing (in one lesson we observed, a student decoded only five total words during 10 minutes of worksheet work—that's only one word every 2 minutes!).

- *Establish routines.* Routines save time. Pick a lesson routine, teach it to your students, and stick to it. Only change the routine for a good reason.

- *Get reading!* Generally, students should be reading within the first minute or so of the intervention lesson (unless you are modeling/thinking aloud or have a very good reason).

- *Keep reading!* In a 30-minute fluency lesson, students should actually be reading for about 20–24 minutes. What's happening the remaining 6–10 minutes? Perhaps a quick teacher model/think-aloud at the beginning, stopping points during reading to ask questions and discuss, and asking students what they learned at the end. During these 6–10 nonreading minutes, students should be talking at least as much as the teacher. Remember, every minute counts.

- *Don't forget the 20/80 split.* Across a week of intervention, remember the 20/80 split in explicit instructions versus implicit practice. For example, if you are doing fluency work with an intervention group, meeting 5 days a week, for 30 minutes a day, that means of the overall 2.5 hours of weekly intervention time, your students should be *reading in context for at least 2 hours!* For many teachers and schools we work with, this is both an eye-opener and a game changer. The students and schools that make the most progress actually read more than this (60–90 minutes per day of reading practice, translating to 7.6 hours per week).

- *Log the amount your students read.* One teacher we worked with logged a student's reading volume who was in a structured intervention plan that placed a premium on explicit instruction (I Do), but who wasn't making much progress. The student was actually reading less than 5 minutes per day! It is no wonder that there was so little growth.

Principle #9. Engagement: Get Your Students to Buy In When They've Already Checked Out

Engagement and motivation are often the very first things many fourth- through eighth-grade teachers mention when talking about their students who struggle to read. What, exactly, is engagement? How important is it? And how can we foster engagement in our students, many of whom are disengaged readers and writers?

According to Guthrie, one of the leading experts on reading engagement, engagement entails much more than simply being motivated. Engaged readers share the following characteristics (Guthrie, 2004):

- *Reading stamina and focus*—Engaged readers not only read much more than disengaged readers, they can sustain this effort over time, even with challenging texts.

- *Actively focused on making meaning*—Engaged readers are not simply trying to "get through" a text. They are actively trying to make sense of it. If something doesn't make sense, they reread, look to another resource, or ask someone else. They use cognitive strategies (such as questioning) and are focused on deeply processing the content.

- *Enthusiasm*—Engaged readers are often enthusiastic when reading and learning. For example, they have strong opinions on what they read, excitedly sharing their favorite books and unabashedly pointing out very specific reasons they dislike certain texts.

- *Purposeful*—If you ask them why they are reading, and what they're trying to learn while reading, engaged readers can give you very specific answers. They are goal-oriented.

- *Socially interactive*—While they may do a lot of reading on their own, engaged readers also enjoy discussing what they've read with peers and are interested in what their peers are reading. They love talking about their reading.

- *Intrinsically motivated*—Engaged readers don't just read for gold stars, grades, or reward points in a reading program. Instead, they read because they are curious about a topic, like the way reading makes them think and feel, and see how reading allows them to participate in a wider world.

For those of us who work with middle-grades students who struggle to read, these bullets above describe the opposite of many of the students we work with every day. Many students who struggle to read are disengaged readers. They often don't read a lot. They may not have a favorite book. Many don't see the point of reading. For many, "school reading" is difficult and frustrating.

Because they haven't had much success in reading in their past, they may have started to give up on ever becoming skilled readers. And it's not hard to understand why. If you've ever tried a diet or workout routine and didn't get decent results after weeks and even months of effort, there's a good chance you gave it up. Now imagine trying something for 4 years or more, with little to show for your efforts!

However, there is hope. The research on reading engagement is convincing. It shows that by employing some common-sense, doable instructional practices, we can significantly improve our students' reading engagement and reading achievement (Guthrie, 2004).

Take Action **Principle #9**

To take action on principle #9, consider employing the following instructional strategies, which we explain in more depth in Chapter 9:

- *Provide choice.* As much as possible, provide choice in reading materials and tasks. Even small choices can make a big difference in motivation.

- *Foster social collaboration.* We can greatly increase our students' engagement when we provide them opportunities to read together and share their thoughts and reactions with their classmates during group work.

- *Demonstrate growth.* We are much more motivated to work hard when we see the fruits of our labors. Showing students their concrete growth toward a literacy goal can be a powerful motivator.

Principle #10. Active, Not Passive: Take a Critical Stance and Read with a Purpose

Perhaps the most common characteristic we see among middle-grades readers who have literacy challenges is a *passive stance* toward reading. Because reading has been such a struggle for so many years, many students we work with don't expect school textbooks and class novels to make much sense. Some are just reading to "get through" the text, calling out the words. Others don't engage with the text, not because they are "lazy" or "don't care about learning," but because despite their best efforts, they haven't seen much in terms of results over the years.

So, how do we inspire and guide *passive readers* to become *active readers?* Readers who expect the text to make sense, who are willing to dig into difficult text and figure it out, who have some reading strategies in their "toolboxes" that they can confidently use when their comprehension begins to break down? Readers who think critically about the texts they are reading and who can critically question what they are learning, including what the author has written?

Take Action Principle #10

Throughout our case study chapters, we will be demonstrating how to reset our middle graders' passive mindsets, helping them develop an active, critical stand toward reading that includes reading with a purpose and engaging with text. While we will give specific examples of this type of teaching and learning in the following chapters and in our sample lessons, you can begin to take action on principle #10 by doing the following:

- *Ask higher-level questions that require students to think critically.* "Why do you think that? What evidence in the text supports your answer?"

- *Model your own critical thinking about text.* "This made me think of something else I read . . ."

- *Teach your students to ask their own questions of the text and author.* "I don't think the author was very clear here. I wonder why he didn't give us more examples of different math problems that are like the ones we have to do for homework?"

- *Provide opportunities to discuss and debate.* "Who agrees with Jalen's point of view? Why? Who disagrees? Why?"

- *Provide tools and opportunities to make sense of text.* "While reading, you can either use *sticky note summaries* or create your own *graphic organizer* to make sense of what you learned. But choose one strategy to use while reading and we'll share in class tomorrow."

CONCLUSION

We don't see the 10 intervention principles we've discussed in this chapter as add-ons or "nice extras" to our work with middle-grades readers. Instead, these principles lie at the very heart of what we do, inspiring us, guiding us, and providing us a North Star to follow as we try to navigate the often difficult waters of literacy intervention work. You'll see them incorporated throughout the rest of this book. At the end of each case study chapter, we will also include a North Star principles table in which we will explicitly lay out how we might apply each of the 10 principles to intervention work with Aliyah, Zach, and Andres and to students with similar literacy profiles.

CHAPTER 3

Start with Assessments

Do you ever feel that you are drowning in data? That you administer too many tests or spend too much time gathering information that you often don't use? You are not alone. Overtesting is a common problem in education. Schools tend to adopt new assessments that are then added to the assessment agenda because administrators are sometimes unsure which assessments are still needed and which ones need to be eliminated (Nelson, 2013).

Our intervention principle #3 says to start with assessments. But which assessments? And for which students? How many assessments are enough? When can you start teaching? As teachers, we are consumers of these assessments, so it's incumbent upon us to consider the purpose of each assessment and how it can inform our instruction to better support student learning. This helps us be efficient with assessment so we can focus our time on instruction.

Our goal in this chapter is to offer you a streamlined assessment plan of action using easily accessible assessments we've leaned on over the years in our work with middle-grades students with literacy challenges. We start with *screening assessments* but target *diagnostic assessments* so we can confidently (1) rank order areas of need (e.g., decoding is priority #1, fluency is priority #2), (2) group students, and (3) choose instructional strategies, appropriate content, and appropriate texts. We'll introduce you to our assessment flowchart and describe how to use the flowchart to choose different assessments that target different areas of literacy for different students. Specifically, we walk you through how to use assessments to target the three different pathways of the cognitive model for readers like Aliyah, Zach, and Andres:

- Assessments that target Pathway #1: decoding, word recognition, and fluency (for readers with profiles similar to Aliyah)
- Assessments that target Pathway #2: vocabulary, prior knowledge, and text-structure knowledge (for readers with profiles similar to Zach)
- Assessments that target Pathway #3: purposes for reading, strategy use, and engagement (for readers with profiles similar to Zach and Andres)

Aliyah, Zach, and Andres have each demonstrated difficulty comprehending grade-level texts, but they each struggle for different reasons and, therefore, have different instructional needs. Moreover, all too often adolescents have accumulated years of difficulty, leading to significant gaps in their achievement.

Assessments play a critical role in helping us identify the cause of their difficulty so we can intervene appropriately, especially when time is of the essence. As Stahl, Flanigan, and McKenna (2020) put it, "when these students leave the [early elementary] grades with significant academic problems, they present grave challenges . . . they struggle, regardless of the cause, until they either catch up or give up" (p. 1). Assessment is the first step in addressing the diverse needs of our students as we work to help them "catch up" and *not* "give up."

MATCHING ASSESSMENT TO YOUR PURPOSE

Using data to inform our instruction pulls together four types of assessment: (1) screening, (2) diagnostic, (3) progress monitoring, and (4) outcome. *Screening measures* are designed to efficiently and effectively identify students who need intervention. *Diagnostic assessments* are designed to provide in-depth information about a student's understanding and skills to inform instructional planning. *Progress monitoring* tools are designed to be used once a student has been identified for intervention and are brief, so they can be given frequently, as well as sensitive to change over shorter intervals. *Outcome measures* are summative assessments that we typically think of as end-of-year accountability tests or end-of-unit tests. Each of these types of assessments answer different questions that help us fine-tune our instruction to better meet the needs of all students (see Figure 3.1).

In the early elementary grades, screening assessments provide the first opportunity for us to identify students in need of intervention support. Students in the upper grades, however, often begin the school year already identified by their school as at-risk. In other words, we already know who many of our intervention students are when we begin the school year in upper grades. Typically, middle school readers with literacy needs are identified when they fail to demonstrate adequate reading comprehension proficiency on high-stakes tests or standardized achievement tests. When at-risk readers are identified at the end of the school year, schools can make decisions about scheduling accordingly. Schools also screen any new students who come into the school district after school has started. Although middle-grades teachers might not need to administer screening measures to decide who needs reading support, it is still important for them to conduct diagnostic assessments as needed. Diagnostic assessments can provide teachers with valuable information about how to group students and guide instruction.

In the early elementary grades, we use screening assessments that will measure students' knowledge and skills in phonological awareness, the alphabetic principle, letter–sound correspondence, and word reading. We assess young students in a sequence that reflects the developmental model, beginning with skills such as letter recognition, sound recognition, and word reading. Then, as students progress along the developmental continuum, we turn to more complex skills such as reading fluency and comprehension. In this way, we usually test students in the early grades from the "bottom up."

As students move into the upper grades, we reverse this "bottom up" process. We start by assessing students' oral reading fluency and comprehension to determine whether further assessments are necessary in decoding or word recognition. So, students in the upper grades, in contrast, are assessed from the "top down," starting with comprehension (Denton et al., 2007; see Figure 3.2).

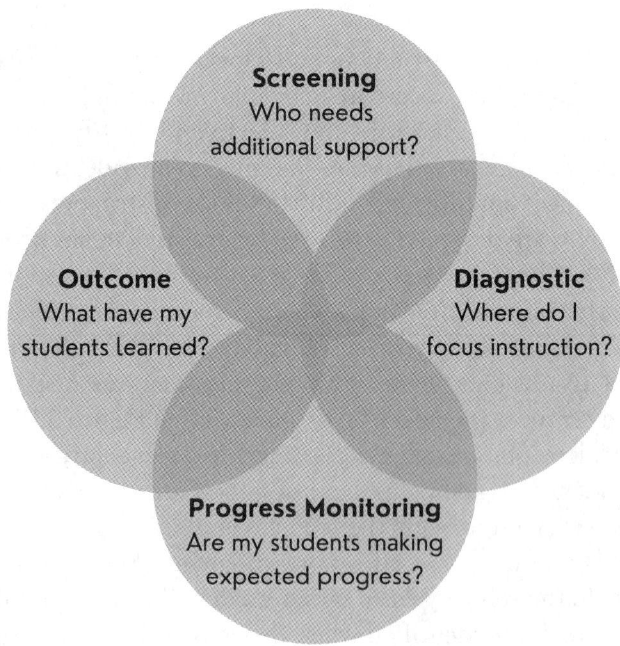

FIGURE 3.1. Types of assessments.

Early Elementary Grades	Upper Grades
Comprehension Strategies	Comprehension Strategies
Vocabulary/Prior Knowledge	Vocabulary/Prior Knowledge
Fluency	Fluency
Word Reading/Decoding	Word Reading/Decoding
Phonemic Awareness	

FIGURE 3.2. Early versus upper grades.

OUR ASSESSMENT FLOWCHART

Our assessment flowchart is designed to help you efficiently identify students who need intervention support and help you decide which diagnostic assessments to use and which ones you can skip. We move from screening to diagnostics measures. Here is the general sequence of steps we follow.

1. Screening
   - All middle-grades students take screening assessments at the beginning of the year.
   - For middle grades, (1) an oral reading fluency task (individually administered) and (2) a Maze comprehension task (group-administered) are commonly used.
2. Brief Diagnostic Assessment to Identify the Pathway
   - This step is only for students who do not meet benchmark on the two screening assessments and further information is needed.
   - We administer an informal reading inventory, including both the graded word lists and one oral reading passage to get a measure of reading accuracy, reading rate, reading prosody, and reading comprehension.
   - Based on results, the intervention team identifies pathway(s) for further exploration.
3. In-Depth Pathway Exploration
   - Based on the pathway(s) identified in Step 2, we administer follow-up diagnostic assessments.
   - These follow-up assessments vary based on the target pathway(s). We unpack options in upcoming sections organized by the target pathway (e.g., assessments to follow up on Pathway #1).

4. Intervention Plan
   - The intervention team analyzes all assessment information and designs an intervention plan, including goals and ways to monitor progress.
   - Each case study chapter (Chapters 4–9) starts off with the intervention team's analysis, discussion, and intervention plan for Aliyah, Zach, and Andres.

Step 1: Screening

Our assessment flowchart begins with a typical two-task screening (see Figure 3.3): (1) an oral reading fluency (ORF) task and (2) a Maze comprehension task. An ORF is probably one of the most commonly used screening assessments in grades 1–8. It is individually administered and involves a 1-minute oral reading of a grade-level passage (e.g., our eighth grader, Aliyah, would read an eighth-grade passage). Students receive a words-correct-per-minute (WCPM) score and an accuracy percentage. In grades 2–8, a Maze comprehension task is added. Maze is group

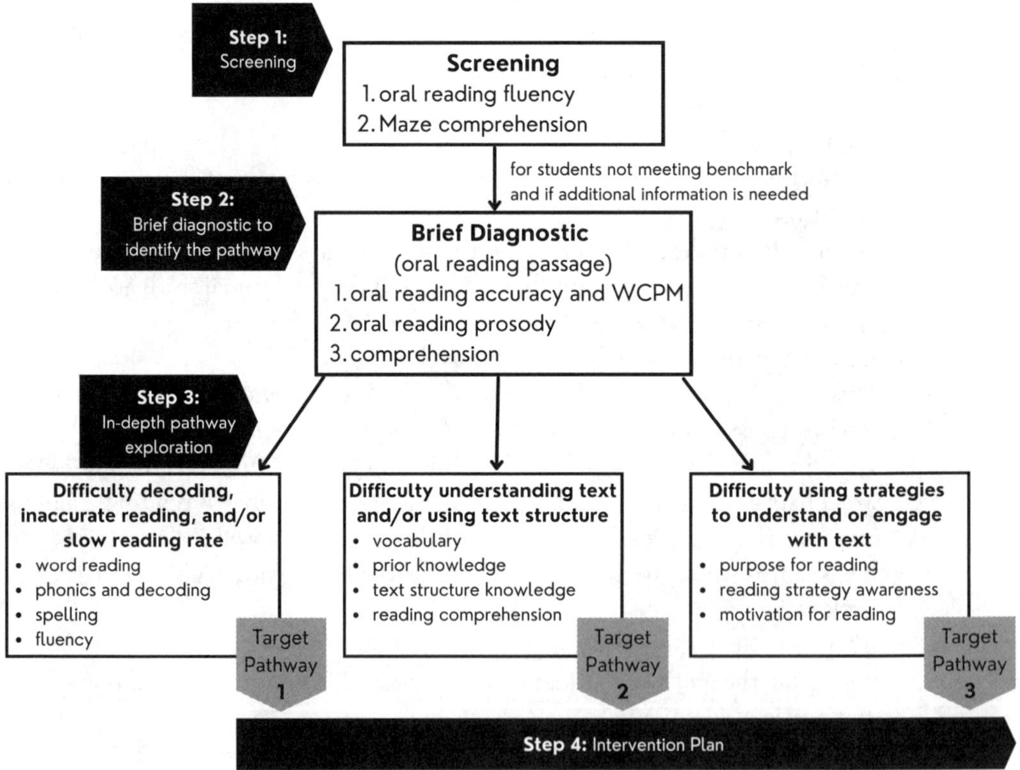

FIGURE 3.3. Assessment flow chart.

administered and involves a 3-minute silent reading of a grade-level passage with missing words (i.e., a cloze procedure), where students choose from three options to supply the missing word. Students receive a score that pulls together the number of items they correctly answered with the ones they incorrectly answered. For both of these, we use grade-level benchmarks that will indicate a level of risk—risk of not meeting end-of-year benchmarks. These screening assessments are available commercially (e.g., Aimsweb, Fast Bridge, DIBELS Next), but there are also free options like DIBELS-8.

These two tasks help us answer an important initial question: *Who needs intervention support?* Screening allows us to identify students who met the benchmarks and those who didn't. Most upper-grade readers who struggle have needs in reading comprehension, and we see this trend in our screening data. This begs the question: Why are these students struggling with comprehension? and brings us to Step 2, diagnostic assessments. Diagnostic assessments help us start "peeling back the onion" for those students who did not meet the screening benchmarks or have not made progress during interventions, as we try to identify: (1) Which pathway(s) is the underlying cause of the reading difficulties identified on the screening tasks, and (2) how should we prioritize the different areas of need?

Step 2: Brief Diagnostic Assessment to Identify the Pathway

We have found informal reading inventories (IRIs) to be especially helpful as a first step in answering the question about why a student has difficulty reading. An IRI provides you with an additional oral reading passage plus measures of reading prosody and comprehension. In this chapter, we use the *Qualitative Reading Inventory, Seventh Edition,* as an example IRI (QRI-7; Leslie & Caldwell, 2021) to walk you through our process using graded word lists, graded passages, and the passage's corresponding comprehension questions.

Graded Word Lists

Starting our diagnostic assessment with graded word lists helps us determine our target passage level and gives us an indicator of their word recognition. We use a timed PowerPoint slide presentation with a single word on each slide and the timing set to 0.25 seconds. We've found the 1-second guidance from the QRI-7 insufficient in gauging automatic word recognition in the middle grades. We have our slide presentation set up for each word slide timed at 0.25 seconds and a blank slide between each word slide set for 1 second. This allows for ease of administration, letting the slide show run if students know words and giving you time to toggle back to a word if it's not automatically recognized or is misread.

1. Begin with the graded word list approximately 2 years below the current grade level (this is common guidance for students in upper grades). You can adjust this if needed; for example, if you know the student is likely significantly below grade level, then you might want to begin three or more grade levels below.

2. Administer the timed slide show of your first graded word list. If the student reads the word right away (i.e., as soon as it appears on the screen), then record it as automatically recognized. If the student doesn't read the word right away or misreads the word, toggle back to the word and allow the student time to read the word (we usually limit this to 5–10 seconds) for "untimed" word identification. We advise toggling back with each word misread or not automatically recognized rather than waiting until the end of the list just for ease of administration. Always write down substitutions or phonetic representations of incorrect responses (this often speaks to a student's decoding skills). This administration allows you to gauge automatic word recognition as well as monitor words identified when given more time.

3. After a word list is finished, we decide if we want to administer the previous list, administer the next list, or stop. The automatic word reading score is the most valid predictor of later contextualized reading (Morris et al., 2011), so we use this score to make these decisions. Morris et al. suggest 50% as a benchmark.

- If the automatic score is 50% or more, administer the next level.
- If the automatic score is below 50%, stop administration. However, if this is your first graded word list, then administer the previous list.
- We've found that students in upper grades can sometimes experience difficulty with a list but then rebound. So, with middle grades and up, we often administer one more list once we've gone below 50% to be certain.

Let's consider Aliyah's performance on the word list reading as an example. Mr. Jackson (one of the school's reading specialists) decided to begin with the fifth-grade word list (three grade levels below her current grade rather than the suggested two). Since she read the fifth-grade list with 90% automatic word reading, Mr. Jackson administered the next list (using the Morris et al., 2011, guidance). She read 75% of the sixth-grade list automatically, so Mr. Jackson moved to the seventh-grade list, where her score was 35% automatic word reading. At this point, using Morris et al.'s guidance, Mr. Jackson decided to stop (notice we don't have data for eighth grade in Figure 3.4). Notice how her decoding ability ("untimed" score) is stronger than her automatic word reading at each grade level, indicating her word knowledge is not fully automatic. Notice, too, how her automatic word recognition drops below 50% at the seventh-grade level, indicating she likely does not have sufficient automatic word recognition to fluently read texts at this level or beyond.

Grade Level	Automatic Score (quick accurate word reading)	Untimed Score (decoding)
5th Grade	90%	95%
6th Grade	75%	90%
7th Grade	35%	65%
8th Grade	----	----

FIGURE 3.4. Aliyah's word list reading.

Graded Passage Reading

Once we've completed the graded word lists, we choose a grade-level passage to administer. Use the student's graded word list results to decide which grade-level passage to administer (see #1 below). Administering this grade-level passage allows us to get another indicator of accuracy *in context*. Oral passage readings also allow us to assess prosody (i.e., expressive, phrasal reading) and get another measure of comprehension using open-ended questions.

1. Choose a passage to administer. Morris (2014) suggests the passage at the highest grade level where the student automatically reads approximately 80% of the words. In Aliyah's case above, we would choose a sixth-grade passage because her automatic score at this level was 75%.

We have two additional considerations: (1) Passage length matters; we aim for longer passages (e.g., 300-plus words) if possible because this is more aligned with the length of texts they might be required to read in their content classes. (2) We are careful about navigating levels in IRIs, especially for older students. We always consult the manuals and check Lexile levels of the passages. For example, in the QRI-7, there are passages in the 500 Lexile range across three grade-level sets. For our purposes, we've identified "go-to" passages with the IRIs we use most. These "go-to" passages help us in terms of using lengthier passages with levels that reflect a grade-level band and/or demonstrate a gradation of difficulty from one passage to the next.

2. Prepare your student for the reading. Ask a topic-related question or identify the topic to assess their background knowledge on the topic. For example, one of

the QRI-7 narrative passages is about a child's birthday, so you might ask a question about birthday celebrations or simply say the passage is about a child's birthday. Before the student begins reading, let the student know you'll ask questions about the reading afterward. We also like to let them know up front that we'll be making notes as they read and respond to the comprehension questions.

3. Have the student read aloud and make sure to time the reading. We usually record these passage readings just in case we need to revisit anything about the reading. A recording also allows us to reflect on reading prosody, which can be especially useful for students with fluency needs.

4. As the student reads aloud, code errors (see Figure 3.5). If the student hesitates, have them continue reading after 5 seconds by saying "go ahead." This short cue usually gets them to move on and continue reading.

5. Reflect on the student's reading prosody and decide on a fluency rating. The QRI-7 provides a fluency rating guide with a 4-point scale.

6. Calculate the student's oral reading accuracy percentage and WCPM. See Figure 3.6.

7. Remember, at this point, we are using the IRI to determine our pathway for in-depth exploration, so you likely won't administer another passage at this point. This said, we still consider the oral reading accuracy and WCPM scores. Using guidance across resources, we use the following: (1) oral reading accuracy benchmark of at least 90% or better and (2) at least 100 WCPM. Our purpose here is

Types of Oral Reading Errors

- **Substitution**: the student substitutes another word (or nonword) for the printed word (e.g., says option for opposition or /ĭl ər sē/ for illiteracy
- **Insertion**: the student inserts a word or phrase that isn't in the text
- **Omission**: the student omits a word
- **Reversal**: the student changes the order of the printed words (e.g., says "said he" instead of "he said")
- **Self-correction**: the student makes any of the above errors (i.e., substitution, insertion, omission, reversal) and corrects their mistake; this type of error is sometimes not included in the error count when calculating oral reading accuracy

  Note: We don't include self-corrections in our error count, but we do make note of them (e.g., a student doesn't monitor reading and doesn't self-correct consistently or the student has many self-corrections because of inaccurate reading)
- **Teacher-provided word**: the student hesitates and will not move forward after encouragement, so you provide the word

FIGURE 3.5. Oral reading errors.

Oral Reading Accuracy	Words Correct Per Minute
$\frac{\text{total \# of words - errors}}{\text{total \# of words}}$	$60 \times \frac{\text{total \# of words - errors}}{\text{total \# of words}}$

FIGURE 3.6. Words correct per minute (WCPM).

twofold: We want to make sure that (1) decoding or word recognition difficulties aren't getting in the way of comprehension, and (2) the student reads at a comfortable pace where they can sustain their effort.

- While we use 90% accuracy as a general guideline, some researchers recommend at least 95% accuracy (e.g., Morris et al., 2014). We shift our thinking to 95% when it is instructionally appropriate, such as during prosody work when we want attention on phrasing and expression rather than accuracy.
- Denton, Bryan, Wexler, Reed, and Vaughn (2007) outline characteristics of fluent middle-grades readers as: reads 100-plus words correct per minute, has automatic word recognition skills, groups words into meaningful phrase units, reads with expression and intonation, makes few word reading errors and usually self-corrects when meaning is compromised, and understands what they read.
- When it comes to thinking about reading rates for middle-grades readers, we follow the guidance offered by Denton et al. (2007): (1) Readers who have comprehension challenges, but who read above 100 WCPM and 90% accuracy in grade-level texts, likely don't need a prioritized fluency intervention and would benefit from instruction highlighting vocabulary, comprehension, and background knowledge. In other words, the most important consideration is whether they can understand and learn from what they read, so students who have below-grade-level oral reading fluency (but still reach at least 100 WCPM) and good comprehension may not require heavy attention to improving their reading rate. (2) Always think about a student's interest in reading and their motivation when you consider oral reading fluency performance.

Mr. Jackson asked Aliyah to read a sixth-grade passage as described above. Afterward, he calculated Aliyah's sixth-grade reading accuracy and speed and determined her prosody rating. Aliyah read the passage with 94% accuracy and 90 words correct per minute. She self-corrected her reading errors occasionally. Mr. Jackson scored her prosody at a level 2, indicating some awkward phrasing and limited expressive interpretation. What does this tell us about Aliyah's passage reading performance? Aliyah's word reading accuracy met our benchmark of at least 90%, but her reading rate falls short of our benchmark of at least 100 WCPM or faster. So, she can accurately read sixth-grade level material but slowly. Our next question is: Did her slower than expected reading rate impact her comprehension?

Comprehension Questions

Directly after the oral passage reading, gauge the student's understanding. The QRI-7 includes open-ended questions, including both explicit (facts found in the text) and implicit (inference) questions.

1. Record student responses regardless of whether they are correct or not. We've found the practice of writing each answer eases anxiety.

2. Prompt students as needed. For example, sometimes rephrasing a question or reminding them to use what the author said is helpful. We always make note of when we prompt because it can be helpful later.

3. Allow students to "look back" to the text as needed. While you could make note about questions answered with and without "look-backs," we give greater weight to a student's comprehension scores *with look-backs*. For most of our reading in school and in life, we are able to look back to find information we just read. If you focus on *the non-look-back comprehension score,* you may be assessing a reader's memory more than their comprehension.

4. Reflect on the student's responses. Did they generally understand the passage, or did they have marked difficulty? Did you have to prompt multiple questions? Were they able to use look-backs to their advantage?

Aliyah's comprehension of the passage demonstrated a pattern noted by her teachers—she consistently demonstrates good understanding of orally presented material or in texts that are "comfortable" but has difficulty understanding grade-level texts. On the sixth-grade passage, she answered 100% of the questions (including look-backs). In other words, she demonstrated strong understanding of the concepts in the sixth-grade passage.

Selecting Texts for Instructional Purposes

In an intervention, we believe it is critical to find texts that students can read with good accuracy and appropriate fluency. This is critical because we want students to focus on the task at hand (e.g., making sense of the text, applying multisyllabic word reading strategies, or reading with a phrasal quality with appropriate intonation) rather than struggling to decode the words. As one way to identify appropriate texts, informal reading inventories (e.g., the QRI-7) provide criteria teachers can apply to the assessment data to identify the different levels at which a student can read with independence or an appropriate level of challenge (traditionally called the *instructional* range). One thing to keep in mind as we move into the upper grades: It becomes increasingly difficult to identify precise reading *levels* and how they relate to the passages from an IRI. For example, is there as clear a difference between a seventh- and eighth-grade reading passage as there is between a first- and second-grade reading passage?

As we move into the upper grades, the interaction of multiple pressure points—such as a reader's background knowledge, motivation, academic vocabulary, text-structure knowledge—plays an increasingly greater role in a reader's success (Stahl, Flanigan, & McKenna, 2020). This is why we believe that with middle-grades readers, it is instructionally more useful to identify a *range of possible appropriate levels* (rather than one level) that a student could successfully read and work with, along with a *range of possible supports*. So, throughout this book, instead of focusing on finding one reading level, we emphasize applying benchmark criteria, which are the minimum criteria needed to read a text with adequate fluency. See Chapter 10 for a more detailed discussion about selecting texts for a specific instructional purpose.

Step 3: In-Depth Pathway Exploration

Does the student read slowly or inaccurately? Are they not monitoring whether the words make sense? Or does the student have difficulty decoding unknown words? Does the student struggle with reading prosody? Or does the difficulty mostly lie with understanding the text? These questions will help you decide about the pathway you'll explore in more depth.

In-Depth Diagnostic Assessment: Taking a Closer Look at the Pathways

As we consider the brief diagnostic assessment using an IRI, we use the following guidance to identify a pathway for more assessment.

- *For some students, are assessment Steps 1 and 2 enough?* Sometimes, you can stop after Step 1. Other times brief diagnostic assessment combined with information from a screening may be needed to identify our intervention priorities. We always want to maximize instructional time, so we'll begin interventions as soon as possible and revisit additional diagnostic assessments as needed.

- *How do I know which pathway to explore?* Sometimes we need additional information to unpack a student's reading and/or writing more fully. Figure 3.7 details how to choose a pathway.

How do I know to explore Pathway #1?
Automatic Word Recognition

Go with Pathway #1 if:

- graded word lists: automatic word reading below 50% on student's grade-level list and the passage determination is below their current grade placement
- oral passage fluency: oral reading accuracy falls below 90% and WCPM below 100 WCPM (note again: passage is below their current grade placement)
- oral passage comprehension: may or may not be affected by word reading difficulty

How do I know to explore Pathway #2?
Comprehension

Go with Pathway #2 if:

- graded word lists: automatic word reading above 50% on student's grade-level list and the passage determination is their current grade placement or perhaps one grade level below
- oral passage fluency: oral reading accuracy is at least 90% and rate is at least 100 WCPM
- oral passage comprehension: despite adequate oral passage fluency, student has difficulty with comprehension (e.g., few correct answers or difficulty with implicit questions)

How do I know to explore Pathway #3?
Strategic Knowledge and Engagement

Go with Pathway #3 if:

- graded word lists, oral passage fluency, and oral passage comprehension may or may not be affected but there is —
- evidence of limited strategic knowledge (e.g., couldn't utilize look-backs) and/or reading engagement

FIGURE 3.7. Choosing a pathway.

- *Does this mean we will always only explore one pathway?* No. Along the way, we consider whether we need to add some assessments from an additional pathway. For example, you might decide you need to explore Pathway #1, but you also made note that the student had particular difficulty with implicit questions during the comprehension portion of the IRI. In which case, you might decide to supplement your Pathway #1 exploration with an assessment from Pathway #2 to unpack implicit questions more thoroughly.

- *How much time should I take on this in-depth exploration?* Generally, we keep this to about 30 minutes of individual student work. One thing to remember, we don't do this level of in-depth testing with all students; as noted previously, sometimes the screening and the brief diagnostic assessment provides us with sufficient information to get rolling with our intervention planning (e.g., prioritize targets, group students, set goals). Plus, there are ways to develop some efficiencies. First, use your brief diagnostic assessment to put students in groups for assessment, so you can administer your spelling assessment in a group setting. Second, follow administration efficiencies built in the assessments. For example, a CORE word reading task suggests you administer the list that corresponds to the student's grade level and move to a lower level if they miss three words. Finally, many of the assessments are meant to be short (e.g., CORE suggests the phonics survey will take approximately 10 minutes).

Remember, the purpose of diagnostic assessment is to provide us with necessary information for prioritizing intervention targets, grouping students, and planning for our interventions. We don't want to over assess, but at the same time, we want to have enough information to appropriately intervene. Sometimes a few informal diagnostic assessments give us what we need to plan and get to our intervention work, and students make adequate progress without the need for additional assessment.

In the upcoming sections, we focus on easily accessible informal diagnostic assessments that will directly inform your instruction. Sometimes, though, we have students who don't make expected progress. If you find yourself at a point of exhausting the tools in your toolbox, consult with another specialist in your school who may have other diagnostic measures in their repertoire to unpack other factors at play (e.g., school psychologist and executive function).

Pathway #1. Diagnostic Follow-up Assessments: Automatic Word Recognition

"Word recognition and fluency issues often occur together; a reader who has difficulty accurately and automatically recognizing individual words is also likely to have difficulty reading words effortlessly and fluency in context" (Stahl et al., 2020, p. 274). It's critical to have a battery of assessments that address word-level skills not only because they are foundational to overall literacy success but also because studies have found that one-third or more of older students who struggle with reading have difficulty in this particular area (e.g., Catts et al., 2005; Deshler et al., 2007; Leach et al., 2003; Valencia & Buly, 2004).

Over the years, we've seen many older students who have fluency issues work only on fluency; fluency practice alone will not help a student move forward if word-level skills are the root cause of the fluency issues. Accordingly, this pathway provides us with information across word reading, phonics and decoding, spelling, and fluency. See Figure 3.8 for a list of possible assessments that target the components along Pathway #1: (1) word reading, (2) phonics and decoding,

(3) spelling, and (4) fluency. The following walks you through our general course of action as we explore Pathway #1 with students in upper elementary through middle school.

Word Reading. Two options we've used are graded word lists from an IRI like the QRI-7 and the San Diego Quick Assessment. Both give us an indicator of text levels that will be easier and more challenging for the student. The good news is that we've already administered graded word lists with our brief diagnostic assessment using an IRI. So, we can "re-purpose" this assessment information, analyzing it more deeply, but not costing us any additional testing time. These are the questions we ask as we "look under the hood" a bit more, looking past the initial automatic word reading percentage score:

- How did the student fare on the grade-level list (i.e., the list corresponding to their current grade placement)? What was the automatic percentage? Were they able to increase their scores when given time (i.e., check the untimed score)?
  - This is important information because it allows you to get an idea of how fluently they might read grade-level texts. If you didn't administer the grade-level word list, you might want to administer that word list (as well as any previous ones not already administered). For example, in Aliyah's case, Mr. Jackson decided to stop the word lists at seventh grade in the brief diagnostic assessment, but he revisited the word lists and administered the eighth-grade list (Aliyah's current grade placement). She read 25% of the words automatically and only successfully decoded two additional words when given time. This suggests that Aliyah's decoding skills will not fully support grade-level reading, which will need to be a consideration in her content-area classes (see Chapter 10), as she will need support accessing the grade-level text.
- What kind of words were read automatically and when given time? The QRI-7 graded word lists includes both commonly used words across grade levels (e.g., the third-grade word list includes words like *believe* and the sixth-grade word list includes *emerge*) as well as content words used in the corresponding grade-level passages.
  - This information can help you understand error patterns, such as commonly used words accounted for most errors, or some content words were missed on the word lists but read accurately in the passage.
- How are they decoding unknown words? Are they using vowel patterns or syllabication to help them decode? Are they utilizing morphemic units or adjusting syllable stress? Do they give up easily or guess based on how the words begin?
  - Analyzing their errors can give you some indicators about how students "attack" unknown words. Our knowledge of the developmental model (see Chapter 2)

	What are the assessments we use regularly?	Why?
word reading	• Graded word lists from informal reading inventories like the QRI-7 (Leslie & Caldwell, 2021) • San Diego Quick Assessment (LaPray & Ross, 1969) • High Frequency Word Survey from CORE (Diamond & Thorsnes, 2018) • Fry High Frequency Word Lists (Fry, 2000)	Graded word lists give us information about a student's automatic word recognition as well as some indication of their decoding. High frequency word lists focus on words that occur most often in written English; in other words, these are words our students need to read quickly and accurately to be fluent.
phonics & decoding	• Phonics Survey from CORE • Informal Decoding Inventory (Walpole, McKenna, Philippakos, & Strong, 2020) • Generating Words from Suffixes and Prefixes (Templeton et al., 2015) • Generating Words from Bases and Roots (Templeton et al., 2015)	The first two measures present both real words and nonwords organized either by phonics features or by gradations of difficulty (e.g., one-syllable to multisyllabic words). Measures of morphological knowledge become more important as a decoding assessment for older students.
spelling	• Words Their Way inventories (Bear, Invernizzi, Templeton, & Johnston, 2020) • Developmental Spelling Analysis (Ganske, 2014)	These two measures provide us with information about spelling knowledge organized by features with options by spelling stage.
fluency	• Oral reading accuracy, WCPM, and stamina from an IRI passage like the QRI-7 • Silent reading passage from IRI like QRI-7 • Multidimensional Fluency Scale (Rasinski, 2010)	Oral passage readings help us understand reading accuracy and pace as well as prosody in lengthier texts (as opposed to a 1-minute oral reading fluency passage from the screening).

* Note: this list is only suggestive and not exhaustive.

FIGURE 3.8. Pathway #1 tests.

helps us analyze more insightfully and with greater precision. In Aliyah's case, she omitted or substituted suffixes (e.g., morphemic units such as the ending suffix *-ion* in *precision*) and had difficulty flexing vowel sounds in big words when negotiating syllable stress in multisyllabic words (e.g., the vowel pattern *ai* in *explained* vs. *mountains*).

- Did the student misread highly frequent words? An important distinction here is that we are talking about highly frequent words and not sight words. A sight word is a word you know at first sight; in fact, every word in this book is likely a "sight word" for you. But a high-frequency word is a word that occurs frequently in written English. Automatic recognition of high-frequency words impacts the flow of reading and text coherence and contributes to overall reading fluency.
  - While we don't always include assessments of high-frequency words for older readers, we do draw upon them from time to time when we notice a student has a particular need in this area. For example, we've worked with older students who have basically formed bad habits. They started out misreading these words in previous grades, and they have continued to just read through them, misreading as they go. If we suspect this based on their reading accuracy in the IRI, it is good to get a measure from a survey of high-frequency words to confirm this issue.
  - One note: The CORE High Frequency Word Survey goes up to fourth grade; however, the authors say it can be used in fifth grade and up if applicable. Fry's High Frequency Word Lists come in sets of 100—the first 100 most frequent words, the second 100 most frequent words, and so forth. So, the lists start out with words like *the* and *is* from the first 100 and *actually* and *bought* on the tenth (and last) 100.

Phonics and Decoding. The graded word lists above assess a reader's sight word knowledge. However, what if a reader doesn't recognize a word immediately? Do they have enough "word knowledge" to figure out unknown words? This is where phonics and decoding assessments come in. These assessments target their phonics (the systematic relationship between letters and sounds), syllable (common syllable patterns and the influence of stress), and morphological (the smallest units of meaning, like *pro-* in *proactive* or *-ity* in *creativity*) knowledge to decode words they don't recognize automatically. We've already gotten some indicator of their phonics knowledge and decoding skill using the graded word lists from the IRI. While this is useful information, it is only one indicator. We sometimes follow up with measures of phonics and decoding.

- Considering the error patterns noted from the IRI graded word lists, do we notice similar phonics and decoding difficulties on a measure targeting these two skills?
  - The Phonics Survey from CORE and the Informal Decoding Inventory are

both options you can use in the middle grades; however, we do find that they become less helpful once students are comfortably reading, around a fourth- or fifth-grade level. But for our students who are not able to reach higher percentages of word reading accuracy at these levels, they can provide insight into your students' phonics knowledge and decoding skill.

- Did the student have difficulty reading words with morphemic units? Common phonics and decoding assessments don't typically include focused attention on morphemic units. This is problematic because older students need to build their morphological analysis skill set—their ability to break down words into prefixes, suffixes, base words, and roots. This becomes increasingly important as they engage with more complex texts.
  - Two assessments we've used that provide insight into a student's understanding of the morphological structure of English are from *Words Their Way: Vocabulary for Middle and Secondary Students* (Templeton et al., 2015). Both assessments task students with producing as many words as they can within a given time using a selection of morphological word parts (e.g., words using the prefix *dis-* like *dislike* or the root *tract-* like *traction*). These assessments, however, are most useful once a student is comfortably reading around a fourth- or fifth-grade level.

Spelling. There is a growing consensus that spelling knowledge contributes to overall literacy success. Because spelling inventories can be group-administered fairly quickly (around 15 minutes), some schools we work with use them as part of their screening or brief diagnostic steps. Through spelling, students refine their representations of words and strengthen their ability to store and retrieve intact words. We have always considered spelling to provide great insight into a student's word knowledge, and we continue to see it as a common area of specific difficulty with older students.

- Diving into Pathway #1 always includes an in-depth look at spelling. We use either the spelling inventories from *Words Their Way* (Bear et al., 2020) or *Word Journeys* (Ganske, 2014). These provide you with information about a student's spelling "stage" (see either book for a detailed explanation) as well as insight into the specific features they have yet to grasp. We often note which words they spelled quickly and which ones they took some time on. Sometimes older students quickly spell everything—even if they miss many words. This is also helpful information.
  - We've noticed that sometimes students, especially older students, can decode features they can't spell. So, we always compare across phonics/decoding assessments and spelling. We might have a false understanding of what a student understands if we only consider their phonics knowledge and decoding skill.

- With older students, we've also found that diving a little deeper than the inventories can sometimes provide very helpful data. For example, older students, especially middle-grades students, have been around the block. They have memorized a chunk of words. So, we often probe spelling a little more with four techniques: (1) "why" questions, (2) "what if" prompts, (3) what looks right, and (4) low-frequency words.
  - We sometimes ask "why" questions after a student has spelled a word. For example, many older students will double the consonant in a word like *swimming* because they've read and written that word many times before. We know the concept of consonant doubling is a key concept as students transition to reading and spelling multisyllabic words, so we follow up by asking, "I noticed you put two *m*'s in *swimming.* Why did you do that?" We're looking for them to make note of the short vowel in the base word *swim*.
  - Sometimes we notice a pattern of misunderstanding, such as vowel patterns. We might notice a student spelling words like *pouch* as *powch* or *contain* as *contane*. So, we might use a "what if" prompt. Let's take *pouch*. We might say, "I see you wrote *p-ow-ch* for pouch. What if I told you that wasn't quite right? The /ou/ is actually spelled a different way." We're looking for them to realize they chose the wrong /ou/ pattern and quickly switch out "ow" for "ou."
  - Other times, we might invite them to look through their words and check the ones they think look right and then circle the ones they are not sure about. Then we'll engage them in a conversation about which parts of those circled words they think they've spelled incorrectly. Let's think back to *pouch* as *powch*. Students often quickly note the vowel pattern as the error. Invite them to try it again. Note: We always have them write any new spellings to the side, so we have access to all their spellings to see the ways they are thinking about words.
  - Lastly, sometimes the spelling inventories use words that are just more frequent, and we want to make sure we fully unpack their understandings. So, let's think back to *swimming*. This is a more common word, so we often ask students to spell a couple of less common words that double the consonant, like *trotting* and *shrugged*.

Fluency. We commonly think of three components of fluency: accuracy, automaticity (we sometimes use the term *speed* or *rate*), and prosody. In other words, fluency is the ability to quickly and accurately read words in texts with appropriate expression and phrasing. We think stamina is equally important, especially when it comes to older readers (Stahl et al., 2020). Reading stamina, or endurance, is a student's ability to focus and read lengthier texts and/or for longer periods of time.

- We already have at least one oral reading passage from the brief diagnostic assessment. Now we want to dive into reading fluency a bit more. This can take us in different directions based on the student. A general first step is to administer a grade-level passage even if the student had less than 50% on the graded word list for that level. Why do that? It's important to understand how older students engage with grade-level text, because they will have to do this throughout their school day. Is there ever a scenario when we wouldn't do this? Yes! If the student is reading significantly below grade level (we define this as three or more grade levels below), then do not administer a grade-level passage. In this case, you might want to administer a "challenge" level (we define this as one to two grade levels above their brief diagnostic passage level) to get an idea of how they engage with challenging text.
- We frequently unpack fluency in the following ways, thinking about accuracy, automaticity, prosody, and stamina.
  - *Accuracy*—We complement the passage reading from the brief assessment with a "challenge" passage (grade-level if we can) to see how a student's accuracy might be impacted as the text level increases. As mentioned previously, we use readability levels in the IRI manual (e.g., Lexile levels in the QRI-7) to help us ensure a gradation of text difficulty.
  - *Automaticity*—We generally look at automaticity in two ways: (1) "challenge" texts and (2) silent reading. We can use the WCPM from the "challenge" text to see how automaticity is impacted as text level increases. With older students who truly struggle in Pathway #1, we sometimes see a trend of accurate yet slow reading in "challenge" texts while maintaining reasonable comprehension. While we do not always administer a silent reading passage, it can be helpful to us, especially when we notice a student who seems to not "keep up" with their group. Older students' silent reading rate should be faster than their oral reading rate, so we sometimes shift our oral reading rate to WPM and compare that to their WPM while reading a passage at the same level silently (we also keep to the same genre—both narrative or both expository). Notice that we changed WCPM to WPM here. This is because we will not have a measure of word reading accuracy for silent reads, so we shift our thinking to WPM, or simply, words per minute.
  - *Prosody*—Some older students can read with accuracy and automaticity but with limited prosody. In other words, while they're accurate and read at an appropriate pace, their reading lacks the expression and phrasing we would expect. This may be a sign of inexperience with the advanced language structures of more complex texts (e.g., multiple clauses in a sentence) and/or an issue with comprehension. We sometimes use the fluency rating scale in the IRI we are using, but if the IRI doesn't have one or we want something more robust, we often turn to the Multidimensional Fluency Scale (Rasinski, 2010).

- *Stamina*—This one is a hard one to capture in a passage reading. However, stamina is one reason we shoot for lengthier passages (i.e., 300-plus words). It is also another reason we administer a "challenge" text. With longer texts and challenge texts, we can begin to ask two questions: (1) Can they maintain their focus in longer texts that might take them 5 minutes or more to read, and (2) how do they maintain their focus when the going gets tough in a "challenge" text? While these passage readings only provide us with some insight into the student's reading stamina, they can alert us to this as an area to prioritize and help us identify materials for our interventions.

Pathway #2. Diagnostic Follow-up Assessments: Oral Language Comprehension Plus Reading Comprehension

As Stahl, Flanigan, and McKenna (2020) put it, the reading demands for older students become increasingly more about the "what"—vocabulary and prior knowledge. The texts older students are grappling with in school have an increased challenge of: (1) domain-specific vocabulary and related concepts, (2) general academic vocabulary and phrases that tie these domain-specific words and concepts together, such as *however* and *in other words*, (3) prior knowledge related to the vocabulary and concepts, and (4) unfamiliar academic language or turns of phrase common within a discipline like *characteristic of*, *density*, or *hypothesize* in science. "The interaction of multiple pressure points—prior knowledge, academic vocabulary, genre, text structure, working memory, self-regulation, and motivation—plays an increasingly greater role in reading success for older students" (p. 277) and Pathways #2 and #3 help us explore these "multiple pressure points" in more depth.

See Figure 3.9 for a list of possible assessments that target the following components along Pathway #2: (1) vocabulary (2) prior/background knowledge, (3) text structure, and (4) reading comprehension. In the following section, we unpack these assessments and discuss their purposes.

Vocabulary. Vocabulary knowledge is crucial to understanding texts. Even if a student has automatic word recognition and can decode words with ease, they will have difficulty comprehending what they read if they don't have adequate vocabulary knowledge.

- Vocabulary Recognition Task (VRT; Stahl & Bravo, 2010) provides a yes–no framework for a formative vocabulary assessment. While it's only been studied with elementary grades, we've found it useful through the middle grades as well. We've adjusted it for our purposes slightly. First, we choose 15–25 target vocabulary words we think will be critical to understanding a text. Then we choose 6–8 foils, or words unrelated to the main concept of the text (e.g., reading about ancient civilizations, we might have target vocabulary like *Mesopotamia, Egypt, pharaoh,*

	What are the assessments we use regularly?	Why?
vocabulary	• Vocabulary Recognition Task (VRT; Stahl & Bravo, 2010) • Vocabulary Screening Test (VST) from CORE	The VRT provides a framework we use to assess vocabulary knowledge prior to reading about a specific concept while the VST is a proxy for the vocabulary knowledge needed to engage with a target grade-level text.
prior knowlege	• Prior knowledge questions or discussions from an IRI like the QRI-7	Prior knowledge is situation-based, making it difficult to unpack. So, we use prereading questions to make a general assessment of a student's prior knowledge of a topic.
text structure	• Informal questions and discussions about sentence and text structure during or after reading a passage from an IRI	One of the best ways we've found to assess text structure is to engage students informally through questions and discussions while reading a variety of texts.
reading comprehension	• Open-ended questions after reading a passage from an IRI and "looking back" to the text as needed • Embedded questions like the think-aloud protocol and inferential passages from the QRI-7 • Contrast with listening comprehension • Writing in response to reading	Comprehension is multifaceted and dependent on many factors; we use passages from IRIs to help explore this comprehension. In fact, in a review of comprehension assessments, the QRI was determined to be an "excellent diagnostic" (Morsy, Kieffer, & Snow, 2010).

* Note: this list is only suggestive and not exhaustive.

FIGURE 3.9. Pathway #2 tests.

empire, and *chariots*, with foils like *United States*, *president*, and *trains*). List the words in three columns and invite students to circle all words they are sure they can read and are related to the main concept. After they've circled words, we often have them sort the words into categories and then explain their choices/categories (similar to List-Group-Label; Tierney & Readence, 2005). While we could score this, we usually use it more as a formative measure to help us understand patterns of vocabulary knowledge across texts. Not only do we get an idea of words we should explicitly teach, but we also start to get a better understanding of whether vocabulary knowledge is a typical obstacle for specific students.

- Vocabulary Screening Test (VST) from CORE uses grade-level lists of vocabulary words alongside three answer choices. Students read each target word silently and underline the word that means the same or about the same as the target word. CORE suggests beginning with the student's corresponding grade-level list. If a student gets less than 50% of the words correct, then they are likely to have significant difficulty understanding grade-level texts—either because of the vocabulary load or because of decoding limitations. Scores between 50 and 74% indicate the student may have some difficulty. While this is just an indicator of possible difficulty, we've found the VST is a useful tool to unpack potential obstacles.
  - There are two forms; the authors suggest they are not to be given at the same time and should be used as pre/posttests to gauge student progress in building generalized vocabulary knowledge.
  - We've adapted this process to administer the previous grade-level list until the student scores at least 75%. Another adaptation is to use Form A for reading vocabulary and Form B for listening vocabulary; this means students read the words when they respond to Form A, and we read the words and choices aloud when they respond to Form B.

Prior Knowledge. Closely tied to vocabulary is prior knowledge. Students with greater prior knowledge not only have increased vocabulary knowledge in the topic, but they also have better comprehension as opposed to texts where they have limited prior knowledge. Older students are often asked to read texts about topics for which they don't have prior knowledge. In fact, a main goal in school is learning about a new topic by reading. So, it's helpful to know how well a student can use their prior knowledge when reading about topics for which they have rich prior knowledge and to know how well they can understand texts when they have little to no prior knowledge.

- We sometimes use the prior knowledge questions or discussions from an IRI like the QRI-7 (or you can create your own if your IRI doesn't include them). We've found three to four questions to be sufficient to get a general understanding.

Score student responses holistically using a 3-point scale: 3 points = strong relevant prior knowledge, 2 points = adequate/some or mixed relevant prior knowledge, and 1 point = little to no relevant prior knowledge. For example, before Zach read *Building Pyramids*, a sixth-grade level passage from the QRI-7, he was asked what a *pharaoh* is and he responded, "A pharaoh is like a president." He was also asked what an *archeologist* is, and he said, "An archeologist is someone who works in a museum." Both of these answers would yield a score of 1 point.

Text Structure. Text structures are the organizational structures used in written texts. These can be within paragraphs or longer texts. They inform us of an author's purpose (e.g., compare/contrast or describe) and support our understanding of that purpose. They often have key academic language associated with them (e.g., *although, as well as, either . . . or* are common in compare/contrast texts); these words or phrases are often called "signals," as they give us clues to the text structure.

- During or after a passage reading (either oral or silent), we engage students in a brief discussion about sentence and text structure. We'll pull out a sentence with complex structure and ask a follow-up question. Or we'll focus on a paragraph and ask questions that require the student to connect across sentences. For example, imagine Zach read the following sentence from a fifth-grade passage from the QRI-7: "The homesteaders faced many obstacles, such as harsh weather conditions and deadly natural disasters." We might follow up by asking Zach, "What obstacles did homesteaders face?" Or in this same passage, we might ask what a *homesteader* is after reading the second paragraph, because defining this term requires connecting across multiple sentences.
- After reading a text, we sometimes ask students to identify the text structure and justify their thinking. Or we show them graphic organizer options (e.g., Venn diagram, semantic web), have the student choose the best option for the text, and then talk us through their reason for that choice. Sometimes we've found it useful to have students underline "signal" words that help them determine the text structure.
- The way students "look back" can sometimes indicate their text-structure knowledge. Students who look back in the text and go right to the section in the text needed to answer a question likely have at least adequate text-structure knowledge. Students who have to go back and start rereading from the beginning likely don't have as strong a sense of text structure.

Reading Comprehension. While Pathway #2 is about language comprehension, we've included reading comprehension here as well. As clearly mapped out in

Chapter 2, reading comprehension is the ultimate goal of reading and the outcome of the pathways of the cognitive model successfully working together. Comprehension assessment is a snapshot of how well a student comprehends that one text at that one moment. Moreover, comprehension can be impacted by many factors, such as limited or rich prior knowledge, limited or successful decoding skill, and minimal or optimal engagement.

Even though comprehension assessment can be considered a bit of a moving target, it does provide us with estimates about: (1) how well a student can generally comprehend and (2) how well a student comprehends a specific text. We always use open-ended questions and look-backs and sometimes bring in embedded questions or compare reading comprehension with listening comprehension. Lastly, we often invite students to write in response to reading, especially in the middle grades.

- We use the open-ended questions after reading a passage from an IRI, and we already have some information from the questions in the brief diagnostic assessment. We can think about the amount of prompting necessary or differences between explicit and implicit questions. If we find a student has particular difficulty comprehending texts, we might decide to unpack this more by administering an additional passage using an expository passage.
  - It's common for older readers to have more success reading and comprehending narrative texts and more difficulty with expository texts, depending on their familiarity with the topics. Learning from what you read is a main goal of schooling, so getting an estimate of how well a student can "learn" from an expository passage is instructionally useful.
- "Looking back" to the text provides valuable diagnostic information. As stated previously, looking back to a text is a more accurate estimate of older students' reading comprehension. Otherwise, we might be assessing memory and recall rather than reading comprehension. Think about it this way—as adults, even we must look back to texts after we've only had one reading, especially if we are reading about an unfamiliar topic. Looking back to text to remember what we've read and to clarify our understanding is how we read in life.
  - Pay attention to how students use the text. For example, do they start at the very beginning and start reading again? Or do they remember that the question was answered toward the end, or do they scan for a key word? Comprehension is an "in-the-head" process, so sometimes we have to explicitly ask how they found the answer.
  - Previously, we talked about having students read a "challenge" text (see fluency section). Using look-backs is especially useful with challenge texts, since students may expend more energy and thought on reading the words as opposed

to understanding them. Providing them the opportunity to look back will give you a more accurate sense of what they have taken away from the text.

- Embedded questions like the think-aloud protocol and inferential passages from the QRI-7 can also provide insight. For example, a sixth-grade inferential expository passage from the QRI-7 dynasties of ancient Egypt embeds questions within the passage that require students to infer meanings of words (e.g., "What is the meaning of *stable* in the context of the paragraph above?"); identify a central idea (e.g., "What is the central idea of the above two paragraphs?"); or use text evidence to substantiate an inference (e.g., "What evidence in the text indicates that ancient Egyptians were probably afraid to go against or oppose the pharaoh?").
- Contrast reading comprehension with listening comprehension. Many older students have a higher listening comprehension level relative to what we might think of as their "reading level." So, we assess listening comprehension for students who have difficulty understanding texts they read.
  - To assess a student's listening comprehension, we *read aloud* an IRI passage to them. Choose a grade-level passage and make sure it's one the student hasn't previously read. Ask comprehension questions as you normally would. Listening comprehension lets us know if the student can understand grade-level texts. If a student does well with listening comprehension but struggles to understand texts they read, then it's the reading burden that's impacting comprehension. This information helps us prioritize our intervention targets, group students, and set goals.
- We also regularly have students write in response to reading. This is a task we often pair with note-taking (see Pathway #3). Writing in response to reading to demonstrate your understanding of a topic is a common task for older students in school.
  - To mimic this process, we have students silently read an expository text at a level aligned with the passage level from the brief diagnostic assessment. So, if the student read a passage around a 700 Lexile level in the brief assessment, we'll choose an expository text close to that level. After the student silently reads the passage, we direct them to write a summary to outline the main ideas from the passage.
  - We like to time how long the student spends on this writing. Then we evaluate their summary. Were the main ideas represented? Were relevant details included? Does the summary demonstrate how ideas are related and does it reflect the text structure of the passage? Notice, these questions are about summarizing and not about composition. For this particular task, our main questions are about comprehension and articulating their understanding of something they read in writing.

Pathway #3. Diagnostic Follow-up Assessments: Strategic Knowledge

When it comes to older students, it is not just the *texts* they are required to read that are becoming more difficult. The *tasks* we ask them to perform are also more difficult than in the primary grades. For example, we frequently ask them to *summarize* their reading or *source texts* for evidence to support an argument. Open-ended questions after a passage reading provide us with an estimate of a student's understanding, but as students move across the grades, it becomes important for us to consider how they engage in the types of thinking they'll be expected to do in school. Moreover, as grade levels increase, students are expected to work with increasingly lengthier, more challenging texts across longer periods of independent work time. The assessments we draw upon to unpack Pathway #3 mirror everyday classroom tasks or examine their strategy knowledge and motivation.

See Figure 3.10 for a list of possible assessments that target the following components along Pathway #3: (1) purpose for reading, (2) strategy awareness, and (3) motivation for reading. We describe each assessment and its purpose here.

Purpose for Reading. When working with older students, we usually ask them to talk about what makes someone a good reader. Students who have struggled as readers usually say things like "They know a lot of words," "They read fast," or "They can read longer books." Or we've asked what makes something hard to read. These answers follow suit, with the most common being "big words." Students who have experienced success as readers usually focus on comprehension. For example, a good reader understands what they read, or something is hard to read when the vocabulary or topic is unfamiliar. With this focus on understanding, these more successful readers tend to adapt their purpose of reading and apply strategies to increase engagement and understanding as needed. In contrast, as stated earlier, it is not uncommon for students who struggle with reading to view the act of reading as something to get through rather than something to do with purpose and engagement.

- A common reading purpose in upper grades is *taking notes* and using those notes to prepare for quizzes and tests. We can easily get some understanding of students' note-taking strategy using an expository passage from an IRI.
  - Have the student silently read an expository passage. As with writing in response to reading in the reading comprehension section in Pathway #2, we usually choose a passage level aligned with the level chosen for the brief diagnostic assessment. Tell the student they will read to themselves and take notes as they normally would. We usually time how long they take reading and note-taking. After they finish, we let them use their notes as we ask the open-ended questions, making note of when they reference their notes. Finally, we ask them about their note-taking strategy.

	What are the assessments we use regularly?	Why?
purpose for reading	• Note-taking while silently reading a passage from an IRI	Taking notes while reading an expository passage is an easy way to get a gauge of how a student determines main points.
strategy awareness	• Metacognitive Awareness of Reading Strategies Inventory (MARSI; Mokhtari, Dimitrov, & Reichard, 2018) • Embedded questions like the think-aloud protocol from an IRI passage • Textbook interview (Stahl et al., 2020)	The MARSI is brief and gives us a look at strategy awareness while embedded questions take a bit longer but give a more detailed look. A textbook interview provides an authentic context to unpack strategy use.
motivation for reading	• Motivation to Read Profile-Revised (MPR-R; Malloy et al., 2013) • Reader Self-Perception Scale (RSPS; Henk et al., 2012) • Survey of Adolescent Reading Attitudes (SARA; McKenna et al., 2012)	These three measures provide us with information about a student's self-concept and attitudes as a reader.

* Note: this list is only suggestive and not exhaustive.

FIGURE 3.10. Pathway #3 tests.

- While we often do this with individual students, it can be administered with a small group. For example, you can provide students with passages to read silently and take notes, skip the open-ended questions (since note-taking is your main question), and engage the small group in a sort of focus group discussion about note-taking strategies.

- Another common reading purpose is *summarizing* a topic to demonstrate your learning in content-area classes. Summary writing also helps assess whether a student can determine essential ideas and consolidate important details of support. When we ask students to summarize, we invite them to read a passage to themselves (silently or aloud—their choice) and then write a summary paragraph. This can also be a follow-up to the note-taking task; we ask them to write a summary after they've written their notes and answered the open-ended questions. Andres's homeroom teacher recently scored one of his summaries using a fifth-grade rubric (see Figure 3.11). Andres did not accurately identify the main idea and included irrelevant details. Perhaps more importantly, he took very little of the allotted time writing a summary of two sentences and one fragment. His teacher wondered if Andres didn't understand what he read, didn't know how to write a summary, or was unmotivated or disengaged with the task.

Strategy Awareness. Insight into a student's strategy use gives you a glimpse into how they navigate "challenging" texts as well as their reading engagement. In other words, we want to understand students' metacognitive reading strategies as

3	2	1	No Score
Main idea clearly stated	Main idea is mentioned	Main idea is not present	No response or response does not relate to the text
Essential, relevant details included	Important details included but some missing	Contains irrelevant details	
Understanding is clearly demonstrated	Understanding is adequately demonstrated	Little to no understanding is demonstrated	
Main idea and details are in own words	Main idea and details in own words with some exact language from the text	Exact language from text that is copied seemingly indiscriminately	

FIGURE 3.11. Summary rubric.

they relate to understanding what they read. Metacognition (or thinking about our thinking) and strategy use are critical to comprehension and learning.

- The Metacognitive Awareness of Reading Strategies Inventory (MARSI; Mokhtari, Dimitrov, & Reichard, 2018) uses self-report to assess students' metacognitive awareness or perceived use of reading strategies. Students make note of how often, using a scale, they use strategies such as "stopping from time to time to think about what I'm reading." MARSI probes across global reading strategies, problem-solving strategies, and support reading strategies. The MARSI can be used with students in sixth grade and up.
- Sometimes we'll opt for embedded questions rather than something like MARSI because they can provide us with a specific reading context (e.g., science text or social studies topic). The QRI-7 uses a think-aloud protocol starting at the sixth-grade level, but you can do this with any passage. The QRI-7 advises to model thinking aloud first, have the student read the passage through one time, and then have the student reread while thinking aloud. Ask nonspecific questions to probe their thinking before, during, and after reading. Stop at key points of the passage and ask questions like, "What are you thinking right now?" The QRI-7 also provides a think-aloud scoring grid, which is generic and can be used across passages. For example, Ms. Hauser (one of the school reading specialists) recently had Andres read word lists from the QRI-7 and read aloud a fourth-grade passage about early railroads. After reading the first two paragraphs, she asked him, "What are you thinking right now?" To which Andres replied, "I rode on a train once." After reading the next paragraph, she stopped with the same prompt. Andres replied with another tangentially related response but not specific to the information provided in the passage. Not surprisingly, his comprehension of the passage was limited.
- Not all of our content classes use textbooks, but if we know a student will need to engage with a textbook (or if a student is having difficulty in a class that uses a textbook), we can get a detailed look at how a student navigates textbooks using the textbook interview (Stahl et al., 2020). This interview explores both narrative and expository texts. The textbook interview can help us think more globally about how students are navigating texts.

Motivation for Reading. As teachers of older students, we all know how difficult it is to engage readers who have a history of reading difficulty. These students often see reading as something to get through rather than something to enjoy or learn from. As the grades increase, the demands of texts and tasks increase as does a reader's disengagement. In fact, disengaged readers read 500% less than engaged readers (Guthrie, 2004). Reading less means students have less practice to build their skills, which often results in diminished reading skills, motivation, and engagement. As a result, a reader's self-efficacy decreases. When we have concerns about a reader's self-concept or motivation, we often turn to the Motivation to Read Profile—Revised (MPR-R; Malloy, Marinak, Gambrell, & Mazzoni, 2013), the Reader Self-Perception Scale (RSPS; Henk, Marinak, & Melnick, 2012), or the Survey of Adolescent Reading Attitudes (SARA; McKenna, Conradi, Lawrence, Jang, & Meyer, 2012).

- MPR-R was developed to be used in the second through sixth grades. It measures a reader's self-concept as a reader and their value of reading. There are two parts: (1) a survey you can administer with groups and (2) an individual follow-up conversational interview. Students respond to questions/prompts like "I am a ____________ reader (reader self-concept) and "My friends think reading is . . ." (value of reading). The authors describe how teachers can use the tool to identify potential development areas for individual students as well as potential areas for instructional reflection/improvement. For example, Ms. Hauser gave the survey to all of her fifth-grade intervention students. On an item about what happens when the teacher asks a question about the reading, many students said they can either almost never or sometimes think of an answer. But no student said they can always think of an answer. The students' responses to that item made Ms. Hauser reflect on how she can support them more with answering questions but also how she can boost their confidence.
- RSPS is designed for students in seventh through tenth grades and gauges how students feel about themselves as readers. Students self-report as they respond to statements like "I am more confident than other students about my reading"; "Deep down, I like to read"; "My teachers think my reading is fine"; and "Vocabulary words are easier for me to understand when I read now." These are loaded into four dimensions of self-efficacy: progress, observational comparison, social feedback, and physiological states. When we've given this in the past, we sometimes have read the statements aloud, and we always implore the students to be honest and thoughtful about their responses.
- For sixth through eighth grades, SARA is another self-report survey where students respond to questions like "How do you feel about reading a textbook?" and "How do you feel about texting or emailing friends in your free time?" SARA is interested in how students feel about reading across academic and recreational settings as well as with print or digital texts.

Step 4: Intervention Plan

The last step in the assessment flowchart brings the intervention team together to analyze all assessment information. The intervention team can be comprised of reading specialists, literacy coaches, classroom teachers, content-area teachers, and special educators as needed. This step confirms the pathway priority and leads the group in designing an intervention plan, including goals for the grading period (e.g., 9 weeks) and ways to monitor progress. The beginning of each of the case study chapters (Chapters 4–9) details the team's analysis, discussion, and intervention plan for our three focus students—Aliyah (eighth grader—Pathway #1), Zach (sixth grader—Pathways #2 and #3), and Andres (fifth grader—Pathway #3).

THE ASSESSMENT FLOWCHART IN ACTION

In the International Literacy Association's leadership brief on literacy assessment, Wixson (International Literacy Association, 2017) stated, "Reading and writing are complex areas to assess. No single assessment can include all aspects of these complex processes. What's more, there are multiple purposes for literacy assessment, and no single assessment can serve all purposes. Together, these facts make it clear that literacy assessment is much more complicated than many realize. In short, literacy assessment needs to reflect the multiple dimensions of reading and writing and the various purposes for assessment as well as the diversity of the students being assessed" (p. 2). Assessment is the first step in addressing the diverse strengths and challenges of our students as we purposefully use assessment to build on strengths, identify specific literacy needs, and provide assessment-based interventions.

CHAPTER 4

Building Automatic Word Recognition with Aliyah

Aliyah, our eighth grader introduced in Chapter 1, brings many strengths to the intervention setting. She is a leader in school government, an athlete, and a strong student. She has excellent social and communication skills, a robust vocabulary, and a rich background knowledge that supports her strong oral comprehension of grade-level concepts.

In terms of literacy support, Aliyah has received interventions since fifth grade. All of these interventions focused on either fluency or comprehension; however, they never got to the root cause of her difficulties—automatic word recognition. This root cause became apparent when, as an eighth grader, Aliyah was administered two screening measures at the beginning of the school year: (1) an oral reading fluency (ORF) passage and (2) a Maze comprehension task.

It wasn't a surprise when Aliyah scored below the grade-level benchmarks on both tasks because of her intervention history. The middle school intervention team met to discuss their students to figure out intervention priorities, determine groups, and map out goals with tools to monitor progress. When Aliyah was discussed, the team quickly began unpacking her screening results, her participation during class, and how to best support her.

ALIYAH'S AUTOMATIC WORD READING CHALLENGES: INITIAL SCREENING RESULTS

Following are Aliyah's screening results and her team's initial thinking about her challenges:

- *Maze:* Aliyah's Maze score fell below the benchmark. This follows suit with her Maze history with scores below the benchmark starting in fifth grade.

- *ORF:* Aliyah read the eighth-grade passage with 91% accuracy and 95 WCPM. While she had reasonable access to words in the text (91% accuracy), her reading speed (95 WCPM) was significantly below the benchmark. Aliyah's history of ORF scores shows accuracy percentages always above 90% and a steady, but slow, increase in her WCPM.

- Her core content teachers reported two main points regarding Aliyah's day-to-day performance across her classes:

  - Overall, her teachers described her as an active participant during class discussions, with relevant contributions to topics that have been *orally* presented. Her affect, however, shifts when asked to read for understanding or demonstrate her knowledge in writing. One of her teachers said, "You actually watch her body fold as her shoulders slump and her head goes down." She is compliant during these points of class, but her engaged, active student self is no longer. Aliyah's teachers went on to say that she often doesn't complete these types of in-class activities in the allotted time when the work is independent and not supported in a group.
  - Aliyah's understanding of content appears to be bolstered by oral classroom lessons and discussions. For example, Mr. Allison, her history teacher, shared one of her most recent responses to their chapter reading guides. Not only were Aliyah's responses short, but they also often missed the main points from the readings and were even sometimes very difficult to read given her spelling and grammatical errors. Mr. Allison was quick to say, though, that after their class lectures and discussions on this same content following the chapter reading, Aliyah's document-based question response (DBQ) met the requirements. Aliyah's reading guides are completed on paper, but her DBQs are on her Chromebook where she can take advantage of speech-to-text and spell/grammar check.

- The team was left with the following question: What could account for Aliyah's ability to learn during oral presentations and strength (plus confidence!) in oral communication relative to her difficulties learning from what she reads and expressing herself in writing? They preliminarily ruled out Pathways #2 and #3, leaving Pathway #1 (automatic word recognition) as the most plausible reason for the difficulties she is experiencing. They wanted to explore this more with diagnostic assessments to make sure the intervention was the best fit for her needs.

ALIYAH'S DIAGNOSTIC FOLLOW-UP ASSESSMENTS

Mr. Jackson, one of the school's reading specialists, did a brief diagnostic assessment with graded word lists and a sixth-grade oral passage reading (see Chapters 3 and 5 for more details on Aliyah's assessments). Right away, he made note of Aliyah's limited automatic word recognition, so he decided to explore underlying skills that can impact reading and writing performance (Pathway #1). Mr. Jackson collected Aliyah's reading errors across the graded word lists and the oral passage reading to explore her decoding skills, and he administered the Words Their Way Upper Spelling Inventory (Bear et al., 2020) to better understand her word knowledge through spelling.

- *Decoding*—Aliyah had difficulty using decoding skills expected to successfully read middle-grades texts; for example, when she read words from graded word lists, she often omitted or substituted suffixes and had difficulty flexing vowel sounds in big words when syllable stress comes into the picture. She was, however, much more successful decoding reading passages when she could take advantage of context.

- *Spelling*—Aliyah scored 7 out of 31, indicating she is a within-word pattern speller. She demonstrated challenges in spelling where she even had trouble accurately representing advanced vowel patterns in single-syllable words; in other words, she had difficulty with spelling skills associated with the elementary grades.

In fact, Aliyah seemed to rely on visual memory to read and spell words. For example, on a measure of word reading, she sometimes substituted similar words when reading (e.g., reading *totally* for *tolerate* and *probably* for *problems*). When asked to spell the word *juice,* she started looking up, searching her mind like she was using her mind's eye to find the letter sequence. She wrote *juces* and then said, "That doesn't look right. I know there is an *i* in there somewhere." Figure 4.1 provides a little more detail about her errors when reading and spelling words with notes about what Aliyah demonstrates she knows alongside what she finds difficult.

Aliyah's diagnostic assessment revealed the following about her word recognition:

- Without the support of context (where she can use her strong oral language skills and background knowledge), Aliyah could not successfully decode big words (i.e., multisyllabic words).
- She had significant difficulty accurately spelling words, even single-syllable words. Her spelling challenges resulted in short written responses that often didn't reflect what she knows, because she steered clear of words she couldn't spell, restricting her word choice.
- Taken together, these points target Pathway #1 as her primary area of challenge. In Figure 4.2, we can clearly see how reading fluency depends on word recognition and decoding.

	word	reading	spelling	what Aliyah knows	what she finds difficult
		Aliyah's response		what this shows us	
reading	captive	cap - tive		provides a plausible pronunciation	uses long vowel instead of schwa; doesn't recognize -ive suffix as /iv/
reading	bison	biss - on		provides a plausible pronunciation	uses short sound for beginning syllable; uses short sound for ending rather than schwa
reading	infectious	infecting		recognizes the base word	doesn't recognize the suffix or the "ti" letter sequence shifting "ti" to /sh/
reading	irresponsible	skipped			likely overwhelmed by the length of the word
reading	obtainable	ob - tain; ub - tain		provides a plausible pronunciation	uses short sound for beginning syllable; omits the suffix
spelling	trapped		traped	uses -ed inflected ending and base word	doesn't double to maintain the short a
spelling	strain		strane	includes a vowel pattern to indicate the long a	chooses the wrong spelling option for the long a
spelling	humor		hummer	indicated knowledge of the first syllable u and the r-controlled ending	doesn't think about the open first syllable u; confuses final /er/
spelling	terrible		tearbole	considers an analogy to the known word "tear"	doesn't think about the suffix -ible
spelling	switch		swich	provides a plausible spelling	doesn't consider the consonant pattern "tch" with single-syllable short vowel words

FIGURE 4.1. Aliyah's word reading and spelling errors, plus explanations.

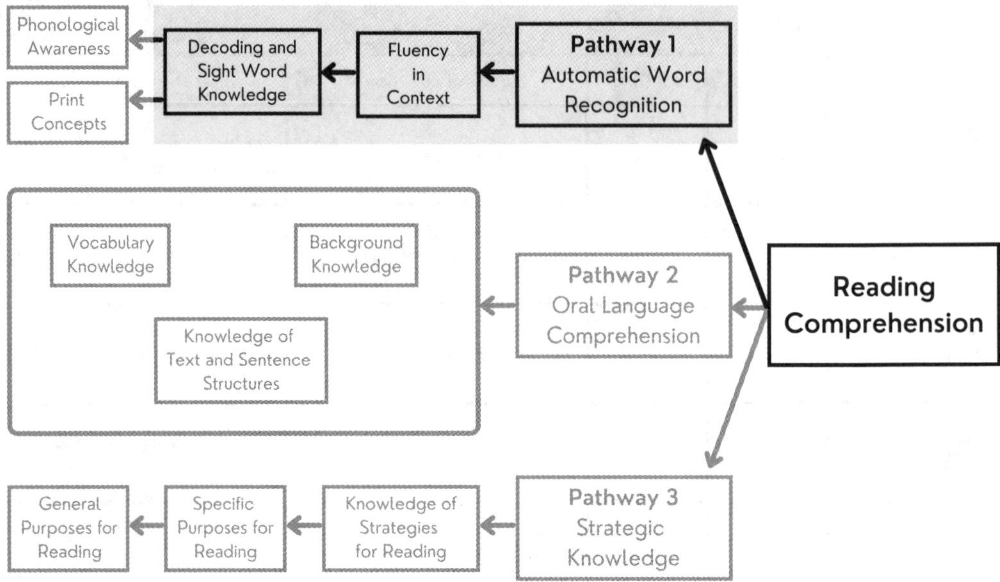

FIGURE 4.2. The cognitive model—Pathway #1. Adapted with permission from Stahl, Flanigan, & McKenna (2020). Copyright 2020 by The Guilford Press.

ALIYAH'S TEAM'S QUESTIONS ABOUT AUTOMATIC WORD RECOGNITION

In the next intervention team meeting, Mr. Jackson shared these results. The team discussed the following questions:

- Aliyah is an eighth grader, so why does she still struggle with decoding and spelling? And why does this persist after she has received interventions in previous years?
- Why does word knowledge matter? I mean, if she can decode more words when she reads in context, isn't that enough?
- What should Aliyah's intervention look like? What does the research say?

Why Does Aliyah Still Struggle with Decoding and Spelling? And Why Does This Persist After Interventions?

Our brains do not have systems designed for reading. Our brains have to repurpose and reorganize the neural circuits for language and visual processing to support learning to read and write (Vaughn & Fletcher, 2021; Wolf, 2018). "The lack of a blueprint for reading circuitry means that its formation is subject to considerable variation, based on the reader's specific language requirements and learning environments" (Wolf, 2018, p. 13). So, if we trace back to early literacy learning, Aliyah needed to take what is an implicit understanding of the sound system of language—at the phonological level—and explicitly apply it to print. "Once this repurposing begins, another neural circuit designed for face and object recognition has to become a rapid letter and word processor; this reorganization of the circuit requires considerable meaningful exposure to print" (Vaughn & Fletcher, 2017, p. 5). At this point, these circuits form a system to process print.

Okay, but what happened to Aliyah? Did her system to process print not form properly? While learning to read in the primary grades, Aliyah likely did not master the alphabetic principle or fully realize the understanding that there is a systematic and predictable relationship between letters/letter sequences and their corresponding sounds. Because of this, Aliyah fell behind in her ability to automatically recognize letter patterns and use that information to recognize words. She found herself trying to "catch up" because her mastery of the alphabetic principle was delayed. Reading became an effortful endeavor. Aliyah did not develop what Wolf (2007) and Dehaene (2009) call the "reading brain" at a critical time in her reading development.

When we look at Aliyah's previous interventions, they sometimes appeared to focus on the wrong pathway or not get to the heart of her struggles. In fifth grade, she participated in a fluency intervention, but this didn't address the underlying word recognition skills inhibiting her fluency growth. In sixth and seventh grades, her intervention primarily focused on comprehension, leaving her needs in automatic word recognition to the wayside.

Why Does Word Knowledge Matter? Isn't It Enough That Aliya Decodes More Words When She Reads in Context?

Starting around fifth grade, students encounter approximately 10,000 words a year in grade-level and content-area texts (Archer et al., 2003). Most of these words are multisyllabic words. Aliyah may know many of these "big" words when conversing with others, but they are not words she recognizes when encountered in print. Decoding these big words has proven problematic for her, and sometimes it can be hard to remember all of the sounds when decoding longer words with more letters. Her word reading accuracy in context, however, increases (e.g., her 75% sixth-grade automatic word list reading versus her 94% sixth-grade passage accuracy).

Here's the problem. Her word reading is bolstered when she reads in context, likely due to her solid oral language skills and her skillful use of background knowledge—a common compensatory strategy for older readers like Aliyah—but that work takes time and requires cognitive energy. When speed and accuracy are compromised and cognitive energy is disproportionately placed on word reading, comprehension can also be negatively impacted. In the end, Aliyah needs to decode with automaticity (i.e., without conscious effort) so that she can put her cognitive energy on the higher-level processes of reading comprehension. As Stahl and Hiebert noted, "comprehension is built on a foundation of words" (2005, p. 182).

Aliyah lacks fluency, reads slowly, and often stops to sound out words. She frequently has to reread sections of text to support understanding. This causes her to get bogged down while reading and spend exorbitant amounts of time on reading tasks. This limited word recognition can lead to exhaustion, discouragement, and even disinterest in reading (Curtis, 2004). Nagy and Anderson (1984, p. 328) maintained students "in the middle grades [who struggle] might read 100,000 words a year while the average children at this level might read 1,000,000. The figure for the voracious middle-grades reader might be 10,000,000 or even as high as 50,000,000." As a result, Aliyah isn't exposed to the language structures and vocabulary of grade-level, more complex texts—at least not to the extent she needs.

What Should Aliyah's Intervention Look Like? What Does the Research Say?

Using the cognitive model, we know automatic word recognition, including decoding, issues lead to fluency difficulties. Aliyah's assessment data aligns with Pathway #1—fluency difficulty rooted in word recognition issues. We use a three-pronged intervention plan for most students like Aliyah who have needs in this pathway—(1) decoding and spelling to build (2) automatic word recognition, which leads to (3) overall fluency. This chapter zeroes in on the first two; see Chapter 5 for details about the complementary fluency portion of Aliyah's intervention. So, let's get started thinking about Aliyah's word-recognition-focused intervention with some of our must-have ingredients: (1) data-based instruction, (2) intervention informed by "the system," (3) explicit instruction with ample opportunities to practice with feedback, and (4) decoding + spelling = big results.

Data-Based Instruction

We strategically use data to ensure instruction is strategically planned and continually adapted to meet Aliyah's needs. One of our principles is starting with assessment (see Chapters 2 and 3) to rank priorities and set goals. Diagnostic assessments, like those outlined in Chapter 3, help us to identify student strengths and needs that inform our intervention priorities or targeted skill areas. One method that provides critical information about these skill areas is error analysis (Filderman, Austin, & Toste, 2019). An analysis of Aliyah's reading and spelling errors (see Figure 4.1 introduced earlier) identifies the following priorities:

- *Decoding*—multisyllabic decoding strategies using division principles and syllable patterns (e.g., *bison*—first syllable is open and stressed and with a long vowel), common prefixes/suffixes (e.g., *irresponsible*—base word

response with *ir-* prefix and *-ible* suffix), and flexibility (e.g., *captive*—the second syllable isn't pronounced /īv/ despite the vowel-consonant-e pattern)
  - Priority 1: explicitly teach and practice basic principles for dividing words, common syllable patterns, and common affixes as well as flexibility
- *Spelling*—advanced vowel and consonant patterns in single-syllable words (e.g., the *ai* vowel pattern in *strain,* the *tch* consonant pattern in *switch*), common syllable patterns in multisyllabic words (e.g., the open first syllable and the unaccented final syllable in *favor*), and common prefixes/suffixes (e.g., the *-ible* suffix in *terrible*)
  - Priority 2: explicitly teach and practice patterns in single- and multisyllabic words including inflected endings and common suffixes (e.g., single-syllable *plain* leading to multisyllabic *explain* and adding the inflected ending for *explaining*)
- *Application*—Aliyah tends to draw upon her compensatory strategy of using the context combined with her oral language and background knowledge, which helps increase accuracy but at the cost of automaticity
  - Priority 3: provide multiple opportunities to apply decoding and spelling study to reading and writing tasks

Intervention Informed by the System

"An effective intervention approach flows from a master plan that understands the architecture of the reading system that it is helping to build. And if there *is* a unified blueprint (or set of blueprints) for building a fluent reading system—one that produces optimal functionality—it is important to have a deep understanding of the learning processes necessary to become a skilled reader" (Lovett, 2016, pp. 9–10). So, we make sure our intervention is designed to reinforce the "reading circuitry" necessary to process print and to teach the regularities of the English written system through incremental, systematic, and cumulative presentation of word parts alongside strategies to use them while decoding and spelling.

The written English system has many "exemplary regularities" (Perfetti, 2003, p. 12). In fact, many consonants are pronounced as we expect in almost all words. We can even add short vowels to that list. Consider the grapheme (or letter) *b*. When we see it, we know it is pronounced /b/. In fact, it's /b/ 97% of the time (e.g., *bulb, block, lobster, carbohydrate*). Or the phoneme /ă/. When we hear it, we know we can spell it with the single letter *a* (e.g., *fast, spasm, abstract*). We take advantage of this system when we teach these regularities one by one as we slowly expand Aliyah's understanding. "By carefully leading students through the complexities, students learn to trust the letters" (Kearns & Whaley, 2019, p. 214). That's what we want—for Aliyah to trust the letters.

For older students, one piece of the system that is extremely important to understand and get plenty of guided practice with is multisyllabic word reading and spelling. Once we move into the world of multisyllabic words (which account for more than 90% of new words in texts starting at the upper elementary level, according to Kearns et al., 2016), we must negotiate how vowel sounds can change. Let's think about this concept with these three words: *fever, never,* and *comedy*. The *e* across these three words has three different sounds: the first syllable in *fever* is /ē/, the first syllable in *never* is /ĕ/, and the second syllable in *comedy* is /ə/. While there are some tips to help cue us to the sound (e.g., two-syllable words with one consonant between the vowel can split either before or after that consonant: *fe-ver* versus *nev-er*), there are no hard and fast rules governing all possible vowel sounds in multisyllable words. However, there are common spelling patterns that can be very useful. Building a "trust" in the system and a healthy bit of confidence in flexibility helps students deal with this issue.

Explicit Instruction with Ample Opportunities to Practice with Feedback

Explicit instruction increases learning time, which is strongly linked to student achievement (Archer & Hughes, 2011), and creates a "diagnostic teaching space" that helps us accelerate or slow down our instruction based on progress monitoring. Explicit introductions are followed by "We Do" opportunities to practice with scaffolds and immediate feedback. We think about feedback in three ways. For example, if Aliyah reads *shiny* as "shin-ee," we might provide the following feedback:

- *Correcting*—"That word is shiny. What's the word?"
- *Coaching*—"Find your vowels and rethink your syllable division."
- *Modeling*—"*Shin-ee*. That's not a word I'm familiar with, so I know sometimes when I have one consonant between my vowels, I divide after the consonant. But if that doesn't work, I should divide before the consonant (pointing out this guidance on our anchor chart). Now I have an open vowel, an open *i* . . . so I have 'shy-nee.' *Shiny*. That's a word I know."

Practice is monitored to phase out the scaffolds over time as Aliyah masters the steps of the skill or strategy and becomes more automatic.

Decoding + Spelling = Big Results

Word reading and spelling depend on the same underlying knowledge. So, it makes sense that instruction in one will impact the other. We teach regular word features (i.e., features that are pronounced and spelled as we expect) and use them in words for both decoding and spelling practice, because focusing on these constituent parts improves not only decoding (e.g., Bhattacharya & Ehri, 2004) but also spelling (e.g., Tsesmeli & Seymour, 2008). However, students also encounter irregularly spelled words (e.g., those that deviate from what we expect, like the *o* in *from*) when reading and are faced with needing to use them when writing. These students need explicit instruction and additional practice with words that don't follow the regular rules for pronunciation or spelling (Shaywitz & Shaywitz, 2020). I (Tisha) am reminded of a middle schooler who identified her number one goal for the semester—to finally spell words like *thought* and *brought* correctly. She said she was tired of not being able to quickly and correctly spell words like them when she needed to use them and was embarrassed to misspell them for someone else to see. She isn't alone. We're sure Aliyah has her own *thought* and *brought* words.

ALIYAH'S INTERVENTION PLAN

With questions answered and a plan starting to emerge, the team places Aliyah in an intervention group targeting the skills and strategies of Pathway #1 (automatic word recognition). They put pen to paper and map out her goals as well as the ways they plan to monitor Aliyah's progress. They look to measures of decoding and spelling as they plan frequent, ongoing assessments (or what we like to call check-ins) using mastery tests that are closely tied to instruction and can be used frequently. This way Aliyah will be able to see how well she is doing and experience academic success; for some of our students, this is the first time for success. See Figure 4.3 to see their plan of action.

We've found mastery testing for progress monitoring to work best when we partner long-term and short-term goals. Let's think about our goals for Aliyah. We have a goal for Aliyah to correctly represent all studied long vowel patterns over the course of one 9-week grading period with a predetermined criterion level like 80%. A short-term goal might identify specific patterns every 2 weeks. These short-term goals can be more motivating to students so they can keep up with their progress as

By the end of 9 weeks, Aliyah will:	This will be measured with:
• Accurately read 80% of a list of 20 unfamiliar, multisyllabic words. • Demonstrate use of decoding strategies for big words.	• Teacher created lists of multisyllabic words that follow the patterns/skills practiced in the lessons. • Teacher created observation checklist.
• Accurately spell 80% of a set of words with the following spelling features: long e, long a, long o, and long i. • Accurately add the -ed and -ing inflected endings to words with doubling, e-drop, and no change to the base.	• Teacher created lists of single- and multisyllabic words including long e, a, o, and i. • Teacher created lists of words including -ed and -ing endings that require doubling, e-drop, and no change to the base.

FIGURE 4.3. Goals and progress-monitoring plan of action.

they work toward their 9-week goal. Finally, we pair these mastery check-ins with cumulative practice and assessment to ensure maintenance of her learning.

Aliyah needs to work on both automatic word recognition *and* fluency as part of Pathway #1. When she meets with Mr. Jackson in her intervention group, they spend:

- about 15–20 minutes devoted to automatic word recognition, including both decoding and spelling (this chapter); and
- about 25–30 minutes focused on building fluency (see Chapter 5).

This chapter is devoted to the first 20-ish minutes of the intervention—automatic word recognition. It might account for a little less than half of the intervention, but it packs a punch when it comes to Pathway #1.

EFFECTIVE INTERVENTION FOR AUTOMATIC WORD RECOGNITION

In the next few sections, we'll outline the key elements of interventions focused on building automatic word recognition. We'll cover:

- Decoding big words
- Spelling words with regular features
- Spelling words with irregular features
- Practicing quick, accurate word reading

The chapter ends with two sample lessons: one on *decoding big words* and the second on *spelling words with regular features.*

Before we get started, there are four considerations to point out when it comes to our approach to interventions prioritizing Pathway #1. First, time is valuable, so we continually reflect on the purpose of our work to maximize instruction. We concentrate on teaching essential highly frequent, high-utility word features and word parts. For example, we concentrate on the most common suffixes (e.g., *-ion* like *creation* and *-ly* like *gladly*) rather than low frequency suffixes (e.g., *-eer* like *engineer* or *-ward* like *awkward*) students might not encounter much. See Figure 4.4 for the most common prefixes and suffixes (White, Sowell, & Yanagihara, 1989).

Second, while we focus on highly frequent prefixes and suffixes, choosing words for practice works differently. One thing we've learned over the years is older students, especially eighth graders like Aliyah, know a lot of words. To have productive lessons, we look for example words for modeling and practice that are lower frequency or longer (i.e., two or more syllables). At the same time, we know we don't want to complicate matters by using obscure vocabulary. It's a balancing act—a word the students likely won't recognize (meaning it's a good choice for

These 20 prefixes account for 97% of all word prefixes:

- un-
- re-
- in-, im-, ir-, il- (not)
- dis-
- en-, em-
- non-
- in-, im- (in or into)
- over-
- mis-
- sub-
- pre-
- inter-
- fore-
- de-
- trans-
- super-
- semi-
- anti-
- mid-
- under-

un-
re-
in-, im-, ir-
dis-
account for 58%

These 20 suffixes account for 95% of all word suffixes.

- -s, -es
- -ed
- -ing
- -ly
- -er, -or
- -ion (-tion, -sion)
- -able, -ible
- -al, -ial
- -y
- -ness
- -ity, -ty
- -ment
- -ous
- -ic
- -en
- -er
- -ive
- -ful
- -less
- -est

-s, -es
-ing, -ed
-ly, -y
-er, -or
-ion,
-able, -ible
account for 82%

FIGURE 4.4. Common prefixes and suffixes.

decoding practice) but is still at least partly familiar (meaning familiar in terms of oral vocabulary).

Third, we also recognize the power of frequent reviews and cyclical learning and have found 1- or 2-minute "burst" reviews to be helpful. A burst review is quick and provides students with a mini-review of a skill, a strategy, or content; an opportunity to practice word reading or spelling with feedback; or a chance to demonstrate what they know with targeted feedback. You'll notice these burst reviews in our sample lessons at the end of the chapter.

Fourth, our sixth principle in Chapter 2 calls for a 20/80 split to indicate most of our lessons are about the guided practice with immediate feedback. When it comes to word work, practice with feedback is especially critical. We strategically select words for targeted practice, but the real practice comes during reading and writing. We include short selections during our lessons where students are reading texts of interest that require them to use our decoding strategies in real time. For example, we might have students read a newsela.com article about scientists teaching goldfish to operate a vehicle, where they have to decode words like *surroundings, navigational,* and even a word like *spurt.* Or we dictate sentences using our target feature and previously studied features to force them to use our spelling features and strategies when writing sentences. For example, we might dictate "My mom cut my screen time for the remainder of the day. The referee explained the delay to calculate the remaining seconds" during a study of vowel patterns. These opportunities for practice lead to valuable feedback moments, as illustrated in Figure 4.5.

Decoding Feedback

student reads "demonstrate" as /dē mŏn strāt/

"You found your vowels and looked at the consonants between. Let's check step 2. (point to anchor chart) This word has one consonant between the 'e' and 'o.' (point to the word) You broke the word before, but it's not a word we know. Be flexible. What can you try next?"

student says "numeratOR" and quickly self-corrects "numerator"

"Nice work being flexible. You moved your break before the consonant and changed your vowel. That got you close to the word, so you knew it was numerator!"

Spelling Feedback

student spells "screen" as "screne"

"You thought about the vowel sound /ē/ and then thought about your spelling options. Which spelling options are more common for /ē/? (point to anchor chart). That's right: 'ee' and 'ea.' Try each one and see which one looks right to you." After a final spelling is chosen, remind student that e-consonant-e is not a common spelling option for /ē/.

student writes "explane" and self-corrects for "explain"

"Nice work being flexible. You went back to the /ā/ and rethought your spelling option. Since you heard it in the middle of /plān/, you chose 'ai.' Now you have explain spelled right!"

FIGURE 4.5. Feedback moments.

Decoding Big Words: It's All About Flexing

Our main goal when working with students to build their decoding skills in big words (i.e., multisyllabic words) is building their understanding of words and how we can break up big words into smaller, more manageable parts or units. We break words based on two big units: *syllable* and *morphemes*. In the end, it's about building their confidence in decoding big words so they can be flexible about breaking words and trying out different pronunciations.

All of the upcoming strategies are getting at how to do different things with these two units in order to decode big words. The strategies we focus on for *syllables* are:

- Identifying syllables in words using common principles
- Knowing different pronunciations of single-letter vowel sounds
- Reading multisyllabic words using a flexible strategy
- Staying "in it to win it" as we practice correcting mispronunciations

The *morphemes strategies* we focus on are:

- Practicing pronouncing affixes in words
- Reading words by identifying affixes, base words, and roots
- Reading words in meaning word families

The good news is research has provided us with instructional practices based on syllable- and morpheme-based decoding strategies that improve word recognition—our ultimate goal. Figure 4.6 summarizes several approaches that we've leaned on over the years.

You can see how these approaches work together and even build on each other. We've used these in combination but often begin with syllable-based strategies and

approach	brief description
ESHALOV — every syllable has at least one vowel (decoding strategy)	1. Underline all of the vowels in a long word (e.g., <u>u</u>n<u>a</u>v<u>o</u>id<u>a</u>bl<u>e</u>) 2. Join any vowel teams into one vowel sound (i.e., oi) 3. Identify known word parts (e.g., un-, -able) 4. Count the number of word parts to expect (i.e., 5) 5. Break the word into parts for decoding (i.e., un-a-void-able) 6. Try a pronunciation of the word (O'Connor et al., 2015, p. 408)
Peeling Off (decoding strategy)	1. Circle the prefixes and suffixes 2. Say the prefixes and suffixes 3. Say the root 4. Say the whole word (Lovett et al., 2000; Lovett et al., 2017)
BEST — break, examine, say parts, try it (decoding strategy)	1. Break it apart ("peel" off affixes) 2. Examine the base word 3. Say each part 4. Try the whole word (O'Connor et al., 2015, p. 409)
Syllable-Based Word Building (teaching activity to emphasize syllables)	1. Write the multisyllabic word on the board one syllable at a time 2. Pause for students to read the syllables as they are added 3. Have students read the whole word (Shefelbine, 1990)
Affix Learning (teaching activity to emphasize morphemes)	1. Name affixes (up to 3 a day and define each, include multiple pronunciations, provide sample words, and have students generate words) 2. Write affixes (have students add new affixes to their affix banks) 3. Review affixes (practice daily) (Toste, Williams, & Capin, 2017)

FIGURE 4.6. Research-based approaches for decoding big words.

then incorporate morpheme-based strategies. We're building up to students using both syllables *and* morphemes flexibly as they decode big words. Think about yourself and what you do when you come to an unfamiliar word. For example, I (Tisha) recently read an article about leap years and came across a word I'm not sure I'd seen in print before—*quadrennium*. I quickly "peeled off" *quad-* and *-ium* because I recognized those morphemes, leaving me with *renn*. In other words, I looked for recognizable word parts and used that to help me pronounce *quadrennium*. How do we get our students to this point? Let's start by thinking about syllable-based strategies.

Syllable-Based Strategies

Syllable-based strategy lessons emphasize two concepts: (1) breaking a big word into its syllables and (2) flexibility with vowel sounds based on syllable breaks and syllable stress. We'll start with breaking big words into syllables.

A key concept about big words is (1) they have more than one syllable and (2) *every syllable has at least one vowel*. Armed with this knowledge, students can more easily look for syllables in words, helping them break big words into smaller parts. Students can then take advantage of strategies they already know for decoding single-syllable words. Single-syllable strategies aren't a perfect fit for decoding big words, but they still help. We like the way Kearns and Whaley (2019) explained it: "every part ([or] syllable) has a vowel, and every part has to look okay" (p. 216).

We complement this concept with a brief review of syllable types to support students as they consider if the parts "look okay." Teaching the basic syllable types can help students recognize pronounceable word parts, or syllables. Following are the most commonly taught syllable types:

- Open (*fe-ver, ma-ple*) and closed syllables (*bas-ket, nev-er*)
- Silent *e* syllables (*ex-plode, com-pete*)
- Vowel team syllables (*com-plain, em-ploy*)
- *r*-controlled vowel syllables (*mar-ket, en-ter*)
- Consonant-*le* syllables (*ma-ple, goo-gle*)
- Final, unaccented syllables (*out-age, act-ive, mo-tion*)

Notice how the first four bullets include syllable patterns that are also common in single-syllable words (e.g., *go*—open, *that*—closed, *make*—silent *e*, *out*—vowel team, and *start*—*r*-controlled). Showing students how the syllable types of shorter, easier words work in big words can increase their awareness of what looks okay—remember, it's about finding vowels to find the parts (or syllables) and making sure each part looks right.

Some programs teach open-vowel syllables (e.g., syllables that end with a vowel like *pa-* in *paper*) with long vowels and closed-vowel syllables (e.g., syllables that end with a consonant like *mot-* in *motto*). We start our study this way, but then we introduce the need for flexibility through the variable sounds of single-letter vowels like the *e* in *fever* and *never*. Flexing our syllable break helps us shift our vowel sound in *fe-ver* and *nev-er*.

Knowing each syllable has a vowel and we can break big words into syllables goes a long way. We have to also consider single vowel letters can be long, short, or schwa (e.g., *fever, never, comedy*). It can be very challenging to decide which sound to say. Starting with a study of words like *fever* and *never* is a comfortable way to introduce this concept. Having students practice reading syllables containing single letter vowels also helps. We often refer to lists of common syllables for practice, having students practice reading syllables (see Figure 4.7) and extending to words where students have to shift the vowel sound. This allows us to practice flexibility with single vowel pronunciations in a controlled, supportive way.

For example, we'll practice *ma* in *maple* (and other words such as *major* and *matrix*) like in the chart, but then we'll pull in other words that also begin with *ma* (e.g., *manor* and *manage*). Here, we are shifting our syllable break *ma-ple* to *man-or* with *ma* open-vowel syllable to *man* closed-vowel syllable. We'll also practice

Common Syllables for Practice

'ter' as in after
'ty' as in sixty
'ry' as in blurry
'ver' as in over
'ma' as in maple
'in' as in incorrect
'ny' as in pony
'ture' as in creature
'fa' as in favor
'ent' as in present
'ex' as in exit
'ble' as in bubble
'an' as in ankle
'to' as in total
'im' as in important

'ten' as in often
'vent' as in invent
'tle' as in little
'ple' as in simple
'com' as in common
'di' as in diner
'der' as in powder
'ta' as in table
'pa' as in paper
'ber' as in October
'son' as in lesson
'fer' as in offer
'af' as in affix
'wa' as in wafer

(Kearns & Whaley, 2019; Zeno, Ivens, Millard, & Duvvuri, 1995)

FIGURE 4.7. Common syllables for practice.

com as /kŏm/ in *common* as noted in the chart, but we'll bring in a word like *computer* where the *com* is pronounced as /kəm/. Here we are thinking about how the vowel shifts due to syllable stress with the first syllable stressed in *common* but not stressed in *computer.*

So far, we've started with big words and worked on *breaking them down* into smaller parts. We can also work from the inside out, starting with smaller word parts so that our students can *build* bigger words, syllable-by-syllable (see Figure 4.6, Syllable-Based Word Building). This activity is a good option for "burst" review. For example, we might write the word *compromising* on the board one syllable at a time like this: com, compro, compromise, compromis~~e~~ing.

It's a lot to juggle for a young person working through a word with three to four syllables, trying different sound options for vowel sounds and thinking about different syllable breaks. Take the word *comedy.* See Figure 4.8 to see Aliyah in action as she decodes *comedy.* She first thinks about where syllables break to identify the word parts. Then she tries different vowel sounds but remains persistent. The hope is that landing in "the ballpark" of the pronunciation of a known word will help her successfully read *comedy.*

Morpheme-Based Strategies Lesson

Morpheme-based decoding lessons are a natural hybrid of a decoding and vocabulary lesson. In Chapter 6, we lay out a vocabulary strategy we call "break it down." The steps for "break it down" reflect the steps we'd use to decode a word, starting with explicit instruction of common prefixes and suffixes. Just as we practice with common syllables (see Figure 4.7), we practice with common affixes (see Figure 4.4).

"Peeling off" is a good place to start when it comes to leveraging what you know about common prefixes and suffixes for decoding (see Figure 4.6). We've found older students might have used this strategy when they were younger with the extremely common *-ed/-ing* inflected endings, but they don't keep using it. Peeling off affixes can be extremely helpful. Remember Aliyah skipping *irresponsible*

FIGURE 4.8. Decoding *comedy.*

in Figure 4.1? Building her awareness of, and knowledge about, affixes would get her to a place where she might feel more confident. If she "peels off" *ir-* and *-ible,* she'd be left with *respons/e*—which is likely already a word she can read without decoding.

The BEST strategy is a multistep plan of action for decoding big words (see Figure 4.6). We've found having a consistent strategy for reading words is helpful. We've both used BEST and have seen our middle-grades students learn to apply it with success. The first step is to break it apart; we encourage our students to "peel off" prefixes and suffixes in this step. The second step has you examine what's left. This might get you to a manageable word part to decode or you might have to break what's left into syllables. The third step is to say each part, and finally, the fourth step is trying out the whole word.

How might this work? Take a look at Figure 4.9 to see how Aliyah decodes *unavoidable* using BEST. When decoding *unavoidable,* she breaks it apart as she "peels off" *un-* and *-able*. Then she recognizes *avoid* straight away as she examines what's left. She quickly says each part and easily lands on *unavoidable*. Sometimes, though, "peeling off" the affixes doesn't leave Aliyah with a word she knows. For example, she might come across the word *vulnerable.* She sees *-able* and "peels" it off. Then she uses syllabication principles to break up *vulner*—something she does quickly because she's getting good at scanning for vowels and seeing common syllables like *ner.*

Both syllable-based and morpheme-based practice is essential to decoding big words. In the end, though, it's about (1) quickly looking for parts you recognize (i.e., affixes or syllables), (2) pronouncing those parts, (3) putting them together to say the whole word, and (4) being flexible with vowel sounds until the word sounds right. See the end of the chapter for an example of a syllables-based lesson.

Spelling Words with Regular Features

When we think about the importance of spelling in interventions targeting the automatic word recognition pathway, we think about three points:

Break off prefixes and suffixes. I see **un-** and **-able**.
Examine what's left. Oh, it's **avoid**.
Say each part: /ən/ /əvoid/ /əbəl/. Say the word: **unavoidable**.
unavoidable

FIGURE 4.9. Decoding *unavoidable.*

1. Reading words *and* spelling words are like "two sides of a coin" (Ehri, 2000) with "each bolstered by awareness of the linguistic elements represented in print: phonemes, syllables, morphemes, and aspects of syntax" (Moats, 2020, p. 67).
2. "Learning to spell is more difficult than learning to read" (Moats, 2020, p. 67).
3. "Knowing the spelling of a word makes the representation of it sturdy and accessible for fluent reading" (Snow, Griffin, & Burns, 2005, p. 86).

The main idea here is that spelling requires a complete and accurate memory of a word, and children who experience difficulties with automatic word recognition tend to experience even more difficulties quickly and accurately spelling words. So, if learning to spell words supports automatic word recognition (i.e., makes a word accessible for fluent reading) and we know spelling is particularly difficult, then interventions should foster the connection between reading and spelling words, making these processes "mutually facilitative and reciprocal" (Ehri, 2000). As Bear et al. (2020) put it, "the key to literacy is knowing how . . . written language represents the language [we] speak" (p. 3). See the end of the chapter for an example lesson on the common spelling options for /ā/.

We structure our intervention work around the "logical framework" of written words (Moats, 2005); we call this "logical framework" *the system*. We (1) study sets of words intentionally chosen by shared features following a scope and sequence that introduces features in a cumulative manner, (2) devote a significant amount of time to writing target words in meaningful contexts, leading to transfer to other contexts and maintenance over time, (3) include as much in-the-moment, actionable feedback as possible, and (4) incorporate cumulative review. To facilitate a study of the system and identify patterns, our lessons discuss words and features using these basic ways to think about spelling:

- *Frequency*—sounds can be spelled with single letters or combinations of two, three, or even four letters, and some of these spellings are more frequent than others.
- *Position*—the spelling of any sound can vary based on where we hear it in a word (e.g., *ui* is a typical spelling for /ū/ but not at the end of words in English).
- *Letter sequences*—some sound spellings are governed by conventions of letter sequences (e.g., words don't end in *v* or *j* in English), and some letter sequences are highly frequent (e.g., *-ake* in words like *shake, bake,* and *take*).
- *Meaning*—a word's meaning and even part of speech can help determine its spelling (e.g., the *t* in *eventual* sounds like /ch/ but spelled with *t* due to a meaning connection to the base word, *event*).

One way we might follow up an introductory lesson is using structured word sorts—a mainstay instructional strategy we use. Word sorts are a valuable visual tool to compare words (Bear et al., 2020). A structured word sort uses explicit instruction techniques to clearly unpack the logical framework. For example, we might think through spelling options for /ā/ using a sort. To do this, we'd set up our sort to be a visual representation of our thinking. Our superordinate category would be "ways to spell /ā/" with the subordinate categories being "I hear it at the beginning," "I hear it in the middle," and "I hear it at the end" (See Figure 4.10). We sort words like *aim, ace, shake, strain,* and *sway* to emphasize the idea that *a*-consonant-*e* and *ai* are both used to spell /ā/ at the beginning and end of words (and syllables) and *ay* is at the end.

Reading and Spelling Words with Irregular Features

What about words with irregular features? In addition to building proficiency with words comprised of regular features, many students continue to struggle with quick, accurate reading and spelling of irregular words (Shaywitz & Shaywitz, 2020). Skilled readers with solid decoding skills, on the other hand, tend to build their quick, accurate recognition of these words more readily. This is an important skill because many of these irregular words are among the most commonly used in the English language (Crystal, 2002). So, we want these words to be recognized "at first sight."

Why do skilled readers have an easier time with these words? It's likely because they are more aware of phonemes, have formed solid understandings of letter-sound connections, and get more reading practice. This means they encounter many words, including irregular words, and notice these irregularities. So, when we practice these irregular words, we pay close attention to the regularities as well as their irregularities. We also make sure we spend time analyzing, reading, and writing these words. See Figure 4.11 for some activities we use to practice these words (all activities are from *www.reallygreatreading.com* and slightly adapted for older students).

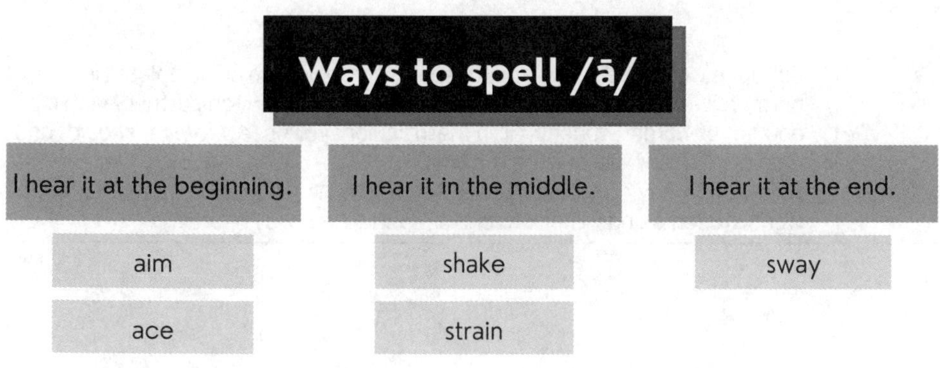

FIGURE 4.10. Structured word sort.

Activity	How to use it
Heart Words	1. Teacher identifies a set of words to target based on lists of highly frequent words and student data, including both reading and spelling words. We've found words like *through, thought, although*, and *should, would, could* are often good choices. Even a word like *different* is often a choice even though it is not "irregular," because many older kids have developed a habit of spelling this word *diffrent*. 2. Teacher explicitly analyzes each word one at a time noting regular features and calling attention to the part to "know by heart." • Write the target word and then a series of boxes underneath—one box per sound. For example, *should* has three boxes. You'd set it up like this: should [ ] [ ] [ ] • Analyze the word by noting the regular sound–spelling correspondence (in this case, /sh/ with *sh* and /d/ with *d*). Then call attention to the irregular part, or the part to know by heart - /o͞o/ with *oul*. Usually, the irregular part gets a heart drawn by its box, but for older students, you can circle it or highlight it. You might end up with: should sh | oul | d 3. Continue analyzing each word similarly. Usually, a small set of three to five words is enough. Note: This is often thought of as an activity for beginning readers, but we've found this level of analysis and attention to irregular features helpful for older students who struggle as well.
Spelling the Part to Know by Heart	1. Complement the above activity with this follow-up spelling activity. Take the set of previously analyzed words and set up a sheet to highlight irregular spellings. Each word would have a series of boxes—one box per sound—with the regular spellings already filled in and a line underneath to write the whole word. *Should* would be set up like this: sh | | d __________ 2. Call out a word for the students to spell. This could also be completed in partners with one partner calling out a set and then switch partners with a new set of words. Students fill in the irregular spelling (e.g., *oul* for *should*) and then write the whole word on the line. 3. Follow up by having students spell the words one more time. After writing each word, students underline or circle the "part to know by heart."

(continued)

FIGURE 4.11. Irregular words activities.

Activity	How to use it
Flip It	1. Create a page with two columns. One column is set up with lines for students to write words. The second column is a list of the target words the students have been studying recently, a set for cumulative review, or a set previously studied to revisit. On the back side in a column that can fold to cover the second include sentences for each word with the target word missing. • The front of the page might look like this (only two words shown as an example): 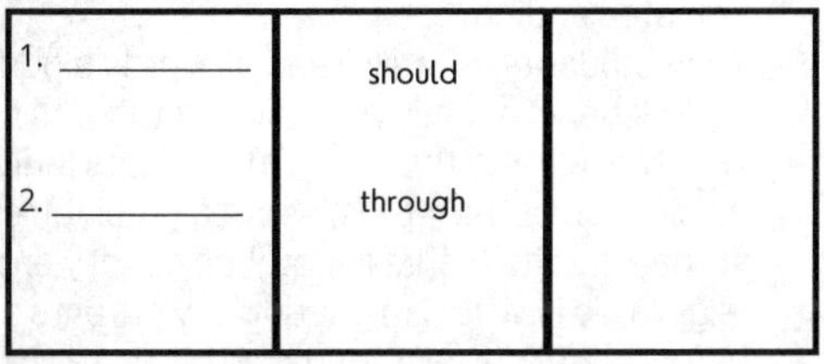 1. ______ should 2. ______ through • The back of the page would look like this: 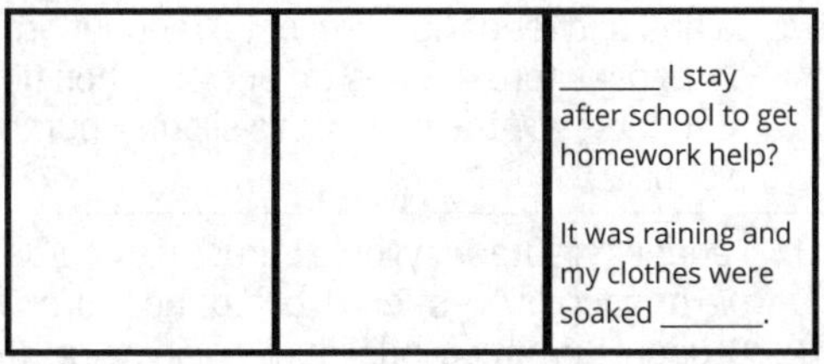 ______ I stay after school to get homework help? It was raining and my clothes were soaked ______. 2. Present the pages to students folded so they see the sentences with missing words and the blanks to write in their words. 3. Students read the sentences and write the missing word in the first column. 4. Once all words are written, the student unfolds to check their spelling.

FIGURE 4.11. *(continued)*

Practicing Quick, Accurate Word Reading

All this work is in service of building automatic word recognition (see Figure 4.2). We've found many of our older readers misread common words (i.e., highly frequent words—and as we noted earlier, many of these have irregular features) due to years of inaccurate practice. So, we pull in regular doses of word reading practice to complement our decoding and spelling practice. We practice words with regular features in our decoding and spelling work as well as high-utility words with irregular features. But always, we are looking for words with high impact, meaning they'll see them and use them a lot. It's important to point out we suggest lessons that target specific skills within a lesson that extends to practice in connected, meaningful texts (see Chapter 5 on fluency). Figure 4.12 presents some of our most used activities to encourage quick, accurate word reading.

Activity	How to use it
Word Reading Plus (Hasbrouck & Glaser, 2019)	1. Teacher chooses a set of words and creates a list of the words either written on the board or projected on an interactive display board. 2. Teacher points to each word and reads aloud and students chorally repeat. While reading each word, teacher provides instruction (or reminders if this is a previously taught word) about word parts (and meaning if applicable). For example, for the word *complained,* the teacher might underline the first two syllables, box the *ai,* and circle the *ed* inflected ending. 3. Then students chorally read all words aloud as teacher points, followed by teacher randomly pointing as students chorally read. 4. We often extend this with: (a) students individually read the list, or a selection of the words, to check their quick, accurate reading; (b) students write words in notebook or dry erase and we provide a clue (e.g., "This is what I might do if my parents say I have to clean my room before I can see my friends." OR "I ____________ [says 'blank'] when my parents made me clean my room before seeing my friends.") for students to find and read the word; or (c) teacher provides words in phrases or sentences for students to read and then highlights the target words—students read the sentences silently, but the target words are read aloud.
Speedy Syllables (Florida Center for Reading Research website)	1. Teacher creates "syllable cards" (i.e., cards with common syllables like *ble* and *ter*), a "yes" card, and a "no" card. 2. Students practice individually or in pairs. Students place the header cards face up on the table along with their timer. 3. They set the timer for 1 minute and then get a syllable card, start the timer, and read. If the student reads a syllable quickly and accurately, they place it with "yes," and if not, it goes with "no." 4. Once the timer is off, they count their "yes" cards and set a goal for their next go. They might practice their "no" cards before giving it one more go. 5. Note: This can also be played with affixes and roots as you study them (e.g., *re-, -able, vis*).
Give Me Five (Florida Center for Reading Research website)	1. Teacher creates cards with five-word sets per card (e.g., *provide, example, interesting, particular, compare*). 2. Students can play this individually or in pairs. Students place word cards face down in a stack and set the timer for 1 minute. 3. If the student is reading and gets stuck on a word, their partner counts to five and then says to move on. If all words on a card are read correctly, the card goes in the discard pile. If not, the card goes back in the deck. 4. As soon as a card goes into the discard pile, the next student goes. They continue to read cards in this manner until the timer goes off. 5. They count the number of cards in the discard, practice any cards that went back in the deck, and then give it another go trying to get one more card in the discard pile.

FIGURE 4.12. Word reading activities.

Big Kids Love Games, Too

Games can help increase student participation, encourage social interaction, and help motivate students to take risks. They also lead to additional practice opportunities. See Figure 4.13 for a list of some of our favorite games. While students can play games alone, we like to play collaborative games where students work in teams as they move through the game. For example, we'll build a Kahoot as a review of recently studied features and have students work in teams. Sometimes the competitive factor is fun but often we work toward a collective score as a whole group to celebrate.

Game	How to play
Don't Be Greedy (Kearns, Lyon, & Kelly, 2021)	1. Teacher creates cards with a variety of multisyllabic words or syllable types for the deck and includes at least one "don't be greedy" card. 2. Students read cards as quickly and accurately as possible. 3. Teacher encourages students to use their strategies when needed and correct errors as they arise. 4. Students keep cards they read correctly within the allotted time.
I'm Out	1. Teacher creates cards with shared target features such as vowel patterns (e.g., words with *ai, oa, ee, ea*). 2. Cards are dealt so each player has the same number of cards. 3. The first player places a card down, reads the word, and designates the vowel pattern to be followed (e.g., *rain* with *ai*). The next player must play a card with the same pattern and read it aloud. 4. If a player doesn't have a match, they must pass. 5. Play continues until all players are out of the designated pattern, and the player who played the last pattern card begins a new round. The object is to be the first player to play all cards in their hand.
Taboo with a Twist	1. Teacher (or students) create cards with a collection of words with target features. 2. Students pair up with one as the speller and the other as the reader. 3. The speller picks a card without looking and holds it up to their forehead so the reader can see it. The reader reads the card, and the speller has to spell it aloud. The speller can write it first to use their strategies and see what looks right. 4. Players switch off between speller and reader.

(continued)

FIGURE 4.13. Some of our favorite games.

Game	How to play
Slap Jack (Bear et al., 2020)	1. Teacher creates 52 cards with 26 cards focused on one feature and 26 on another (could make 60 cards with 20 cards per 3 features). For example, you might contrast V-CV like *pilot* (open-vowel in the first syllable) and VC-CV like *basket* (closed-vowel in the first syllable). 2. Deal cards (usually a two-person game) until the deck is gone. 3. Each player turns a card face up in a common pile. When the two cards have the same feature (e.g., *pilot, diner*), the first player to "slap" the pile takes the cards. 4. Play continues until one player has all of the cards.
Prefix Spin (Bear et al., 2020)	1. Teacher creates a spinner with around six prefixes (e.g., *re-, dis-, un-*) and word cards (e.g., *cover, test, able*). Main thing is to make sure you can make plenty of real words (e.g., *retest, disable, uncover*). 2. Put all word cards face down in a pile and turn one over at a time. 3. The first player spins for a prefix. If their prefix can be added to the word card's base word to make a real word, then the player takes the card and records the whole word on paper or a dry erase. If a real word can't be made, play moves to the next player. 4. The winner has the most words.
Online tools like Quizlet	1. Teacher creates card with a sentence and the target word missing with a hint: "The baseball player had a (fr______n) on her face because she lost her favorite glove." 2. Students then have to type in the word with the correct spelling—and target pattern. 3. Students practice until they reach a goal of number of words correctly spelled.
Incorporating games kids love like Minecraft	1. Teacher creates a journey. Tasks might be: (a) use these three words in one silly sentence, (b) brainstorm at least 10 words with the *ain* letter sequence, (c) provide a picture (e.g., face frowning) and word with the target pattern missing for the student to fill in (e.g., "fr______n)", or (d) what's the most common way to spell /ā/ and write a word with that pattern and use it in a sentence 2. Students move through the teacher-created maze, visit rooms, and find out their next task on their journey. 3. Students work together or alone to complete the specified number of tasks.

FIGURE 4.13. *(continued)*

CONCLUSION

Aliyah has been in an intervention with a small group focused on Pathway #1 (automatic word recognition). Her intervention included explicit instruction and ample opportunities to practice with feedback as she learned to (1) decode big words, (2) spell words with regular features, (3) read and spell words with irregular features, and (4) build her quick, accurate recognition. We check in on her progress toward her goals in Figure 4.14.

The North Star guiding principles in Chapter 2 informed our intervention decisions and helped Aliyah achieve her goals. How did they play out across the interventions to build her automatic word recognition? See Figure 4.15.

By the end of 9 weeks, Aliyah will:	This will be measured with:	Progress at 9 weeks:
• Accurately read 80% of a list of 20 unfamiliar, multisyllabic words. • Demonstrate use of decoding strategies for big words.	• Teacher created lists of multisyllabic words that follow the patterns/skills practiced in the lessons. • Teacher created observation checklist.	• She read all 20 words correctly (allowing for self-corrections) on her most recent decoding check. • An observation checklist shows she is doing well "peeling" off parts she knows and applying the syllabication principles. She continues to work on flexing vowel sounds as needed, especially the schwa in unaccented syllables. Her strong oral vocabulary continues to be a big help to her, because she can fairly consistently increase her decoding success when in context.
• Accurately spell 80% of a set of words with the following spelling features: long e, long a, long o, and long i. • Accurately add the -ed and -ing inflected endings to words with doubling, e-drop, and no change to the base.	• Teacher created lists of single- and multi-syllabic words including long e, a, o, and i. • Teacher created lists of words including -ed and -ing endings that require doubling, e-drop, and no change to the base.	• She scored 85% on a recent spell check across these 4 long vowels. • She represented all 3 spelling conventions (i.e., doubling, e-drop, no change) accurately when adding -ed and -ing on a recent spell check.

FIGURE 4.14. Aliyah's progress toward her goals.

Principles	An example of how we used it:
1. What Do You Stand For? Articulate Your Literacy Beliefs	We used the cognitive model from Chapter 2 to pinpoint a pathway and the developmental model to fine-tune our specific goals.
2. Don't Forget Your Map! Choose and Use an Intervention Model	Aliyah's team used the cognitive model to target Pathway #1 and the developmental model to target specific features for spelling and strategies for decoding.
3. Start with Assessments Get to Know Your Students	The screening assessment provided some information, but the diagnostic assessments homed in on Aliyah's needs, especially in decoding, spelling, and quick, accurate word reading.
4. Keep the Main Thing the Main Thing Design a Focused, Flexible, Doable Intervention Plan	Aliyah's intervention included a streamlined lesson with a repeated routine with a relentless focus on the "main thing"—using strategies to (1) decode big words and (2) spell long vowels as well as use spelling conventions adding inflected endings.
5. Make the Invisible Visible Use the "I Do" to Be Explicit and Systematic	Each lesson sample included an "I Do" section with explicit, systematic instruction such as the syllabication lesson (see upcoming decoding lesson example).
6. Practice, Practice, Purposeful Practice Leverage the "We Do" and "You Do" for Long-Term Transfer and Independence	Sample lessons included ideas for additional practice such as the dictated sentences following the spelling lesson (see upcoming spelling lesson example).
7. One Size Does Not Fit All Differentiate and Scaffold When They're Not "Getting It"	Anchor charts were used to support the concepts, reinforce during guided practice, and support independent application.
8. Time Where Does It All Go and How Can I Get Some Back?	One example would be the review burst activity at the start of the spelling lesson (see upcoming spelling lesson).
9. Engagement Get Your Students to Buy In When They've Checked Out	Aliyah's longer-term goals for 9 weeks were broken down into shorter-term goals every 2 weeks so Aliyah could see her progress more frequently.
10. Active, Not Passive Take a Critical Stance and Read with a Purpose	Aliyah practices flexibility when decoding (e.g., shifting the sound of single-letter vowels like n<u>e</u>ver and f<u>e</u>ver) and spelling (e.g., navigating spelling options for /ā/).

FIGURE 4.15. North Star guiding principles.

APPENDIX: SAMPLE LESSONS

The following lessons are examples of lessons we might use with Aliyah and her intervention group, using guidance from syllabication principles and the common spelling patterns for long *a*. They walk you through the "I Do" and "We Do" portions of the lessons, including anchor charts. After each lesson, we give a few ideas about how we might provide additional practice with feedback and how we could use formative assessment to inform our next steps.

Lesson 1—Syllabication Principles (Figure 4.16)

Aliyah's group has previously covered:

- *Peeling off*—students have already learned to look for prefixes and suffixes to take off so they can analyze a more manageable chunk before blending all parts for the whole word (e.g., *impossible* = *im*- and -*ible* are "peeled off" leaving *poss* which is much more manageable: im+poss+ible= *impossible*)
- *Every syllable has a vowel*—students know that all syllables have one vowel sound, which might be a single vowel letter (e.g., *beg, pilot, fantastic*), but it might also be a string of letters (e.g., *rain, explain, mountaineer*)
- *Syllable types*—we've connected the basic syllable types to single-syllable words (e.g., open as in the first syllable of *fever,* closed as in the first syllable of *never,* vowel-consonant-*e* as in the second syllable of *explode,* vowel teams as in the second syllable of *employ,* and *r*-controlled vowels as in the second syllable of *fever*); note: we don't teach syllable types for coding purposes but rather to help focus on vowels
- *Flexibility, persistence, and confidence in the system*—students have been working toward these skills, and so far, we've kept it contained to single vowel letters as long, short, or schwa (e.g., *fever, never, comedy*)

"I Do"—
Directly and explicitly teach your concept

Make the Objective Public:

This lesson is focused on basic syllabication principles: find vowels, check consonants between—if one consonant, divide before and shift if needed; if two, divide between; if more than two, look for consonants that go together, say each part and blend for the whole word.

Here's our anchor chart:

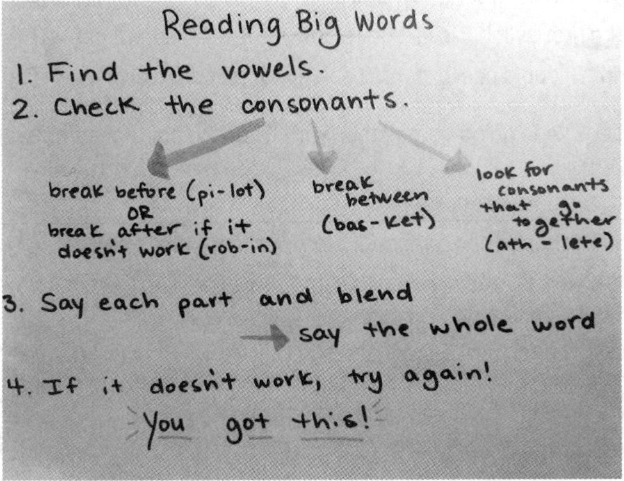

Introduce the Lesson:

Teacher: Today we are going to use what we know about big words to practice more. I'm going to show you how to divide words into smaller chunks. Just like our practice peeling off prefixes and suffixes, what I'll show you today will help you get big words into smaller chunks.

What does every syllable have? Let's say it together:

Students: Vowels

State the Secret and Model Your Thinking:

Teacher: You got it! Vowels. We've practiced finding vowels and thinking about how many syllables a word has. Now we're going to use those vowels to help us think about how to break words up into smaller chunks. I'm going to show you how this works.

[Teacher writes the word *incubate* on the board.]

Teacher: Okay. Let's look at this word. Remember, you might know a word I have chosen for us to practice. If you do, stay quiet. It will still help us think about how to break words up.

We already know one of the first things we can do when we get to a big word we don't know! Find the vowels. You can see that's my first step here [points to the anchor chart], so I'm going to do that here. I'm going to underline the vowels.

[Teacher underlines (1) *i*, (2) *u*, (3) *a* with the *e*.]

(continued)

FIGURE 4.16. Sample lesson 1: Syllabication principles.

Teacher: *i*, *u*, and here I see an *a*-consonant-*e*, so I know that goes together. Three vowels mean we have three syllables. Let's think about how to break them apart.

To do this, we'll think about how many consonants come between our vowels. Like here between the *i* and *u*. There are two consonants.

[Teacher points to the anchor chart.]

Teacher: Look here—it says "two equals break between." So, I'm going to break between *n* and *c*.

[Teacher makes a slash between the *n* and *c*.]

Student 1: Wait. The first syllable is *in*. That's one of the prefixes we peel off.

Teacher: That's right. I could peel that off. Looking for places to divide will also help you. Good connection!

Okay. Let's keep going across this word. There's 1 consonant between the *u* and *a*-consonant-*e*.

[Teacher points to the anchor chart.]

Teacher: Now look—If there's one consonant, break before first. Let's do that here.

[Teacher makes a slash between the *u* and *b* and points back to the anchor chart to indicate the third step.]

Teacher: Now let's say each part. Blend. And say the whole word. /în/ /kyū/ /bāt/—*incubate*. That's what you do with baby chicken eggs. They incubate in an incubator. Have you heard this word before?

Student 2: Yes. But I forgot about it!

Continue Modeling:

The lesson continues with two more intentionally chosen words:

- *liberate:* This word will demonstrate the principle of breaking before the one consonant and then after when it doesn't work (encourages flexibility); it also brings in *r*-controlled vowels and reinforces the vowel-consonant-*e* pattern as one vowel sound.
- *substitute:* This word will demonstrate the principle of looking for consonants that go together when you have more than two consonants between your vowels; it also continues to reinforce the vowel-consonant-*e* pattern as one vowel sound.

"We Do"—
Provide opportunities for scaffolded practice

Five Words for Guided Practice:

The teacher presents one word at a time for the group and uses the anchor chart to prompt the students as they decode and say each word.

- *embrace:* provides a more manageable start with only two syllables but has three consonants between the vowels; likely unknown in print but familiar when they hear it
- *demonstrate:* provides a syllable break with four consonants, so we need to look for consonants that go together like the common letter string *str* in words like *stride, string,* and *street;* encourages flexibility with the first syllable break

(continued)

FIGURE 4.16. *(continued)*

- *numerator:* has four syllables so plenty of opportunity to practice the syllabication principles; encourages flexibility with the final syllable where the *or* sounds like /er/
- *inconsistent:* has four syllables and is straightforward in terms of breaking; encourages flexibility with the *o* in the second syllable shifting to schwa and saying /ĭn kôn sĭs tənt/ will get them in the ballpark
- *tenderizer:* also has four syllables and is straightforward in terms of breaking; meaning likely unknown but a good word to connect to a known word—*tender*

Once a word is decoded, a companion sentence using the word is presented and the students read the sentence in unison. Sentence options might be:

embrace	She smiled warmly and stood to **embrace** them with a hug.
demonstrate	Please **demonstrate** how to multiply fractions.
numerator	Is the **numerator** the top or the bottom of a fraction?
inconsistent	The weather has been **inconsistent**, so I keep an umbrella with me.
tenderizer	Do you use a **tenderizer** when you cook meat?

FIGURE 4.16. *(continued)*

Lesson 2—Common Spelling Patterns for Long *a* (Figure 4.17)

Aliyah's group has previously covered:

- *Adding inflected endings*—focus on the base word as we double (e.g., *rubbing*), drop the final *e* (e.g., *baking*), or make no change at all (e.g., *marching, reading, lifting*)
- *Every syllable has a vowel*—students know that all syllables have one vowel sound, which might be a single vowel letter (e.g., *beg, pilot, fantastic*), but it might also be a string of letters (e.g., *rain, explain, mountaineer*)
- *Tap each syllable*—to ensure students represent all syllables, they tap each syllable and focus on spelling one syllable at a time
- *Do what's easy first*—when faced with a part they're unsure of, they get down what they know and then focus on the rest (e.g., spelling *explaining* . . . they tap for /êx/ /plān/ /îng/, write *ex,* leave a space, and write *ing* so they can focus on spelling options for /ā/
- *Common spellings*—long *e* (i.e., open *e, ee,* and *ea* as in *fever, unseen,* and *heater*) and *ea* as short *e* (e.g., *threat*) considering frequency, position, and letter sequences to help
- *Flexibility, persistence, and confidence in the system*—students have been working toward these skills as they write spelling options to see what looks right and adjust if needed

"I Do"— Directly and explicitly teach your concept

Make the Objective Public:

This lesson reinforces the concept that English has sounds that can be spelled in more than one way. We demonstrate this targeting one vowel sound, and its most common spellings—/ā/ is commonly spelled open *a, a*-consonant-*e, ai,* and *ay*. Frequency, position, and letter sequences can help.

Review Burst:

While a 1-minute review might be doable when decoding a small set of words, it's usually not enough for spelling. We often extend this to 2–5 minutes for spelling. For this lesson, we begin with a set of words with long *e* with and without inflected endings.

- The students are directed to their anchor chart with a few quick reminders, "Remember, when we hear /ē/ in words, we have some more common spelling options. If I hear /ē/ in the middle of a word or syllable, what are my common spelling options? What about if I hear it at the end?"
- Then the teacher has the students use their spelling strategy "Stop and Think" to spell: *creeping, between, reached, weakness, sledding.*
- To finish, the students underline or highlight the patterns for /ē/ in each word as they say the words aloud.

Here's our anchor chart for this lesson:

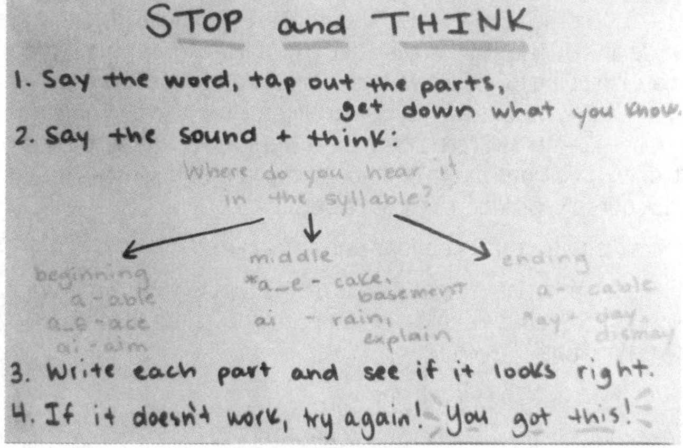

Introduce the Lesson:

Teacher: Today we are going to think about spelling options for this sound in words—/ā/. You already know different spelling options for this sound. Today we'll talk about how we can be more strategic in spelling words with /ā/ just like we have been doing when we hear /ē/ in words like *jeep* and *peach*.

We talked about how some spelling patterns are just more common. Which ones are the most common for /ē/?

Student 1: *ee* and *ea*

(continued)

FIGURE 4.17. Sample lesson 2: Common spelling patterns for long *a*.

Teacher: You got it! Just like in the words we just spelled like *creeping* and *reached.* [Teacher writes these on the board and underlines the *ee* and *ea.*] Any other options?

Student 2: *e*-consonant-*e*?

Teacher: Thanks for bringing that to the table. Let's talk about this one—*e*-consonant-*e* in a word like *these*. This one isn't very common, so you won't use this one very much. I'm thinking about open syllable *e* like in *fever.* [Teacher writes *fever* beside *creeping* and *reached,* underlining the *e* in the first syllable.] So, when we think of our spelling options for /ē/, our go-to options are open-syllable *e, ee,* and *ea.*

State the Secret and Model Your Thinking:

Teacher: We can think about common spelling options for words with /ā/, too. We can think about where we hear it. Like /ē/ . . . I know open syllable *e* and *ea* are my best spelling options for /ē/ at the beginning like *east* and *evolve*. /ā/ works the same way.

[Teacher points to the anchor chart.]

Teacher: We always start with saying the word, tapping the parts, and getting down what we know. Let me show you how this works with /ā/ words.

Here's my word: *exclaim. Exclaim.* I'm going to tap my parts: /êx klām/. I know how to spell the first part /êx/, so I'm going to get that down.

[Teacher writes *E-X* on the board.]

Teacher: Now for the next part. /klām/ I hear /ā/ in the middle.

[Teacher points to the anchor chart.]

Teacher: So, I'm here . . . in the middle. When I hear /ā/ in the middle, my spelling options are *a*-consonant-*e* and *ai.* The star here is saying that if you aren't sure, *a*-consonant-*e* is more common. I'm going to write it with both spelling options.

I know /kl/ is *C-L*, so let's get that down. First, I'll write *C-L-A-M-E*. Now I'll write my next option—*EX—CL—AI—M*. [Verbalizing the letters while writing, the teacher partners them like this—*ex, cl, ai,* and *m*—to emphasize the letter sequences that go together.]

Let's ask ourselves. Which one looks better?

Students: [Students discuss various options and land on *exclaim.*]

Teacher: I agree. The *ai* option looks right. This is a step that won't always work, but we've read this word a lot. Because of that, we can sometimes tell which spelling looks right if we write them both out.

Student 2: But what if we pick the wrong one?

Teacher: That's okay. We all make spelling mistakes. And, I'll help when we practice together, and we'll practice a lot.

Continue Modeling:

The lesson continues with two more intentionally chosen words:

- *bracelet:* This word encourages tapping for syllables and the first syllable follows the *a*-consonant-*e* option when we hear /ā/ in the middle of the word/syllable.
- *underpaid:* This word also encourages tapping for syllables and begins with a familiar word *under*; the last syllable brings in the *ai* spelling option for /ā/ in the middle.

(continued)

FIGURE 4.17. *(continued)*

"We Do"— Provide opportunities for scaffolded practice
Five Words for Guided Practice: The teacher presents one word at a time for the group and uses the anchor chart to prompt the students as they spell each word. • *spray:* provides a more manageable start with only one syllable; reinforces *ay* when you hear /ā/ at the end of a word/syllable • *blazer:* gives an option to apply the open-syllable *a* and connects to their decoding practice • *straining:* has an inflected ending for continued practice as well as practice negotiating the middle /ā/ when considering *a*-consonant-*e* and *ai* • *gateway:* has two syllables with /ā/—one in the middle and one at the end • *sustain:* kept the practice to all words with one or two syllables, so there we stay at two; the *ain* letter sequence will be emphasized in later lessons, so this word begins that practice
After spelling all words, the teacher dictates at least one sentence for students to use the strategy once more. A sentence option might be: "She complained that lately she always strains to get that blazer on."

FIGURE 4.17. *(continued)*

CHAPTER 5

Building Fluency with Aliyah

In Chapter 4, we focused on what Aliyah's assessment results revealed about her *word recognition, decoding, and spelling* challenges and walked you through her intervention plan in those literacy areas. In this chapter, we focus on what Aliyah's assessment results revealed about her *fluency* challenges and discuss how to build an effective intervention, including fluency, for her. It's common for *word recognition* and *fluency* challenges to go hand-in-hand, which is why reading profiles like Aliyah's are often found in the middle grades. Please also see Chapters 1 and 4 for an introduction to the many strengths Aliyah brings to the intervention setting.

ALIYAH'S FLUENCY CHALLENGES: INITIAL SCREENING RESULTS

As we discussed in Chapter 4, Aliyah's initial screening results revealed the following:

- *Maze*—Aliyah's below-benchmark scores on the Maze screener indicated *reading comprehension* difficulties. Aliyah's content teachers confirmed this initial finding, reporting that she struggled to answer the end-of-chapter questions in the social studies and science textbooks. Ms. Taylor, Aliyah's English/language arts teacher, shared that Aliyah was having trouble keeping up with class discussions based on the novel she was expected to read independently. *Reading comprehension* was definitely a challenge for Aliyah.

- *ORF assessment*—Aliyah read the eighth-grade passage with adequate accuracy (91%), but very slow reading rate (95 WCPM), indicating *reading fluency* challenges.

While discussing Aliyah at their weekly team meeting, her eighth-grade teachers noticed an interesting—and initially somewhat confusing—pattern. Aliyah's comprehension of content information was actually quite strong when teachers *orally* presented information during lectures, class discussions, and via video clips. In fact, until seventh grade, Aliyah's grades were generally A's and B's across her core content classes. However, it was when she was asked to *actually read* texts by herself—something that was increasingly required across seventh and eighth grades—that Aliyah struggled to grasp key concepts and make sense of grade-level content. Aliyah's team asked the school reading specialist, Mr. Jackson, to follow up with diagnostic assessments to see if they could pinpoint, exactly, the root cause of Aliyah's reading comprehension difficulties.

ALIYAH'S DIAGNOSTIC FOLLOW-UP ASSESSMENTS

What could account for Aliyah's (1) strong *listening* comprehension versus her (2) weak *reading* comprehension? Mr. Jackson's initial thinking and diagnostic follow-up assessment plan was as follows:

- **Pathway #1: Focus on *fluency*.** Based on her weak fluency scores on the ORF, Mr. Jackson strongly suspected that her difficulty *reading fluently* was a primary cause of *her reading comprehension* difficulties. In short, lack of fluency might be a barrier to her comprehension. To get a closer look at her fluency, he decided to administer (1) a graded word list from the QRI-7 and (2) an oral reading passage from the QRI-7 (as described in Chapter 3).

- **Pathway #2: Focus on *listening comprehension*.** Based on reports of Aliyah's strong listening comprehension skills in the classroom, Mr. Jackson decided to also administer an eighth-grade *listening comprehension* passage from the QRI-7 to confirm this. In a listening comprehension assessment, Mr. Jackson read the passage aloud to Aliyah prior to asking her the comprehension questions (see Chapter 3). With Mr. Jackson "doing the decoding" for Aliyah, this listening comprehension assessment provided a direct measure of Pathway #2: Aliyah's oral language comprehension skills (including her vocabulary, background knowledge, and text-structure knowledge), without the burden of her having to decode the words.

Aliyah's Follow-Up Diagnostic Assessment Results

Fluency

As part of the brief diagnostic, Aliyah read graded word lists, which led Mr. Jackson to choose *Lifeline of the Nile*, a sixth-grade passage from the QRI-7 (two grade levels lower than the eighth-grade passage administered in the initial ORF screening).

Mr. Jackson recorded Aliyah's accuracy, reading rate, expression, and comprehension. See Figure 5.1 for Aliyah's assessment results from this passage.

As the scores in Figure 5.1 indicate, despite the sixth-grade passage being two grade levels lower than her eighth-grade ORF passage, Aliyah continued to experience the same fluency challenges. While she could accurately decode most of the words in the passage (94% on the sixth-grade passage)—a relative strength—she struggled greatly in the other two fluency components:

- *Reading rate*—Aliyah's reading rate was 90 WCPM, which is significantly below even the sixth-grade ORF benchmark for her school's screening measure.

- *Phrasal reading and expression*—Aliyah's prosody scale score was a 2. This means that she was not able to consistently read smoothly, with expression, or in phrases, often lapsing into word-by-word reading and awkward phrasing.

- *Reading comprehension*—Notice how Aliyah's original sixth-grade reading comprehension score (see Figure 5.1) was a 63% (below benchmark), but when allowed to look back in the passage, she improved her comprehension to 100%. Mr. Jackson believed that Aliyah's lack of fluency may have made it initially difficult for her to comprehend the text. However, when given time to look back, she was able to compensate with her strong vocabulary and background knowledge.

Listening Comprehension

In contrast to her struggles with fluency, the listening comprehension follow-up assessment revealed important strengths in Pathway #2 (oral language comprehension) and Pathway #3 (strategic knowledge) for Aliyah.

- **Pathway #2: *Oral language comprehension*.** On the upper-middle school listening comprehension passage that Mr. Jackson read aloud to Aliyah, she was able to answer 100% of the comprehension questions accurately without lookbacks, using her strong background knowledge and sophisticated vocabulary in her answers. (See the bottom right cell under listening comprehension in Figure 5.1.)

- **Pathway #3: *Strategic knowledge*.** On this same listening comprehension passage, Aliyah was able to make sensible *inferences,* using text evidence to support her answers. In addition, when asked by Mr. Jackson, she was able to orally *summarize* the passage concisely. *Inferencing* and *summarizing* are two critical comprehension strategies for middle-grades readers.

Based on these strong *listening comprehension* assessment results, coupled with teacher reports of Aliyah's strong *oral comprehension* skills in the classroom, Mr. Jackson ruled out Pathway #2: Oral Language Comprehension (including

Aliyah's Assessment Results

Grade Level	Passage	Accuracy	Reading Rate	Prosody	Reading Comprehension	Listening Comprehension
6th	Oral passage reading from QRI-7**	94% (met benchmark)	90 WCPM (below benchmark)	2 (below benchmark)	63% (below benchmark) 100% with look-backs	
7th						
8th	ORF*	91%	95 WCPM		Maze* (below benchmark)	
	Listening comprehension passage from QRI-7***					100% (above benchmark)

* Step 1—ORF and Maze from screening
** Step 2—Oral passage reading from brief diagnostic
*** Step 3—Listening comprehension from in-depth diagnostic
(see Figure 3.3 for assessment flowchart detailing these steps)

FIGURE 5.1. Aliyah's QRI-7 assessment results.

vocabulary, background knowledge, and text structure) and Pathway #3: Strategic Knowledge as possible causes of her reading comprehension difficulties. This left Pathway #1 as the primary area of challenge for Aliyah (see Figure 4.2 on p. 70), in particular word recognition, decoding, and fluency challenges.

ALIYAH'S TEAM'S QUESTIONS ABOUT FLUENCY

Mr. Jackson met with Aliyah's content teachers to discuss the follow-up diagnostic assessment results. He reported that Pathway #1, which includes *fluency*, looked to be the main culprit affecting Aliyah's reading comprehension. He also agreed that Aliyah's strong oral language comprehension skills were a real strength. During this meeting, Aliyah's team asked Mr. Jackson the following questions about Aliyah and her fluency challenges:

- What, exactly, is fluency?
- How do Aliyah's fluency issues affect her comprehension?
- Why does Aliyah do so well comprehending *orally* presented information, but struggles when reading it by herself?
- If Aliyah can—for the most part—decode the words on the page, isn't that enough?
- How is reading words in isolation different than reading them in context?
- What, specifically, can the team do to improve Aliyah's fluency? What does the research say?

What, Exactly, Is Fluency?

We define *fluency* as the ability to read in context (1) accurately, (2) with appropriate rate, and (3) with adequate prosody, all in support of comprehension. Let's define each of these three fluency components:

- *Accuracy* (also known as *word recognition in context*)—fluent readers are able to read at least 90% of the words in a text accurately. Some researchers recommend 95% accuracy for fluent reading. Consider this guideline for certain instructional purposes (see Chapter 3).
- *Rate*—fluent readers are able to read with appropriate rate (neither too slow *nor too fast*!). Rate is measured in words per minute (WPM) or words correct per minute (WCPM).
- *Prosody*—prosody is the "musical aspect" of reading and involves reading with appropriate expression, intonation, and smoothness, reading in phrasal units, and pausing at the appropriate phrasal boundaries, which are marked by punctuation such as commas and periods.

Aliyah is relatively strong in one component of fluency: accuracy. For the most part, when given time, she can decode the majority of the words on a page. Isn't simply decoding the words enough? As we see in the next section, the answer is a resounding no. Aliyah needs to work on the other two components of fluency: reading the words not just *accurately,* but also *automatically* and with adequate *expression and phrasing in context.* Aliyah's profile—a relatively accurate, but extremely slow and labored, nonfluent reader—is a common one we see with middle-grades readers who struggle with reading. And very often, this inability to read fluently negatively affects our older students' reading comprehension and ability to keep up with their content reading and class assignments. It's not just about decoding for older students.

How Do Aliyah's Fluency Issues Impact Her Comprehension?

One of our inspiring mentors, Darrell Morris, likens acquiring fluency to learning to drive a stick-shift car (Morris, 2014). We can still remember the very first day our fathers took us out on the road and started to teach us how to drive stick (Kevin in a black Dodge Omni, Tisha in a gray Toyota Celica). We made all the usual mistakes of new drivers learning to drive stick: letting out the clutch at the wrong time, stalling over and over, rolling backward down hills, and forgetting to downshift—all with lots of parental exclamations sprinkled in with the driving instructions!

A few months later, we were shifting smoothly, effortlessly driving our Omni and Celica while listening to the radio and talking to friends. What happened during those 2 months? With enough guidance and practice, we had so automatized all of the skills involved in driving manually, including downshifting and letting the clutch out at the right time, that we didn't have to think about them—at least consciously—anymore. This freed up our "mental energy" to focus on other important things like paying attention to other cars on the road, listening to music, and talking to our friends.

A similar process occurs as beginning readers transition from labored, word-by-word reading to the fluent reading characteristic of skilled readers. In the *Simple View of Reading* (Gough & Tunmer, 1986; Hoover & Gough, 1990), reading comprehension is conceptualized as product of (1) decoding (i.e., accurate and, importantly, *automatic* word recognition) and (2) language comprehension. See the equation below:

$$\text{Decoding (D)} \times \text{Language Comprehension (LC)} = \text{Reading Comprehension (RC)}$$

The main issue here is that our "reading brains" only have *a limited amount of cognitive resources to consciously devote to any one conscious task, particularly tasks that we haven't yet automatized* (like a new driver trying to drive a car while talking to friends). Perfetti's groundbreaking work (1985, 1992) explains how the ability to accurately and automatically recognize words frees up our limited "mental resources" to devote to comprehension.

To make this clear, see Figure 5.2 for the "reading brain" of a nonfluent decoder, like Aliyah. In this figure, the circle represents the finite amount of "cognitive energy" Aliyah has to devote to reading. Inside the circle, the "D" represents her decoding processes, and the "c" represents her language comprehension processes. In Figure 5.2, Aliyah—who is still not yet a fluent decoder, particularly with the more difficult multisyllabic words—must spend the majority of her "mental energy" decoding the words on the page. While she can do this relatively accurately, the effort decoding required leaves her little "mental energy" to focus on making meaning. See how the large, uppercase "D" (decoding) takes up nearly the entire circle, leaving only a little space for the smaller, lowercase "c" (language comprehension). Looking at Aliyah's reading process through this lens, it's little wonder that Aliyah's lack of decoding ability—which affects her fluency—is negatively affecting her reading comprehension.

In contrast, see Figure 5.3 for the "reading brain" of a fluent decoder who we'll call Alex. Alex has so automatized his word recognition skills that reading the words on the page requires little effort or "mental energy" for him, leaving the large majority of his "mental energy" to focus on making meaning. See how the lowercase "d" (decoding) takes up so little space in the circle, leaving a lot of space to focus on comprehension, hence the large, uppercase "C."

Why Does Aliyah Do So Well Comprehending *Orally* Presented Information But Struggle When Reading It by Herself?

If Aliyah's lack of decoding negatively impacts her comprehension, how has she been able to maintain such strong grades up to seventh grade? How is she able to understand class discussions, videos, and orally presented information so well? It's because with *orally* presented information, Aliyah doesn't have to decode any

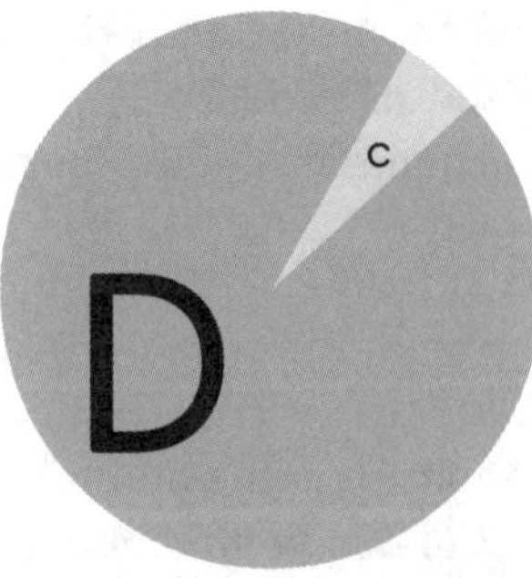

FIGURE 5.2. Reading brain of a *nonfluent* decoder.

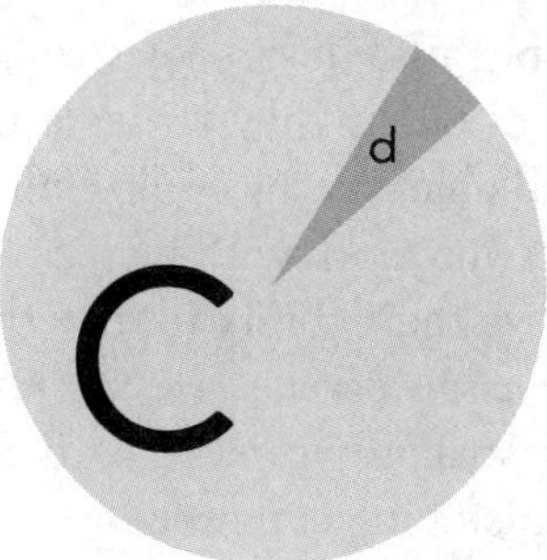

FIGURE 5.3. Reading brain of a *fluent* decoder.

printed words! She simply relies on her strong language comprehension skills and background knowledge. In other words, she doesn't have to use Pathway #1—automatic word recognition—at all.

This is where the importance of the listening comprehension assessment that Mr. Jackson administered comes into play. Not surprisingly, without the burden of decoding, Aliyah demonstrated strong comprehension on the eighth-grade passage Mr. Jackson read aloud to her. In fact, through this assessment, Mr. Jackson saw, firsthand, the ease with which Aliyah could comprehend grade-level text when she didn't have the burden of decoding it herself. Figure 5.4 highlights a common, and important profile of middle-grades readers whose *listening comprehension* is, generally, higher than their *reading comprehension.*

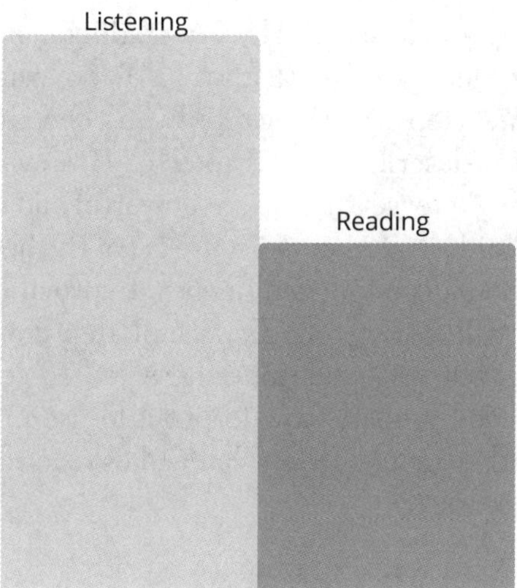

FIGURE 5.4. Listening versus reading comprehension levels.

Think of how many of your middle-grades struggling readers are like Aliyah, carrying around a backpack of books they struggle to decode, but could actually understand if they were available via an audio-enhanced format. Think of how many middle-grades students you work with who can understand orally presented information many grades above their ability to read themselves.

This *listening comprehension versus reading comprehension* discrepancy is incredibly common for older struggling readers, yet we rarely see school districts administering or reporting a listening comprehension level for our older struggling readers. We think this is an incredibly important piece of assessment information, which is why we often administer listening comprehension assessments to our middle-grades readers.

The purpose of a listening comprehension assessment is to determine if your students' reading comprehension difficulties are truly due to language comprehension difficulties or are due to something else. Simply reading aloud a grade-level content passage (e.g., from a science or social studies text or a grade-level IRI passage) with follow-up comprehension questions provides a reasonable estimate of a student's listening comprehension skills. If they score strongly on these listening comprehension assessments and do well during class discussions and activities, like Aliyah, language comprehension (Pathway #2) might not be the issue at all. Start looking elsewhere for the underlying reading problem. For students like Aliyah, the underlying issue might be a decoding and fluency one.

If Aliyah Can—for the Most Part—Decode the Words on the Page, Isn't That Enough?

We now know that the root causes of Aliyah's reading comprehension difficulties are due to decoding and fluency issues (Pathway #1). So, what can we do to improve Aliyah's fluency? The first step is working on Aliyah's decoding and automatic word recognition skills, as we described in Chapter 4. However, this automatic word recognition and decoding intervention, while powerful and essential, is only part of the puzzle for Aliyah. As illustrated in in Figure 5.1 at the beginning of this chapter, Aliyah has issues with both decoding and fluency. Improving Aliyah's decoding and sight word knowledge will take us one important step down Pathway #1 toward reading comprehension, but we're not quite there yet. To get the full benefit of her decoding work, she'll need to learn how to put it to use in context; she'll need to learn how to read fluently in context. So, what makes reading words in isolation different from reading in context?

How Is Reading Words in Isolation Different from Reading in Context?

How will decoding and sight word knowledge fuel Aliyah's fluency? And what else does reading in context require? As Aliyah improves her ability to decode words *in isolation,* she'll be more likely to read those words accurately and fluently *in context.* However, this transfer of skills from isolation to context won't just happen automatically; she'll need explicit fluency instruction and large amounts of practice putting her new decoding skills to work in context. This is because when you move from reading in isolation to reading in context, you have a lot of other mental balls to juggle. Let's consider Aliyah reading the following sentence from her science textbook as an example:

> *Fleas are parasites that live on the outside of the host (exoparasitic), including dogs and, yes, even humans.*

When Aliyah reads this sentence in context, she not only has to read each individual, separate word, accurately and automatically, she also needs to:

- *Monitor meaning at the sentence-, paragraph-, and text-level context.* After Aliyah decodes each word, she must check that each word makes sense based on everything she has read leading up to this sentence. She also needs to connect phrases within sentences, sentences within paragraphs, and paragraphs across the page. This requires a lot of mental energy. For example, does *exoparasitic* make sense when talking about fleas on dogs and humans?

- *Match her phrasing and intonation to the passage meaning.* Aliyah must also read with appropriate intonation, expression, and phrasing to match the author's intended meaning. For example, Aliyah would pause at the comma, after the word *exoparasitic,* and might emphasize the words "*and yes, even humans.*" There is a reciprocal relationship between prosody and comprehension, so discussing the meaning of the larger text can support Aliyah's phrasing.

In sum, a common missing link we see in interventions with older struggling readers is only focusing on either (1) decoding *or* (2) fluency to improve their overall fluency and comprehension. Many middle-grades readers need both. Solely focusing on Aliyah's decoding—without fluency instruction—would be like a baseball team practicing hitting and fielding skills in isolation, but never playing a scrimmage (learning how to apply those skills in context). And, focusing on fluency—without decoding instruction—would be like playing a scrimmage without having the skills work on hitting and fielding. In either scenario, the team would never be ready for the actual game—in our case, reading this science selection and learning about *exoparasites.*

Fluency: What Does the Research Say?

Repeated readings are perhaps the most powerful, well-researched, and widely applicable instructional practice for improving reading fluency. Guided repeated oral readings—with guidance from teachers, peers, or parents—has a significant and positive impact on word recognition, fluency, and comprehension across a range of grade levels (NRP, 2000). Taken together, multiple studies have found that when we ask students to practice rereading a relatively short chunk of text three or four times—and provide these students modeling and feedback on their reading fluency—we see significant positive effects across multiple components of reading. Even more encouraging, this type of repeated readings works for both strong readers and readers who struggle and in both regular and special education settings.

In Aliyah's intervention section below, we describe what these "guided repeated oral readings" might look like in an intervention setting. Before we do, let's note one more point about building fluency. One of the primary reasons repeated readings may work is simply because students are reading more—plenty of scrimmage opportunities as they prepare for the big game! So, is it repeated readings itself, or simply reading volume that makes the difference in fluency? Researchers who compared *repeated readings* versus *wide reading* found that both groups made comparable improvements in word reading and fluency, but only the wide reading group also showed gains in comprehension (Kuhn, 2005; Kuhn et al., 2006). We recommend both approaches *across a week* for building fluency with middle-grades readers: (1) large amounts of wide reading combined with (2) shorter, fluency-focused lessons using repeated readings as the primary instructional strategy in the intervention settings.

ALIYAH'S FLUENCY INTERVENTION PLAN

After their general questions about Aliyah's fluency challenges were answered, Aliyah's intervention team, led by Mr. Jackson, was ready to create her fluency intervention goals for the next 9 weeks (see Figure 5.5).

As a reminder, Aliyah's daily intervention with Mr. Jackson includes both automatic word recognition *and* fluency as part of Pathway #1. When she meets with her intervention group, they spend:

By the end of 9 weeks, Aliyah will:	This will be measured with:
• Read a 6th grade level passage in 100 WCPM	• Calculating Aliyah's reading rate in WCPM from a 6th grade QRI passage
• Improve her reading prosody score from a 2 to a 3, including reading with appropriate expression and in phrasal units	• Observing her prosody on a 6th grade QRI passage, using the QRI prosody scale

FIGURE 5.5. Aliyah's fluency goals and progress monitoring.

- About 15–20 minutes devoted to automatic word recognition, including both decoding and spelling (see Chapter 4)
- About 25–30 minutes focused on building fluency (this chapter)

This chapter is devoted to the types of fluency activities Aliyah would do in the final 25–30 minutes of her intervention class. Combining word recognition and fluency instruction in an intervention for students like Aliyah is a powerful combination.

EFFECTIVE INTERVENTION INSTRUCTION FOR FLUENCY

What, exactly, can we do to improve Aliyah's reading fluency? What will her fluency intervention look like? For most middle-grades students with fluency issues like Aliyah, we follow a three-pronged intervention plan (see Figure 5.6).

1. *Automatic word recognition and instruction.* As you can see from Pathway #1 in the cognitive model, many fluency issues are, at their root, caused by lack of decoding ability and automatic word recognition. If Aliyah can't recognize words in isolation accurately and automatically, that will impact her ability to read fluently in context. We see this decoding work as a missing piece in many middle-grades students' fluency intervention plans, as it's assumed either that (1) most older students can "already decode," or that (2) their slow, labored decoding is good enough. It isn't. To be a fluent, skilled reader, an older reader's decoding must be automatic and relatively effortless. (See Chapter 4, Figure 4.3, for Aliyah's word recognition goals and progress-monitoring plan of action.)

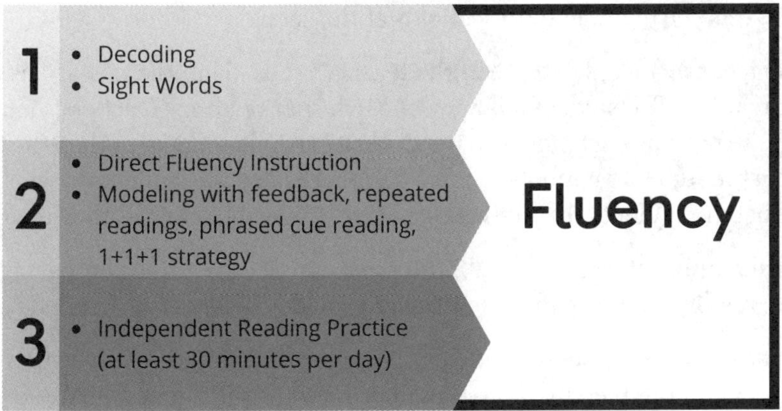

FIGURE 5.6. Three-pronged fluency intervention plan.

2. *Direct, explicit fluency instruction.* In addition to decoding instruction, we need to directly and explicitly teach Aliyah to read fluently. Like all explicit instruction, this includes (1) modeling what fluent reading sounds like and (2) providing opportunities for guided practice with teacher feedback. This direct, explicit fluency instruction can be delivered using: (1) the Gradual Release Model described in Chapter 2, coupled with (2) various research-based instructional strategies and routines such as repeated readings, phrased cue reading, and the 1 + 1 + 1 strategy, all described later in this chapter.

3. *Wide independent reading practice.* Aliyah will also need a lot of practice reading independently to become fluent—at least 30 minutes per day. As with a daily 30-minute walking goal, these reading minutes are cumulative, meaning it's not strictly about 30 minutes in one sitting. This fluent practice should be in texts she can read with adequate accuracy, rate, and prosody.

Core Four-Step Repeated Readings Routine

Following is a core four-step method for repeated readings we use, based on a number of fluency researchers and practitioners (Morris, 2014; Reutzel & Hollingsworth, 1993; Samuels, 1979, 2006):

1. *Student cold read and teacher feedback.* In step #1, the student reads the passage aloud the first time. During this "cold read," the teacher listens and, if they have a copy of the passage, marks any miscues. If a student gets stuck on a word for 3–5 seconds, the teacher provides the word. The teacher and student discuss the passage meaning and the teacher provides specific feedback to the student, including fluency strengths ("You read this part smoothly—well done!"), and notes any missed words. Scooping (visual marks showing where phrases begin and end) and highlighting "golden words" (words that require the extra "umph" like "I just KNEW it was you!") are helpful scaffolds at this step.

2. *Teacher models.* In step #2, the teacher reads aloud the passage as a model of fluent reading. The student follows along, whisper reading. Teachers should make sure they are not reading faster than the student can follow along (perhaps just slightly faster than the student's normal rate). We find that asking the students to whisper read ensures that the students are "actively listening" to the modeling as they read along.

3. *Student practice reading #2.* Student practices reading the passage a second time, reading aloud again. The teacher provides feedback as needed.

4. *Hot read.* The student reads the passage a final time—the "hot" read. The teacher provides final feedback, noting improvement and fluency goals for the next lesson. This hot read can be the reading "performance" for peers, part of a self-evaluation, or the final timed reading (see *timed repeated readings* below).

Consider the following when choosing a text for use with repeated readings:

- Choose texts that are right at, or slightly above, the level at which a student can read with at least 90% accuracy. It's fine to choose slightly more difficult texts, as long as by the "hot" read (usually the third or fourth time practicing a text), your student's accuracy is up to at least 90% or better and their rate and/or prosody has improved from the cold to the hot read. If they are still struggling by the hot read, you've probably chosen a text that's too difficult. Some researchers recommend a 95% accuracy benchmark, which we consider for certain appropriate instructional purposes (see Chapter 3).

- Choose a text that is on a topic the student is interested in (if at all possible). Or perhaps a text recently read in a content class or coming up to revisit or review a key topic. We've also found using a "hook" text can be motivating; this is a selection from a novel we're reading that cues up a good, juicy part.

- Choose a relatively small chunk of text. We recommend starting smaller (perhaps a paragraph) and then moving to bigger chunks as your student's fluency and confidence improve (perhaps a page, but not much more; most fluency researchers and approaches recommend 50–200 words). It's also very motivating to allow the student to choose the short section that they will reread.

- Choose a section of text from a book they are already reading for another purpose. We often ask our students to choose their chunk of text from the last section of a text they have just read for their fluency work. "With your reading buddy, go back to Chapter 4, which we read yesterday, and choose two paragraphs that you're going to practice reading a few times. You might want to choose some text with dialogue so you can really showcase your expression!" Choosing a section from a just-ready text for fluency work is a powerful and efficient routine for a number of reasons: (1) Because your students have just read the text recently (often that day or the day before) they are at least somewhat familiar and hopefully more comfortable with tackling it, (2) it saves you time as a teacher—you don't have to find a different text every time you plan a fluency instruction, and (3) working with a partner (a partner that you must approve of!) is nearly always more motivating for students.

- If you don't have time to model, don't worry. The fluency research shows that repeated readings, without modeling, still builds fluency.

Modifying the Four-Step Fluency Lesson for Accuracy, Rate, or Prosody

We can modify the core four-step fluency lesson described above to target the three different fluency components: rate, accuracy, and prosody. In addition to these three components of fluency, many middle-grades readers with fluency challenges also need support moving from oral to silent reading. In the rest of this section, we describe different fluency activities that target different fluency needs outlined in Figure 5.7.

Is Your Fluency Target Reading Rate? Choose Timed Repeated Readings

Timed repeated readings (Samuels, 1979, 2006) are used with students who need work with reading rate. In Figure 5.8a and 5.8b, see two possible timed repeated reading graphs you can use with either 10-second or 5-second intervals for recording a student's reading time on the y-axis. Choose a chunk of text (50–200 words). On the first "cold read," time the students and record your baseline time in the number of seconds it took your student to read the chunk of text on the y-axis. On the final "hot read," you record the time again on the graph. Remind the students that it's actually a *positive* for the line on the graph to *slant down* (since it's taking you fewer seconds to read the same number of words on the hot read).

Some commercial fluency programs record the number of *words* read in a minute, instead of recording seconds. The problem we find with words is you have to use their materials for fluency work (since the words are precounted), or end up counting the words yourself, which takes time. If you record seconds, you can use any text the student is currently reading and you never have to count the words, since students are reading the same number of words (the same "chunk" of text) with each reading.

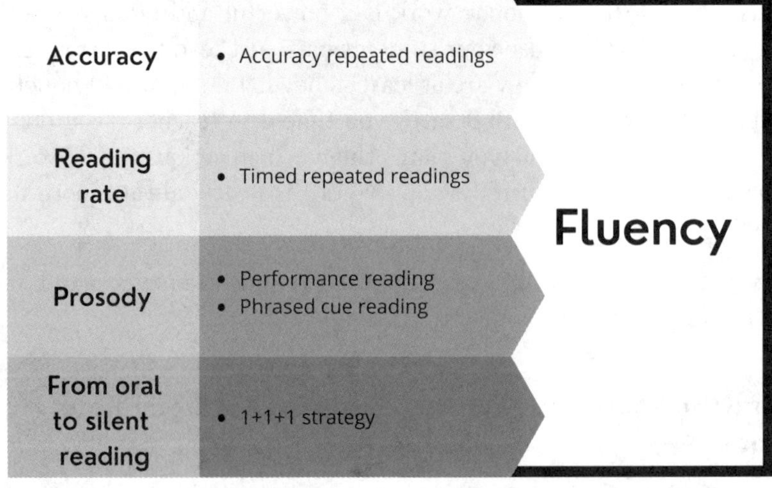

FIGURE 5.7. Different fluency activities for different fluency needs.

(a) Time Repeated Reading Graphs (10-second intervals)

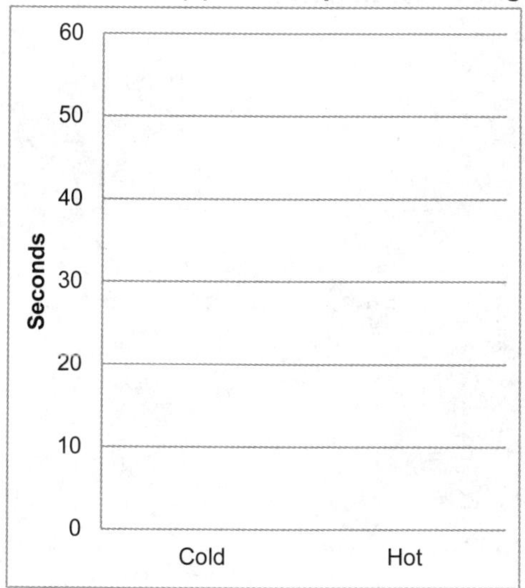

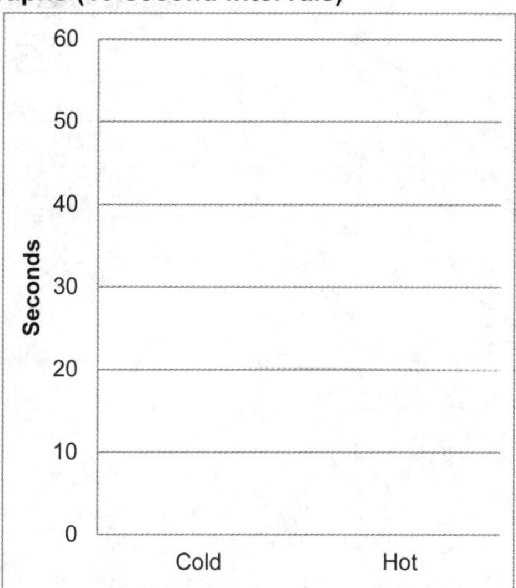

Name:
Date:

Name:
Date:

(b) Time Repeated Reading Graphs (5-second intervals)

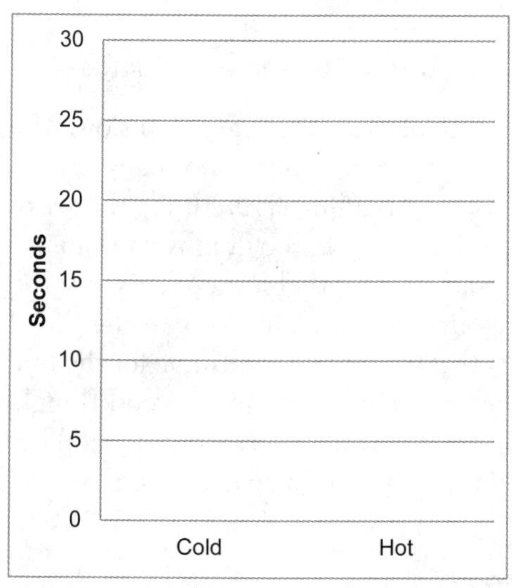

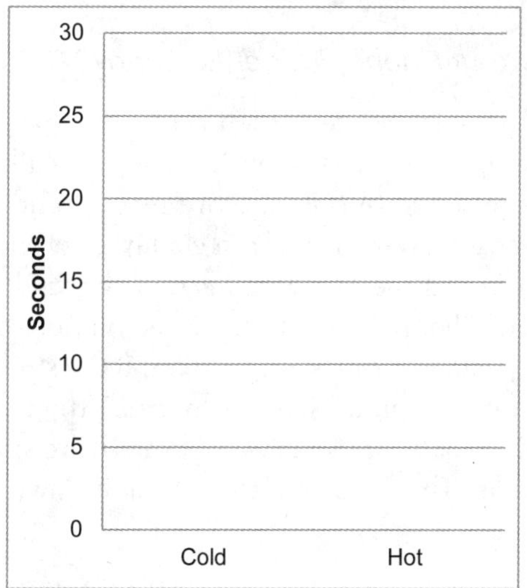

Name:
Date:

Name:
Date:

(continued)

FIGURE 5.8. Timed repeated readings and accuracy repeated readings graphs.

(c) Accuracy Repeated Reading Graphs

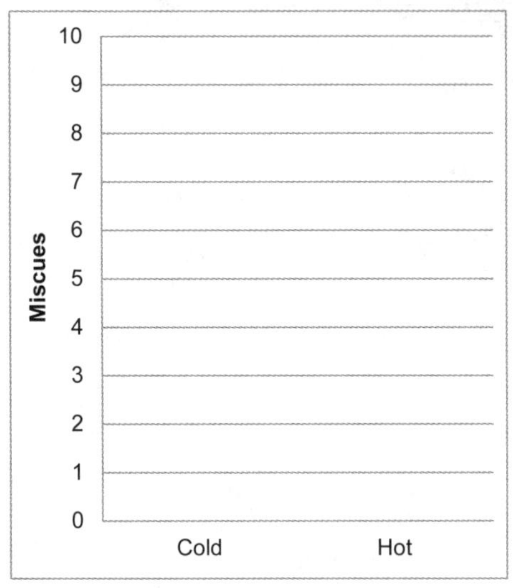

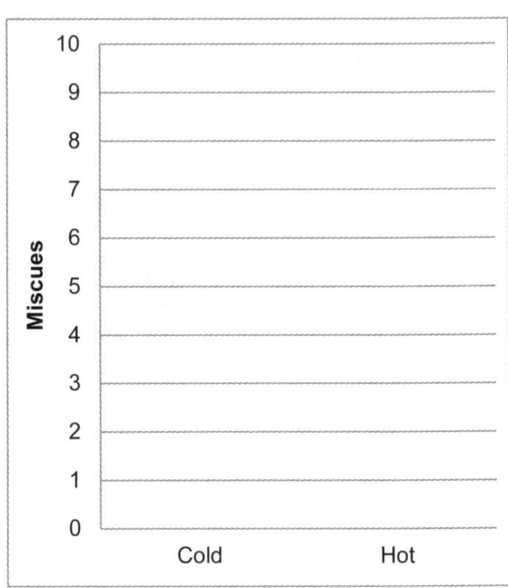

FIGURE 5.8. *(continued)*

Is Your Fluency Target Accuracy? Choose Accuracy Repeated Readings

With some readers, the issue is *not* that the student's reading rate is too slow. The issue is the exact opposite: They're reading *too fast* and making too many errors, or miscues. In this case, we recommend measuring reading *errors* (the number of words read *in*correctly in context), not *time*. In Figure 5.8c, see graphs you can use to record the *number of errors* the student read incorrectly on the *y*-axis. On the final "hot read," you record the number of reading errors again. As with the timed repeated readings graph, remind the students that it's actually a positive for the line on the graph to slant down, since the number of errors decreased (a good thing!). Many older students we work with are surprised at how many errors they regularly make. This motivates them to slow down and focus on reading each word.

Is Your Fluency Target Reading with Prosody? Choose Performance Readings

Performance readings are motivating activities for students who need to work on their prosody, including phrasing, intonation, and overall expression. What's the best motivator for reading and rereading a section of text until you sound fluent? How about the fact that you're going to perform it before a live audience of your peers in about 10 minutes? Or about to perform for yourself as you prepare to record your reading for self-evaluation?

For performance readings, use the core four-step fluency lesson; however, don't time or measure anything. Instead, tell your students that for their "hot read" they are going to "perform" the section of text for their peers in a few minutes or in the next day or so. Performance readings work particularly well when (1) using text with dialogue and (2) pairing students. The pairs can perform for their peers. They can even record it to share with family. To motivate them even further, create a context for their performance. You can also ask students to self-evaluate their fluency growth using the following questions:

- Did I read in appropriate phrases?
- Was my reading smooth?
- Did I pay attention to the punctuation markers, changing my voice and expression as appropriate?
- Did I read the words on the page?
- Did I read at an appropriate speed, not too slow or too fast?

Is Your Fluency Target Reading with Prosody, Particularly Reading in Appropriate Phrases? Choose Phrased Cued Reading

Phrased cued reading (Rasinski, 1990, 1994) is a method to help students improve their ability to read in phrasal units, pausing at the appropriate syntactic boundaries. The idea is that because phrases more or less correspond with "idea units," improving their ability to read in phrases will help your students to literally "see" where one idea ends and the next begins, thus supporting their comprehension of text. Steps for phrased cued reading include:

- Select a 150- to 250-word section of text at or slightly above the student's instructional reading level.

- Make two copies of the text. Keep one original (unmarked) and mark the phrasal boundaries in the second copy: two slashes (//) to mark sentence boundaries and one slash (/) to mark within sentence boundaries. Example:

  After he picked up breakfast at the drive-through,/ but before he arrived at work,/ he must have committed the crime.//

- Say to the student, "The key ideas in a text are often organized by phrases, so it helps to know where these phrases are. We know where phrases begin and end by punctuation markers such as commas and periods. So, if you know where phrases begin and end, you know where the key ideas begin and end." The teacher then points to the pre-marked text, noting the beginning and ending of each phrase.

"Here's a phrase or key idea. Here's another phrase, another key idea. The reason we pause and stop at commas and periods is to give our brains a chance to store one idea in our brains before getting ready for the next idea coming up. If you don't know where one idea stops and the next idea starts, you'll get the ideas in a text all mixed up with each other. This will make it hard to understand what you're reading."

- The teacher reads the marked copy of text while the student(s) follows along, possibly whisper reading. The teacher and student discuss the text meaning and phrasal boundaries, including where and why the teacher paused and stopped.

- The student reads the marked copy of text aloud two or three more times. The teacher provides positive feedback and points out areas to improve after each practice reading. At this step, the teacher might model a sentence or phrase again. Additional possible scaffolds we've found helpful are marking the text with arrows pointing up or down to note a rising voice (such as at a question mark) and highlighting certain words as the "golden" word that get a lot of emphasis; "You did WHAT?"

- The student's hot read is a "performance" of the unmarked text.

Considerations When Using Repeated Readings

When using repeated readings, remember that the end goal is to build your students' reading fluency. Consider the following when using any of the repeated reading variations described above:

- One of the reasons repeated readings work is that students are *getting a lot of reading practice.* So, make sure your students have their "eyeballs on the page" for the majority of the fluency lesson. This critical point can too easily get lost in the mix. For example, we've seen *reader's theater* (an instructional approach for teaching fluency during which students practice reading their assigned or chosen parts from a scripted play), in which the struggling readers get the smallest parts, thus only actually "reading" for a few minutes in a fluency "lesson."

- It's better to do a little a lot rather than a lot a little. If you really want to build a student's fluency, don't do a reader's theater once at the end of the month and then never revisit it. As with anything, purposeful practice makes perfect. For students with fluency needs, they should be doing repeated readings in short bursts, perhaps three or more times per week. The repeated reading four-step fluency lesson plan might take 15 minutes or so. Importantly, your fluency lessons do not have to be a big production—like a reader's theater—every time. In fact, most of the time, your performance reading might just be asking a pair of students at the beginning or end of a small-group reading lesson to (1) choose a chunk of text from a section of the book that the group already read, (2) practice it for about 5–10 minutes while you model and provide feedback, and then (3) perform it for the group right then or the very next time the group meets. It can, and should, be that straightforward.

- We expect the student to show growth from the cold to the hot read. This is a good measure of short-term fluency growth. However, the ultimate test of fluency growth is generalizing these skills to a cold read of a new text.

- As with all intervention work, continuous, precise feedback is critical to building fluency. Between each repeated reading, provide specific, concrete, actionable feedback on a reader's accuracy, phrasing, ability to read punctuation, and smoothness. Make sure to point out positives and growth as well as areas of continued need. For example: "Aliyah, I noticed how you paused at the first comma in this long sentence. It made me realize that you had finished one idea and were ready for the next idea. I'm going to mark two other long sentences where you didn't pause, and we're going to work on those next."

Moving from Oral to Silent Reading: The 1 + 1 + 1 Strategy

Many middle-grades struggling readers find it difficult to move from oral reading to silent reading. Because most of the reading in the middle grades and as adults is done silently, it's important to help our students take this step. The following straightforward three-step strategy (Morris, 2014) is a supportive way to help students make this oral-to-silent reading transition that we've found success with.

- Step #1—The teacher *reads aloud* one "chunk" of text (one paragraph or more, generally 50–200 words). The students follow along, whisper reading if possible.

- Step #2—The students *read aloud* the next "chunk" of text. The teacher listens and provides feedback on the students' fluency. Chunk #2, read by the students, is about the same length as chunk #1, which was read by the teacher.

- Step #3—The students read the next "chunk" of text—chunk #3—*silently*. After chunk #3 is read, the students stop. The students and teacher discuss the meaning of the text.

- These three steps can all be done in small groups. During step two, if students are sitting closely in a guided reading group, ask them to scoot back into their "reading bubbles" and whisper to themselves while the teacher moves from student to student, listening to individual students read aloud.

- If doing this in a small group, for those students who finish early in steps 2 or 3, ask them to (1) start rereading until the other students catch up or (2) write on a sticky note: a summary of what they just read, any questions they have, any interesting/unknown words, or their prediction for the next section.

- Repeat this process. As students gain confidence and skill, increase chunk #3, so students are reading longer and longer sections silently and independently.

- If you can't be right there with your students, ask them to partner-read. Partner one reads a paragraph aloud while partner two follows along silently. They switch roles for the second paragraph. They both read silently for paragraph three and then discuss.

CONCLUSION

Aliyah has been in an intervention for 9 weeks. Her intervention included explicit instruction in fluency, focusing on reading rate and reading prosody. During the intervention lessons, Mr. Jackson used timed repeated readings to target her reading rate and performance readings to target her prosody. Throughout these sessions, Mr. Jackson followed the Gradual Release Model, explicitly teaching and modeling fluent reading, and providing plenty of guided practice with specific feedback. In addition, Aliyah read for at least 30 minutes independently.

Figure 5.9 shows Aliyah's growth after this 9-week intervention. In terms of reading rate, Aliyah made her goal of reading a sixth-grade passage at over 100 WCPM. While she didn't quite make her prosody goal (scoring a 2.5 prosody instead of a 3), she did show progress in this area and will continue to build her phrasal, expressive reading over the next 9 weeks.

The North Star principles we introduced in Chapter 2 informed our intervention decisions and helped Aliyah make progress toward her goals. How did they play out across the interventions to build her fluency? See Figure 5.10.

By the end of 9 weeks, Aliyah will:	This will be measured with:	Progress at 9 weeks:
• Read a 6th grade level passage in 100 WCPM	• Calculating Aliyah's reading rate in WCPM from a 6th grade QRI passage	• Aliyah read the 6th grade QRI passage with 105 WCPM on a cold read
• Improve her reading prosody score from a 2 to a 3, including reading with appropriate expression and in phrasal units	• Observing her prosody on a 6th grade QRI passage, using the QRI prosody scale	• Aliyah read the 6th grade QRI passage with a 2.5 prosody. The majority of the reading was fluent and in appropriate phrasal units. There were only a few sections where the phrasing was awkward.

FIGURE 5.9. Aliyah's fluency goals, progress monitoring, and 9-week growth.

Principles	An example of how we used it:
1. What Do You Stand For? Articulate Your Literacy Beliefs	Based on the research on reading fluency, Aliyah's team believed that direct fluency instruction, use of the Gradual Release Model, and increased volume of reading would result in fluency gains for Aliyah.
2. Don't Forget Your Map! Choose and Use an Intervention Model	Aliyah's team used the cognitive model to target Pathway #1.
3. Start with Assessments Get to Know Your Students	Importantly, Aliyah's team ruled out Pathways #2 and #3 as areas of need using a listening comprehension assessment combined with content teacher reports.
4. Keep the Main Thing the Main Thing Design a Focused, Flexible, Doable Intervention Plan	Aliyah's team focused on two fluency components, reading rate and prosody. They kept improvements in these two areas their main objectives throughout the 9-week intervention.
5. Make the Invisible Visible Use the "I Do" to Be Explicit and Systematic	Each fluency lesson started with an explicit introduction, including why, and a think-aloud modeling of fluent reading. Anchor charts served as explicit visual reminders.
6. Practice, Practice, Purposeful Practice Leverage the "We Do" and "You Do" for Long-Term Transfer and Independence	For the majority of each fluency lesson, Aliyah was reading text, her "eyeballs on the page." In addition to repeated readings, she spent at least 30 minutes a day independently reading a self-selected text. This wide reading was critical to her reading practice.
7. One Size Does Not Fit All Differentiate and Scaffold When They're Not "Getting It"	Aliyah was provided additional scaffolding and support as needed, including posting of fluency anchor charts, reminders to apply fluency strategies while reading, and specific feedback from Mr. Jackson.
8. Time Where Does It All Go and How Can I Get Some Back?	Mr. Jackson was able to save valuable planning and instructional time by asking Aliyah to do many of her performance reads out of the same novel she was reading for independent reading practice.
9. Engagement Get Your Students to Buy In When They've Checked Out	As much as possible, Aliyah was given choice in what she was asked to read, even if it was a limited choice. She was highly motivated by the performance reads because she was paired with a friend and was performing for peers.
10. Active, Not Passive Take a Critical Stance and Read with a Purpose	Aliyah really liked tracking her progress in reading rate on the timed repeated readings graph. Seeing this concrete progress made her feel that she was in the "driver's seat" and was actively engaged in her own learning.

FIGURE 5.10. Aliyah's North Star principles.

APPENDIX: SAMPLE FLUENCY LESSON

Building Prosody

One of Aliyah's primary fluency goals was to build her prosody, including her ability to read with expression and in phrasal units. Figure 5.11 presents a sample lesson that teaches students to use punctuation marks to aid in phrasal reading.

"I Do"—
Directly and explicitly teach your concept

Make the Objective Public:

By the end of the 9-week fluency intervention, Aliyah will improve her ability to read in phrases and with appropriate expression, using punctuation markers as guides. Here's our anchor chart:

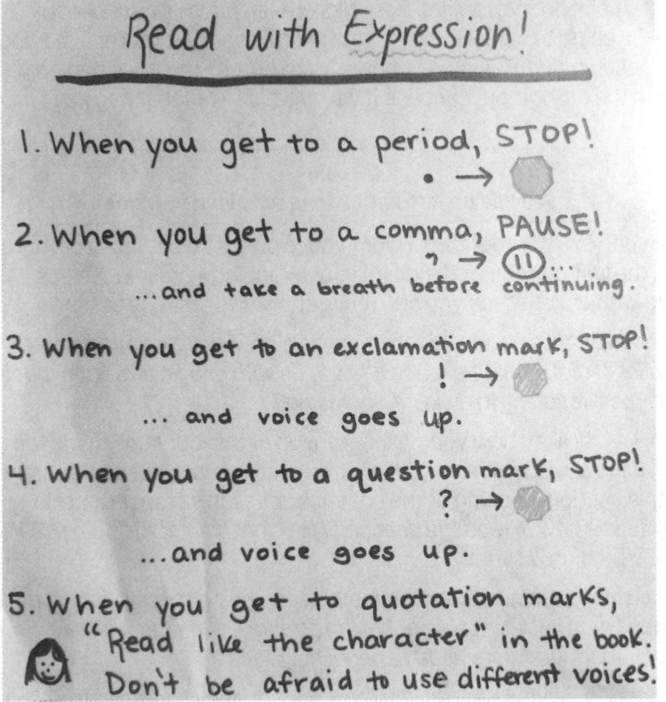

Introduce the Lesson:

Teacher: Today, we're going to work on reading in phrases, rather than reading without pausing or stopping. When you read without ever pausing or stopping, it is sometimes difficult to figure out what the author really means. However, when you know when and where to pause and stop, you know where one idea in a text ends and where the next one begins. This will help you not only read more fluently, but also improve your comprehension.

(continued)

FIGURE 5.11. Sample lesson: Building prosody.

State the Secret and Model Your Thinking:

Teacher: There's a secret to reading in phrases. And that's paying attention to the punctuation. Take a look at our "Read with Expression" anchor chart. It shows you what to do when you come to each type of punctuation marker. When you get to a comma, you pause. When you get to a period, you stop for a longer time and take a breath. When you come to a question mark, your voice goes up.

I'll model how these tips "look and sound" in action, and then you'll try them out using our "repeated readings" strategy that we've used before. We'll always keep our fluency anchor chart posted as a visual reminder of our fluency tips.

Aliyah, now that we've gone over the five tips on the fluency anchor chart, I'm going to model how NOT to read fluently—like a robot. So, I'm going to read this first paragraph like a robot, with no expression at all. *[Teacher reads word by word, not pausing at punctuation markers.]* Now, I know I overdid the "robot reading" a bit to make a point, but did you see how boring that sounded? Do you think I understood what I was reading? What didn't I do? That's right, I didn't pay attention to the punctuation markers. My voice sounded the exact same whether it was a period, question mark, or exclamation point. In fact, sometimes I didn't even pause at the periods!

Now I'm going to model fluent reading of this same paragraph, paying attention to the punctuation markers. Listen to how my voice goes up at the beginning of this first sentence in the paragraph, because it's a question. *[Teacher begins to model fluent reading.]*

"We Do"—
Provide opportunities for scaffolded practice

Teacher: OK, Aliyah. Now it's your turn. I want you to choose a couple of paragraphs to read from the last chapter of the novel you're reading in your ELA class. Maybe pick something with dialogue, so you can really show off your expression!

Student: *[For her initial "cold read," Aliyah chooses a section in the middle of the chapter which includes a lot of dialogue. She reads a few lines with good expression, but fails to pause at two commas, resulting in awkward phrasing.]*

Teacher: Aliyah, I really liked how your voice went up at this question mark! Nice job paying attention to the punctuation. Now, I think you may have missed this comma here. Let me read this section, pausing at the commas. You can whisper read along as I model. *[Teacher models how to read the section of text, pausing at the commas.]* What did you notice in my reading, Aliyah?

Student: I noticed you pausing at this comma here. I'm going to circle it so I remember to pause when I read it. *[After teacher finishes giving his feedback, Aliyah practices reading the text, and then "performs" it on her final hot read.]*

Teacher: Fantastic job, Aliyah! How do you think your fluency improved from the first "cold read" to the final "hot read"? Which punctuation markers were you more likely to notice while reading?

Student: *[Aliyah discusses her fluency improvement, referring to the punctuation markers on the fluency anchor chart. Teacher asks her to try to continue reading in phrases during her independent reading time.]*

FIGURE 5.11. *(continued)*

CHAPTER 6

Building Vocabulary with Zach

Zach, our sixth grader introduced in Chapter 1, brings many strengths to the intervention setting. He is a talented artist and a skilled and avid skateboarder with a small but close group of friends who share his interests. In terms of his literacy skills, he is a strong decoder, which enables him to read grade-level text accurately at an appropriate rate, and with generally solid fluency.

In this and the following two chapters (6–8), we follow Zach, who has a very different literacy profile than Aliyah. As we discussed in Chapters 4 and 5, Aliya had *word recognition* and *fluency* challenges. Zach's challenges center on *vocabulary* and *comprehension* difficulties, which often occur together with many middle-grades readers. We discuss Zach's *vocabulary intervention* in this chapter and his *comprehension intervention* in Chapter 7. In Chapter 8, we show how to further support Zach's comprehension and content learning through writing.

ZACH'S VOCABULARY CHALLENGES: INITIAL SCREENING RESULTS

Zach was administered the (1) Maze and (2) ORF screening assessments in September. Following are his results and Zach's intervention team's initial thinking:

- *Maze*—Zach scored below benchmark on the Maze assessment, indicating *reading comprehension* issues. His teachers confirmed these comprehension problems, reporting Zach's difficulties (1) keeping up with class discussions, (2) writing coherent responses to text readings, and (3) performing adequately on quizzes and tests. Importantly, and in contrast to Aliyah, Zach experienced comprehension issues both (1) when *he read the text himself* and (2) when information *was presented orally.*

- *ORF assessment*—Despite his comprehension difficulties, Zach's fluency score on the ORF was at benchmark: He read the sixth-grade passage accurately and with an appropriate reading rate for a sixth grader (130 WCPM), indicating his overall fluency is likely strong. Based on his strong scores on the ORF, Zach's team tentatively ruled out Pathway #1 (automatic word recognition) as a contributing factor to his comprehension issues. Decoding and fluency did not seem to be the problem for Zach.

- Ruling out Pathway #1 left Pathway #2 (*oral language comprehension,* including vocabulary, background knowledge, and text structure) and Pathway #3 (*strategic knowledge*) as the possible culprits.

Zach's team asked the school reading specialist, Mr. Jackson, to follow up with diagnostic assessments targeting Pathways #2 and #3 to see if he could pinpoint, exactly, the root cause of Zach's reading comprehension difficulties.

ZACH'S DIAGNOSTIC FOLLOW-UP ASSESSMENTS

Mr. Jackson followed up by administering an informal reading inventory to Zach (see Chapter 3 on brief diagnostic assessment). Because Zach demonstrated adequate fluency on the ORF, he asked Zach to read a sixth-grade passage titled "Building Pyramids," from the QRI-7 (Leslie & Caldwell, 2021), using a think-aloud protocol. Based on the results, Mr. Jackson decided to assess Zach's listening comprehension skills by *reading aloud to Zach* another sixth-grade passage, "Clouds and Precipitation," as part of an in-depth exploration of Pathway #2. Figure 6.1 illustrates Zach's results on the reading passage and the listening passage.

Let's start with his oral reading passage. Confirming his grade-appropriate fluency scores on the ORF screener in September, Zach's fluency scores on the sixth-grade passage that he read himself were very strong:

- Accuracy—98% (nearly perfect accuracy)
- Reading rate—*We do not calculate rate when we use a think-aloud protocol*
- Prosody—3 (generally fluent and expressive)

However, Zach's 50% reading comprehension score indicated that, despite solid fluency, he still struggled to adequately understand the "Building Pyramids" passage. As Mr. Jackson dug deeper beyond this number, he noticed that Zach experienced difficulty on a number of other sections of the QRI-7 and made particular note of Zach's vocabulary challenges, including:

Zach's Assessment Results

Grade Level	Passage	Accuracy	Reading Rate	Prosody	Reading Comprehension	Listening Comprehension
6th	ORF*	95% (met benchmark)	130 WCPM (met benchmark)		Maze (below benchmark)	
	Oral passage reading from QRI-7**	98% (above benchmark)	N/A	3 (met benchmark)	50% with look-backs (below benchmark)	
	Listening comprehension passage from QRI-7***					50% (below benchmark)

* Step 1—ORF and Maze from screening
** Step 2—Oral passage reading from brief diagnostic
*** Step 3—Listening comprehension from in-depth diagnostic
(see Figure 3.3 for assessment flowchart detailing these steps)

FIGURE 6.1. Zach's assessment results.

- *Prereading concept questions.* Before reading, Zach struggled to answer questions that tapped his *background knowledge* of key *vocabulary* terms and *concepts* in the upcoming reading, such as *pharaoh* and *archeologist.* He knew *pharaohs* were some type of people back in ancient Egypt, but he didn't know that they were the Egyptian kings. Lack of background and vocabulary knowledge—particularly knowledge of key terms and concepts that an author assumes a reader already has in order to make sense of the text—can significantly impact comprehension.

- *During-reading think-alouds.* At the QRI-7's preplanned stopping points during his reading of the passage "Building Pyramids," Mr. Jackson had planned some additional questions to probe's Zach's vocabulary knowledge. For example, he asked Zach what the word *preserved* meant in the context of this passage. Zach's answer indicated he did not grasp the word's meaning. In addition, Zach showed little evidence of using any comprehension strategies, such as *summarizing* and *inferring.*

- *After-reading open-ended questions.* After the reading, when asked, "Why were *pharaohs* buried with their possessions?" Zach answered, "Because pharaohs were rich and didn't want anyone else to have their stuff." Even when Mr. Jackson probed and reminded Zach that he could look back in the text, Zach wasn't able to infer the correct answer (i.e., the Egyptians believed that the pharaoh took his possessions into the afterlife with him, a major point in the passage). When asked, "What *organ* did the ancient Egyptians leave in the dead pharaoh's body?" Zach answered, "They put oils and perfumes in it." This answer made it clear that he didn't know the meaning of the word *organ.*

On the listening comprehension assessment, Zach's listening comprehension score was the same as his reading comprehension—both only 50%. In other words, Mr. Jackson's reading a passage aloud *to* Zach didn't improve his comprehension. This was further evidence that Pathway #1, word recognition, was *not* a cause of Zach's reading comprehension difficulties.

In sum, Mr. Jackson told Zach's team that Zach's reading comprehension difficulties appeared to stem from issues with:

1. **oral language comprehension** (Pathway #2), particularly *vocabulary* and *background knowledge,* and
2. **strategy knowledge** (Pathway #3), including *summarizing* and *inferring.*

Mr. Jackson met with Zach's content teachers to discuss the assessment results above and then began to develop an intervention plan for Zach. Based on all the assessment information gathered so far, the team felt that they had pretty good sense that they had pinpointed Zach's major areas of difficulty. Figure 6.2 highlights Pathways #2 and #3.

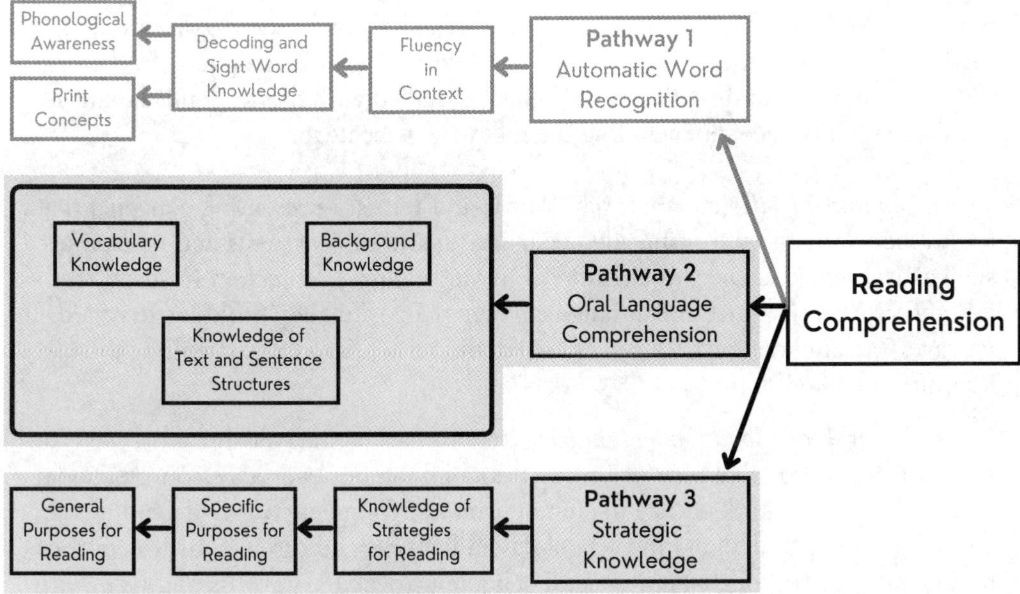

FIGURE 6.2. The cognitive model highlighting Pathways #2 and 3. Adapted with permission from Stahl, Flanigan, & McKenna (2020). Copyright 2020 by The Guilford Press.

ZACH'S TEAM'S QUESTIONS ABOUT VOCABULARY

As Zach's sixth-grade intervention team met with Mr. Jackson to discuss the intervention goals and develop their intervention plan, they had the following questions about vocabulary:

- What, exactly, is *academic language and vocabulary*? Why is it so important for middle-grades students?
- How and why do Zach's vocabulary issues affect his comprehension?
- Since they can't teach Zach every possible vocabulary word he might encounter, which words should they focus on? Which should they skip directly teaching? Should they teach vocabulary before, during, or after reading?
- What can the team do to improve Zach's vocabulary knowledge? What does the research say?

Academic Language and Vocabulary—What Is It? Why Is It So Important for Middle-Grades Students?

According to Nagy and Townsend, academic language is "the specialized language, both oral and written, of academic settings that facilitates communication and thinking about disciplinary content" (2012, p. 92). Think of these vocabulary terms not simply as *words* on a page, but as *tools* that can help our middle-grades students read like historians, think like scientists, and write and talk like poets. In the oral reading passage, "Building Pyramids," Zach struggled with the academic language, vocabulary, and concepts, including the following subcategories:

- *Domain specific vocabulary*—Words and terms representing concepts that are explicitly taught and primarily occur in specific subject areas and disciplines, such as *isotope* in science, *quadrilateral* in math, *push-pull factors* in social studies, and *red herring* in English/language arts (ELA). In the "Building Pyramids" passage, Zach did not have a strong grasp of the term *pharaoh,* particularly the fact that pharaohs were kings.

- *General academic vocabulary*—General academic vocabulary refers to sophisticated words that may not occur frequently in our everyday, conversational language, but that students are likely to encounter frequently in their readings, in any subject area, and across the school day in lectures and discussions. In contrast to domain-specific vocabulary, general academic vocabulary words and terms are likely to occur across any and in all subject areas. For example, the words *reaction, insightful, production,* and *specific* could just as easily be found in a social studies textbook, a science article, or an ELA lesson. Zach struggled with the general academic words *organ* and *archeologist.*

- *Signal words and phrases*—One important subcategory of *general academic vocabulary* are signal words and phrases like *however, in the form of, depends largely on, from which,* and *if . . . because.* Understanding how these vocabulary words work is critical to a reader's comprehension precisely because they "signal" the type of thinking the author is trying to convey and how the key concepts in a text are organized and relate to one another. For example, *however* signals a compare/contrast text structure, and *therefore* signals a cause/effect relationship.

How and Why Do Zach's Vocabulary Issues Affect His Comprehension?

One of the longest-standing findings in the literacy field is the strong relationship between vocabulary and comprehension (Anderson & Freebody, 1981). Intuitively, this makes sense. The larger a reader's vocabulary, the better their overall reading comprehension should be. But what is it, exactly, about a reader's vocabulary knowledge that impacts their comprehension? Stahl and Nagy (2006), Anderson and Freebody (1981), and Stanovich (1986) delved deeper into this relationship. Figure 6.3 highlights some possible explanations for this vocabulary-to-comprehension connection.

Which one of the four hypotheses summarized in Figure 6.3 is correct? Stahl and Nagy's (2006, p. 14) answer: "Probably all of them!" This is because the

Vocabulary-to-Comprehension Connection:
4 Possible Explanations

1 Instrumental Hypothesis
Simply knowing the meanings of more words will improve a reader's comprehension.

2 Background Knowledge Hypothesis
It's not necessarily the knowledge of the words themselves (e.g., humpback whales), but a reader's background knowledge of the underlying concepts that the words represent (e.g., knowing general information about whales such as their diet, habitat, etc.) that makes the difference with comprehension.

3 Aptitude Hypothesis
Vocabulary knowledge and comprehension are related because both are indicators of a general underlying verbal ability. Students with stronger verbal abilities generally have an advantage in learning and reading.

4 Reciprocal Hypothesis
Knowledge of word meanings supports comprehension, making one a better reader. Better readers read more, developing larger vocabularies, which improves comprehension even more.

Comprehension

FIGURE 6.3. Four hypotheses for the vocabulary-to-comprehension connection.

vocabulary-to-comprehension relationship is a complex one. It's important to understand how vocabulary and comprehension relate because it leads us to some important considerations about vocabulary instruction in general and Zach's vocabulary intervention plan, specifically:

- *A multifaceted approach.* Because the relationship between vocabulary and comprehension is so complex, we need a multifaceted approach to teaching vocabulary (see Seven Principles of Effective Vocabulary Instruction, below).

- *Teaching vocabulary in context and with content.* With vocabulary, it's not just about the words per se, it's about the underlying concepts they represent, the context surrounding them, and their relationship to background knowledge and the content our students are learning. Information we learn in a void never sticks. So, Zach's vocabulary intervention work must connect vocabulary *words* and *concepts* to *context* and the grade-level *content* Zach is learning in English, math, science, and social studies.

- *Reading volume.* No vocabulary program, approach, or intervention can substitute for the amount Zach needs to read in connected text to improve his vocabulary, along with the many other cognitive benefits of wide and deep reading.

ZACH'S VOCABULARY INTERVENTION PLAN

Zach's intervention, focused on his reading comprehension, necessarily includes both *vocabulary* and *comprehension*. Now that his intervention team had their general questions about vocabulary answered, they felt ready to work with Mr. Jackson to develop a vocabulary intervention plan. Based on all of the assessment information and their knowledge about Zach, the entire team decided to target the following vocabulary areas as part of his intervention (see Figure 6.4). While this chapter focuses on Zach's vocabulary challenges, we should always be aware of how closely tied vocabulary and comprehension are. For this reason, we continue discussing Zach in Chapters 7 and 8 when we target his comprehension challenges.

Seven Principles of Effective Vocabulary Instruction

Zach's intervention goals give us a destination, but don't necessarily provide us with a guide for how to get there. Figure 6.5 presents seven research-based principles of effective vocabulary instruction (Beck, McKeown, & Kucan, 2013; Graves, 2006; Stahl & Nagy, 2006; Templeton et al., 2015). These principles can guide us as we make the critical day-to-day instructional decisions, such as which words to teach Zach, how to teach them, how often to practice them, and which instructional strategies to choose.

Provide Student-Friendly Definitions Plus Contextual Information about the Word

Definitions aren't useful when they define *a word our students don't know* using *other words they don't know*. Yet, think how often this happens when students

By the end of 9 weeks, Zach will:	This will be measured with:
• Be able to define and explain, in-depth, 20 key domain-specific vocabulary terms and/or phrases in each content area (5 each chosen by the math, science, social studies, ELA teachers)	• A four-square concept map or other appropriate vocabulary map/graphic organizer to demonstrate knowledge of a content-area vocabulary term/concept (as chosen by Zach's content teachers)
• Be able to use a vocabulary map (e.g., concept of definition map, four-square concept map) to learn a new word/concept in one of his content-area classes	• See above

FIGURE 6.4. Zach's vocabulary intervention goals and progress monitoring.

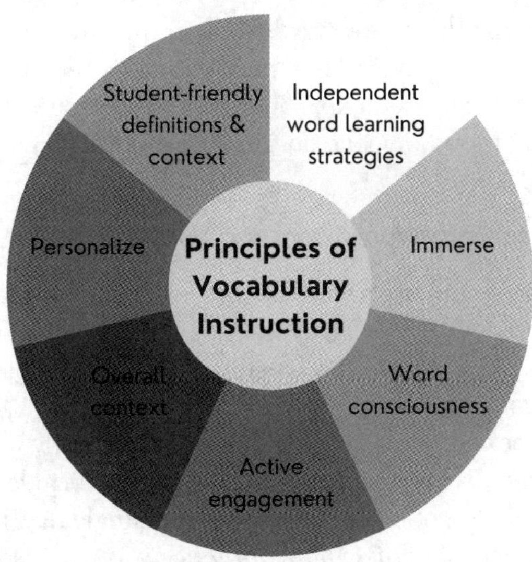

FIGURE 6.5. Principles of effective vocabulary instruction.

look up words in a dictionary. So, a critical first step in introducing new words is to start with a *student-friendly definition,* which means using *familiar* words to define the *unfamiliar* word (Beck, McKeown, & Kucan, 2013). Then, it's critical to follow this up with contextual information about the word. For example, here's a student-friendly definition of *swagger:* to walk proudly in a way that shows you are confident. Then, the teacher could follow up with contextual information and discussion about *swagger,* such as: Who might swagger? Someone trying to show off at a school dance? A bully walking down the hall might swagger, right? Would a shy person likely swagger? Why or why not? What's the opposite of swagger? *Shuffle?* Why's that?

Foster Active Engagement with Words

Effective vocabulary learning is active, not passive. The students are the ones doing the work, not listening to a lecture or passively copying a list of definitions from a dictionary or glossary in a textbook. Instead, they are creating visuals and graphic organizers, discussing and debating words and ideas, trying out words in skits, applying words to their own lives, and presenting to and sharing with their classmates.

Personalize Word Meanings

One of the most powerful learning practices we know is making "new-to-known" connections. When we ask students to find examples of words at work in their own lives, they are anchoring these new words in their own lived experiences, ensuring that they "stick" because they are not simply memorized. Rather, they are connected to who they are. For example, "Share with the group about a time recently you felt *mischievous* or saw someone do something *mischievous*."

Immerse Your Students in Words across a Variety of Rich Contexts

Students must see, hear, and use a word again and again in multiple contexts before it will "stick." How many times? That depends on a number of factors, including the difficulty of the word/concept and a student's ability to pick up words. Based on research, we recommend working with a word at least 10–12 times (Beck et al., 2013) across a week in a variety of contexts. Importantly, just as cramming on Thursday night for the Friday test doesn't result in long-term learning, these 10–12 "practice sessions" should not be crammed into one single day, but rather sprinkled across a week. This concept of *distributed practice* was most eloquently articulated by a yoga teacher I (Kevin) had, who often reminded the class, *it's far better to do a little a lot, rather than a lot a little.* Finally, for some particularly difficult words/concepts and for some students, you'll have to practice more, perhaps much more. This means you must be careful and selective in choosing which words to spend your valuable instructional time on.

Don't Forget about Overall Context

Think of the person in your life with the deepest, broadest vocabulary you know. Chances are they are a voracious reader. This is because the large majority of new vocabulary for middle-grades students and above (including adults) is acquired *not* through direct instruction, but indirectly through context, including (1) wide reading and (2) rich discussions. This is an eye-opener for many. So, an important component of Zach's vocabulary learning will include increasing the sheer volume of reading he will do across a day, week, month, and year. Listening to rich language and engaging with audio-enhanced books will also help boost Zach's vocabulary.

Teach Independent Word Learning Strategies

An old adage goes, "Give someone a fish, they can eat for a day. Teach them how to fish, they can eat for a lifetime." Teaching students individual word meanings, as described above in word-specific instruction, is like giving someone a fish. It's important in the short term, but if we truly want Zach to become an independent word learner, we need to teach him how words work, so he is able to "fish" for words for the rest of his life. One powerful independent word learning strategy is based on knowledge of high-utility Latin and Greek affixes and roots, which we describe later.

Foster Word Consciousness

Word consciousness refers to a positive disposition toward words, including a belief that word learning is important, doable, and simply fun. Unfortunately, when we say "vocabulary," many of our students think of lists of words, copying definitions, workbooks done silently and individually, and Friday quizzes—not a recipe for building a love of words. One engaging way to foster word consciousness is through word games and wordplay, which we describe in a section below.

Choosing Words to Teach: Three Categories

"So many words, so little time," is a common refrain heard from teachers everywhere. Because you often have too much to teach in the time allotted, one of the first decisions you have to make for vocabulary instruction is choosing which words to explicitly teach. While the sheer number of possible vocabulary words you could teach is daunting, remember that most of our students' vocabulary growth comes not from direct instruction, but rather incidentally from context, including wide reading and rich discussion (Nagy & Anderson, 1984).

However, it's still critical to teach the most crucial vocabulary terms and key concepts directly. But how do you decide which words to teach? Which ones to skip? When to teach them: before, during, or after a reading or lesson? Consider the following three categories and guidelines when deciding which words to directly teach (Flanigan & Greenwood, 2007): (1) "deep dive" words, (2) "foot-in-the-door" words, and (3) skipped and "saved for later" words.

"Deep Dive" Vocabulary

These are words that represent the key concepts and big ideas in a discipline. Therefore, they will require a "deep dive" of instructional time, perhaps 15 minutes or more, often much more, sometimes across several lessons. For *deep dive* words, ask yourself, "Which words or concepts do I absolutely want my students to know five years from now when I run into them in the grocery store?"

Deep dive words represent major concepts that students (1) absolutely need to know based on curriculum standards and your judgment and (2) are unfamiliar with or probably have little background knowledge on. You'll likely need to spend some time preteaching them before reading a text and need to further develop them during and after reading. Examples from math include *rational and irrational numbers* and the *Pythagorean theorem,* from social studies *civil rights* and *rights and responsibilities of citizenship,* from English *compound-complex sentence structure* and *symbolism,* and from science *convergent, divergent, and transform tectonic plate boundaries*. Use our "deep dive" strategies described later for words in this category.

"Foot-in-the-Door Words"

Sometimes, for some words, and for some instructional purposes, you may not want or even need to do a "deep dive." In fact, students may only need a "foot-in-the-door" understanding of a word meaning to make sense of a lesson or to read a text. Use the quick, three-step procedure (see below) for introducing these "foot-in-the-door" words. You can always explore these words deeper at some later time. For example, all a student may need to know about *quarry* in an upcoming short story is that, in this particular story, *quarry* refers to something that is hunted or being pursued, *not* a rock quarry.

Skipped and "Saved for Later" Words

Some words you may not want to address at all because, even though they may be unfamiliar to the students, they aren't essential to their understanding of the text. Or perhaps there is enough contextual and morphological information about these words for students to figure them out independently. You can always follow up on these *skipped and "saved for later"* words after the lesson or reading.

Choosing, Categorizing, and Prioritizing Words to Teach

When choosing and prioritizing vocabulary, consider the following questions (Flanigan et al., 2011; Flanigan & Greenwood, 2007):

- What are my instructional goals for the lesson? Without specific goals, all words tend to "look" the same. Your instructional goals will help you answer all the remaining questions below, including words to explore in-depth and words to skip.
- Based on these goals, which words are my "deep dives"? These will likely require significant amounts of instructional time and are often introduced before reading and developed during and after reading, across multiple lessons. For these words, consider the deep dive strategies section below.
- Which words are essential, but don't necessarily require a deep understanding? Consider quickly introducing these using the three-step vocabulary introduction procedure below.
- Which words can I skip or save for later, either (1) because they are not essential or (2) because my students have a good shot of figuring them out based on rich context in the passage?
- Are there words not essential to this particular passage or lesson, but are high-utility words that students will likely need to know, encounter, and use later in

their lives, like *concept, analyze, vary,* and *structure?* If so, consider teaching them directly after the lesson.

- Don't forget about wordplay and the sheer love of language. Are there words that jump out at you, that you have a visceral reaction to, that you love or that disgust you? Share them, discuss them, and play around with them. A wonderful activity is to bring in your favorite and least favorite words and share with the class. This is a crowd favorite that engages even many of our self-avowed "vocabulary haters." Some of our teachers' and students' favorite/least favorite words include the following: *moist, trousers, damp, mold, wallop, puckish, uncanny, shenanigans,* and often the biggest crowd pleaser that never fails to bring a smile when we say it aloud in a group, *brouhaha!*

Introducing Vocabulary Words in Three Easy Steps: Our Go-To Strategy for "Foot-in-the-Door" Words

After you've chosen which words to teach, you need an effective, efficient way to introduce them. The following three-step procedure for introducing new vocabulary words is based on Beck, McKeown, and Kucan (2013) and Stahl and Nagy's (2006) work. This process works particularly well: (1) for general academic words that could be found in any content area, such as *assume, survey, comprehensive, scathing, dote,* and *meticulous,* and (2) with words your students already have the underlying concept of, but may not have the label for. For examples, students may not be familiar with the word *dote* (the label), but they have surely (and hopefully!) experienced someone in their lives (perhaps a grandparent) who showers another person with excessive love and affection, possibly to the point of spoiling them (the underlying concept of *dote*). Words like this generally take less time to teach precisely because the student already has the general underlying concept. Here are the three steps for introducing words:

- Introduce the word using a student-friendly definition.
- Provide contextual information about the word.
- Ask students to make a personal connection.

Step 1: Introduce the word using a student-friendly definition

As we've mentioned in our principles above, it's critical to make sure you introduce words using student-friendly definitions (Beck et al., 2013), which employ words the student *already knows* to define the *unfamiliar* word. While you can create your own student-friendly definitions, this takes time. The free, online version of *Longman's Dictionary of Contemporary English* (*ldoceonline.com*) is an excellent dictionary for this purpose. Importantly, Longman's uses a controlled defining vocabulary of 2,000 high-frequency, "student-friendly" words and their most common meanings to define all the target words in the dictionary, resulting in clear definitions. For example, consider Longman's student-friendly definition for *luminous*—shining in the dark (adjective).

Step 2: Provide contextual information about the word

A student-friendly definition, like the one for *luminous* above, is a good start, but it's just a start. In step #2, provide your students additional, rich contextual information about the word. This includes providing examples of the word being used in a sentence and any synonyms, antonyms, and other words the target word is related to. It's also very helpful to explain to your students things the target word is often associated with, such as *who* or *what* the target word might describe (a bully? a very proper, refined professor?) and *when* and *where* they are likely to encounter the target word (in a mystery novel during a scary scene at night?).

From the *luminous* example above, you could provide the following two sentences and rich contextual information:

- The *luminous* yellow paint seemed to glow in the afternoon sun.
- The mother's large eyes were *luminous* as she held her child for the first time.
- To help students make connections, you might say, "Notice how in both sentences, the thing described as *luminous* is glowing or bright. Why might a mother's eyes seem glowing or bright when she's holding her child? Notice also how *luminous* can describe both inanimate (paint) and animate (mother's eyes) things. You'll often see *luminous* used to describe bright things like the stars, shiny objects like a lighthouse, or something warm and glowing and bright."

Step #3: Ask Students to Make a Personal Connection to the Word

Connecting new information to known ideas or personal experiences is one of the most powerful learning tools we know. These "new-to-known" connections are critical first steps toward cementing a word in long-term memory. Two quick and easy activities we've used countless times to help students make these connections are (1) *Have you ever*? and (2) *Go find it!*

In *Have you ever?* (Beck et al., 2013), you simply ask students to connect something from their personal experiences to the word.

- Have you ever seen something or someone that looked *luminous?*
- What made them *luminous?*
- Why would you say that person's eyes looked *luminous?*

In *Go find it!* you ask your student to go find an example of the word outside the classroom and report it back to the class the next day. This is one of the most engaging methods we've found for getting students to take vocabulary learning outside the classroom walls. For example, "For homework, find three things or people in your life that are *luminous* and report back tomorrow." A middle school science teacher we worked with, during an online class session, said, "Okay everybody, take 10 minutes, search your house, and go find an example of something from the *biosphere, geosphere, hydrosphere,* and *atmosphere.* Bring it back to share on-screen. Go find it!" One enterprising student brought her dog as an example of the *biosphere,* resulting in a rich and lively discussion.

These three steps—(1) student-friendly definition, (2) context, and (3) personal connection—are a powerful, engaging, and relatively quick way to get students to start digging into a word's meaning. What's more, they are "back pocket" strategies that don't require much planning time or teaching time (often just a few minutes) and can be pulled out anytime an interesting word or learning opportunity presents itself: during a read-aloud, during a class discussion, or to break up a lecture. These three steps also establish a strong foundation for further vocabulary study if you want to go deeper.

Instructional Practices for Your "Deep Dive" Vocabulary

After you've introduced a new vocabulary term, you need to decide whether it's a word that requires additional, in-depth instruction required for our "deep dive" words. Our go-to instructional strategies for deep dive words are graphic organizers and vocabulary maps. When done well, vocabulary maps and graphic organizers can be engaging, collaborative, and visually arranged to highlight the key aspects of the word's meaning as students dig deep.

Four-Square Concept Map

Based on the classic Frayer model (Frayer, Frederick, & Klausmeier, 1969), the four-square concept map (Eeds & Cockrum, 1985) provides a visual format for exploring a word/concept beyond the student-friendly definition, including discussing synonyms, antonyms, examples, and non-examples of the word. Figure 6.6 is a four-square concept map generated by a group of students in an ELA class for the word *tangible.*

Consider the following procedures for using a four-square concept map:

- Introduce the target word with a student-friendly definition.
  - *tangible:* something I can touch
- For more support, provide an example of the word and contextual information.
  - My car is *tangible*—I can touch it

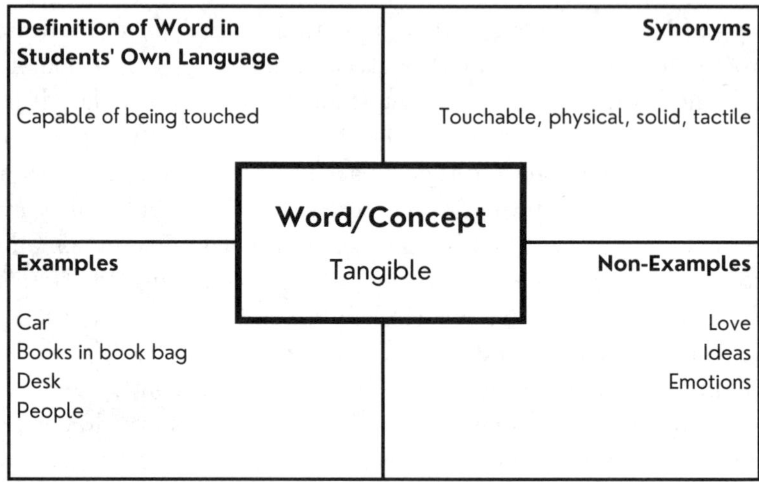

FIGURE 6.6. Four-square concept map for *tangible*.

- Ask the students for examples of the word from their lives and write these in the four-square concept map.
  - What are some tangible things—things you can actually touch—at home? At school?
- During the discussion, add synonyms/antonyms, and non-examples and allow students to use a dictionary or thesaurus.
  - Synonyms—real, touchable, actual
  - Examples—my pencil, a desk
  - Antonyms—unreal, abstract, intangible; non-examples—my anxiety about a quiz
- Ask students to create the vocabulary maps on chart paper. On completion, they can share their four-squares with the group as words are discussed in even more depth. Post or collect four-square concept maps for later reference.
- We often ask students to draw a picture representing the word/concept in a "fifth square," making them "five-squares." Elementary drawings using stick figures are fine. We tell our students who say they aren't artists that the picture isn't meant for an art exhibition. If it helps you remember the concept, then it works.

Concept of Definition Map

A concept of definition map (Schwartz & Raphael, 1985) is another type of vocabulary map. Concept of definition maps lend themselves to domain-specific words and concepts in science, social studies, math, and ELA. See Figure 6.7 for an example

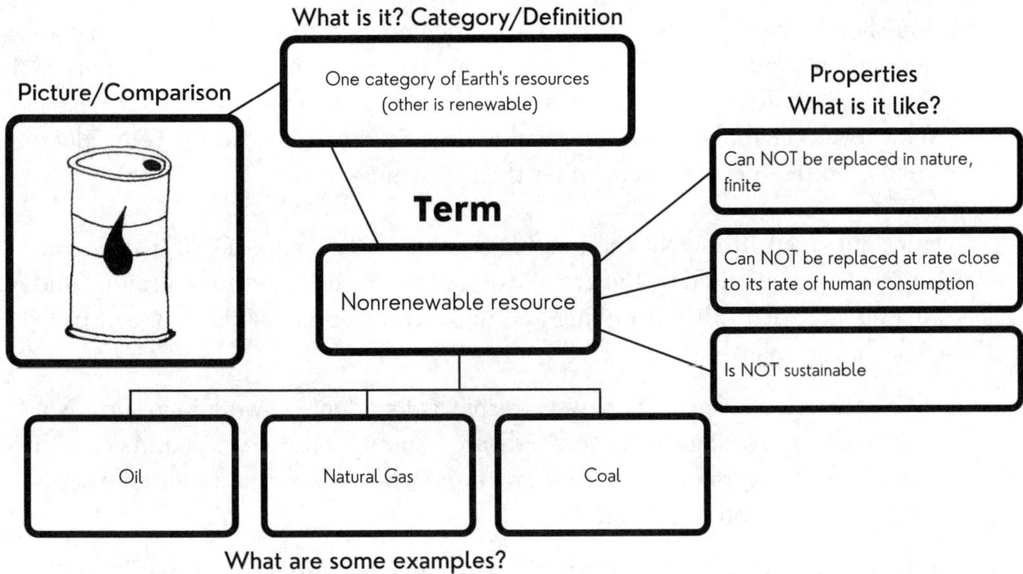

FIGURE 6.7. COD map for *nonrenewable resource.*

of a concept of definition map with the term *nonrenewable resource*. This strategy guides students to consider the following essential questions about word meanings:

- *Category—What is it? To what general category does it belong?* Is it a type of natural resource? Is it a type of government like a democracy or monarchy? Is it a part of speech? Is it a general category of shape, like quadrilaterals, in geometry? Is it a category of solid, gas, or liquid?
- *Characteristics—What is it like?* What are the characteristics of a nonrenewable resource? Are they infinite or finite? What are characteristics of a direct democracy? Is it a government in which the people vote directly, or for their representatives? Who makes the decisions?
- *Examples—What are some examples?* What are some examples of nonrenewable resources? What are some examples of a democracy? The United States? Russia? Argentina? Canada?

Vocabulary Web

Vocabulary webs are graphic organizers that lend themselves to the study of general academic words that can be found in any content area, such as *product, evaluate, resplendent,* and *reminisce.* Intervention teachers can connect to ELA classrooms with vocabulary webs. These are particularly helpful for the types of literary words found in short stories, novels, and poetry. Notice how Figure 6.8 digs deeper into the meaning of *strut* by including "circles" for (1) shades of meaning, (2) part of speech, and (3) context (word used in a sentence).

Whichever vocabulary map or graphic organizer you choose for your "deep dive" into a word or concept, remember the following:

- It's not about filling out the graphic organizer. It's about the *discussion* and *thinking* that are generated by the graphic organizer. So, ask questions, prompt, and get students to explain their thinking and make connections while they construct these vocabulary maps.

- *Collaboration* is key. Whenever possible, get students to work in groups. Not only is it more motivating, multiple heads are usually better than one. Ask small groups to share their graphic organizers with the whole class, sparking rich discussions and, often, humorous comments.

- Like any new strategy, use the *Gradual Release Model*. You may need to model and think aloud the vocabulary learning process using the graphic organizer the first few times before students "own it."

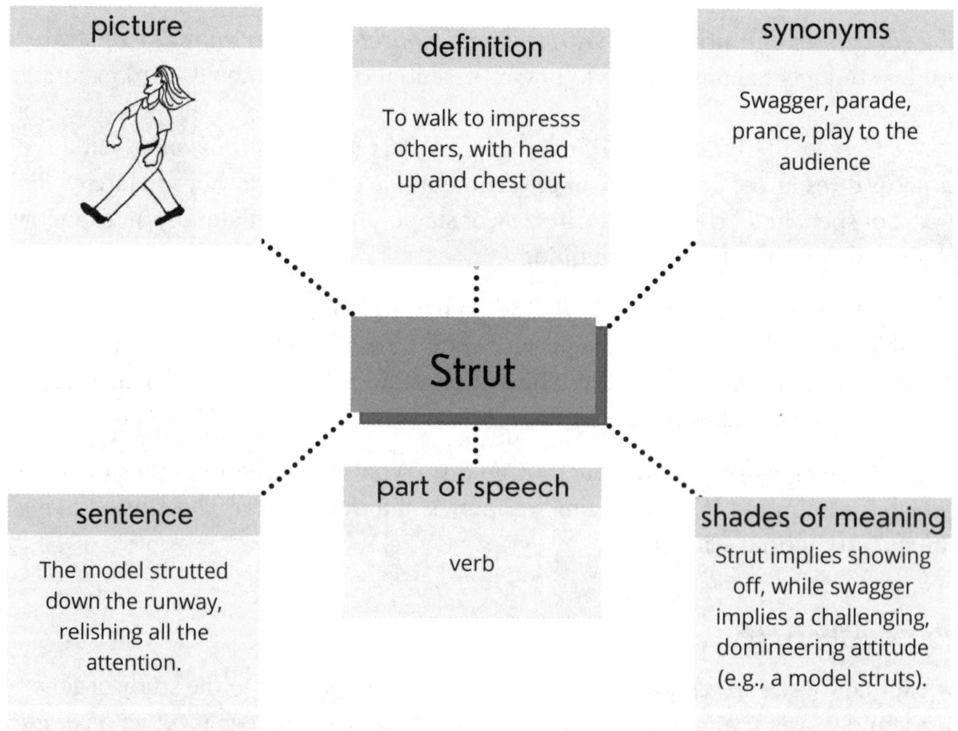

FIGURE 6.8. Vocabulary web for *strut*.

- Because these may take a fair amount of instructional time (perhaps 15 minutes or more), save these vocabulary maps and graphic organizers for your "deep dive" words.

- Consider using these vocabulary webs and maps as assessments. They will give you a much deeper, more rigorous sense of your students' vocabulary knowledge than an "old-school" vocabulary word-definition matching quiz. Moreover, in contrast to a matching quiz, you don't have to spend your Thursday evenings creating a new vocabulary quiz for Friday. Instead, on Friday morning, simply say, "I want you to complete a vocabulary map on the following four terms/words for our quiz. Each cell/circle in a vocabulary map is worth one point."

Vocab Review Games for Practice and Building Word Consciousness

After you've studied and explored vocabulary words and concepts, you will want to periodically review them. Remember, students need at least 10–12 encounters with a word across a week (perhaps three or so encounters per day, on average) for that word to stick. So, how do you get your students to periodically review words in a quick, motivating format? Even 5–10 minutes of review every day is much more effective than a single 30-minute cram session on Thursday night for the Friday quiz. Following are some of our favorite vocabulary review activities. They are all game-like; require little, if any, planning or teaching time; and provide you a lot of bang for your instructional buck.

Applause, Applause

Applause, Applause (Beck et al., 2013) engages students by asking them to clap to demonstrate how much they would like to be described by the target words. *How would you like to be described as frivolous? Luminous? Sophisticated? Diabolical?* Students' answers could include: (1) *not at all* (hands together without clapping), (2) *a little* (a quiet, "golf clap"), (3) *yes, a fair amount* (a regular clap), or (4) *a lot!* (a huge, rousing clap). As with all vocabulary activities, don't forget to ask students to justify their clap/answer. "Zach, why did you give us a 'golf' clap for *diabolical* instead of not clapping at all—is there a small part of you that wants to be seen by others as *diabolical?*"

Word Associations, Situations, and Thumbs Up/Thumbs Down!

In *word associations* (Beck et al., 2013), you simply ask students to associate one of the target words with a word or phrase. As always, don't forget to ask *why*—the student's explanation of their thinking is where the deep word processing really occurs. For example:

> "Which one of our target words this week goes best with a 'criminal mastermind, like the Joker from the Batman movies?' You said, *diabolical*, Jose? Why? Which one of our target words goes best with a man in a tuxedo sipping a glass of expensive champagne? Darrel says *sophisticated*, but Hannah says *frivolous*—OK, each of you, try to convince the rest of the group why *sophisticated* or *frivolous* goes best with tuxedoes and champagne."

As you can see, sometimes there is not a single, clear-cut answer. That's completely fine, as it's the discussion about the word's application that leads to a deeper, more nuanced understanding of word meanings.

For *situations* (Beck, 2013), a related activity, provide a hypothetical situation and ask students to identify the target word that best relates. "A model is walking down a runway—which word best relates? Why did you say *strut* and not *swagger*, Jack?" To get the entire group involved, present a situation or word association and ask the group to agree (thumbs up) or disagree (thumbs down). For example: "Who agrees with this statement: *Frivolous* people have too much money? Okay, I see about two of you agreeing with their thumbs up, and two others with their thumbs down. I'm going to ask a few of you to explain your answers now."

Clue Review and Charades

Clue review (Templeton et al., 2015) is one of our students' favorite vocabulary review activities because it's so fun and fast-paced. All it requires is a deck of "flash cards" with the target vocabulary word on one side and the definition and possible additional information (e.g., a four-square concept map of the target word) on the other. We love it because, in contrast to many review games, every student "plays" every round; there is no downtime, and thus no lost instructional time. This is because students are paired up in one of two roles, both of whom have a job to do every round: (1) clue giver, or (2) "hot seat" (clue guesser). After students are paired up:

- The student in the "hot seat" shuffles the deck of cards, all face up, with the target word showing. Importantly, the "hot seat" student does *not* look at the deck but picks a word from the deck and places it on their forehead, so their partner, the clue giver, *can* see the word, but "hot seat" cannot (because it's on their own forehead).

- The clue giver, who can see the word card on their partner's forehead, facing them, gives a clue to the word. This could be a definition and/or example. For example: "This is a natural substance that is limited, but we can't keep replacing it. Like oil or gas."

- The hot seat student answers, "Nonrenewable resource!" Then the hot seat student puts the card down and draws the next card. If the pair isn't sure of the answer, they check the back of the card.

- Pairs aim to: (1) get through as many words as possible without checking definitions, or, (2) time themselves and see how long it takes to get through the deck.

- Partners switch roles so that both have a turn as "clue giver," which is generally the more difficult job.

- Consider pairing up more and less proficient students and giving the "clue giver" role to the more proficient student the first round. This provides their partner a model of how to construct clues before switching roles.

- We also play a charades version. Instead of giving verbal clues, on the second day of clue review, tell the "clue givers" that they have to act out the word without verbal clues/words, as they would in a game of charades. This adds another layer of fun to the word learning.

Morphology: Tapping into the Vocabulary System in English

We don't just want to teach students words. We also want to teach them how to become independent word learners so they can learn words effectively for the rest of their lives. This is where *morphology* and *morphemes* come in. *Morphemes* are the smallest units of meaning in a language and include high-utility Latin and Greek affixes and roots, such as the prefix *pre-* (meaning "before") in *preview, prevent,* and *predict.* A working knowledge of these Latin and Greek affixes and roots can be a powerful independent word learning strategy.

Now, when you mention "Latin and Greek," many people's first thoughts are of old textbooks, oral recitation of verb conjugations, and the *Iliad* and the *Odyssey.* However, Latin and Greek are not dead languages only used in dusty classrooms but are alive and thriving in modern English. How alive? Approximately 70% of all English vocabulary, and 90% of the vocabulary of science and technology, contains a Latin or Greek affix or root (Green, 2008; Nagy & Anderson, 1984; Padak, Newton, Raskinski, & Newton, 2008).

This vocabulary system is so powerful that knowledge of just one affix or root, like *trans-* (a Latin prefix meaning "across") can be the key to unlocking scores of words. Notice how the following 24 words, each containing the *trans-* word part and found across multiple content areas, all share the core meaning of "across":

- *Transfer of energy* (science)—the movement of energy from one place to, or "across," another place
- *Transcontinental railroad* (history)—railroad built to go "across" the United States
- *Translucent* (English/Language arts)—permitting light to pass "through or across," but diffusing it so the object is not clearly visible
- *Transport, transmit, transplant, translate, transparent, transform, transient, transcend, transaction, transitive property of equality, transgression, transmissible, transatlantic, transcendentalist, transfusion, transfix, transept, transgender, transition, transpose,* and *transpire*

As you can see from this *trans-* example, with root knowledge, *a little goes a long way.* Before you and your students can tap into this system, it's very helpful to explicitly teach them the following word parts:

- *Prefix*—a meaning unit attached at the beginning of the base word/root
  - Examples: *pre-, un-, dis-, anti-*
- *Suffix*—a meaning unit attached at the end of the base word/root
  - Examples: *-ion, -ible/-able*
- *Affix*—a collective term for prefixes and suffixes
- *Base word*—a stand-alone word to which prefixes/suffixes are added
  - Example: the base word *whole* in *unwholesome* (un-*whole*-some)
- *Root*—word parts, often of Greek or Latin origin, that combine with other word parts to form words. Importantly, roots *cannot* stand alone as words. This is why we avoid the term *root word* (because as one of our sixth graders pointed out once, why are they calling it a root *word* when it's not really a *word?*). Instead, we use the term *root* (be aware, however, many programs still use *root word*).
  - Examples: *spect* (as in *retrospect*), *arch* (as in *monarchy*)

After you have introduced these basic word parts to your students, you can employ two of our favorite root activities, *root webs* and *break-it-down* in both classroom and intervention settings.

Root Webs: Building Words from Word Parts

Root webs (Templeton et al., 2015) provide an engaging format for visually organizing all the high-utility words that derive from a single affix or root. Draw a center circle with the affix or root written in it. Ask students to brainstorm words they can think of that contain that affix or root. Write these derived words in the surrounding circles on the web, as in Figure 6.9.

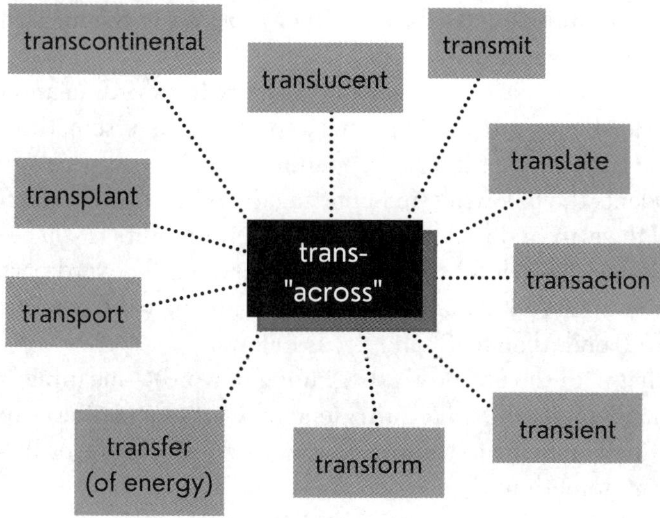

FIGURE 6.9. Root web for *trans-*.

If your students are stuck generating new words from an affix or root and need help, introduce the derived words yourself. Importantly, guide your students to figuring out how the definitions of the derived word meanings all share the core meaning of the affix or root in the center circle. "We know *trans-* means across, so what does a heart *transplant* have to do with 'movement across'? What's being moved in a heart transplant? Right, someone's heart is being transported from one person *across* to another person." We tell our students, when you learn one word this way, you're actually learning 10, 20, or 30 words, or more, because you're learning the root that gave birth to all these words.

Break-It-Down

Once students have a few affixes and roots under their belts, teach them how to use their newfound "root knowledge" to break down vocabulary words that contain these roots. Break-It-Down will help them not only decode the *pronunciation* of these words, but also decode and store their *meanings* (Flanigan et al., 2011). To introduce them to the "break-it-down" process, start with a familiar word that contains an actual base word, like *unavoidable*.

- Target word: *unavoidable*
- Ask your students to circle the prefixes and suffixes. Write the meanings of each word part underneath that word part.

- Ask them to underline the base word or root. Write the meaning of the root or base word underneath it.
- Put the meaning parts together to construct the word meaning. *Un* = not, *able* = capable of, and *avoid* means to prevent. So, if something is *unavoidable,* you can't prevent it from happening.
- Tell students the following tip in putting the parts together: Do not *necessarily* read the affix and root meanings from left to right, as you read words in a book. Rather, it's helpful to analyze and combine the word parts more flexibly. For example, with *unavoidable,* we "read" the word parts from (1) beginning, to (2) end, then to (3) middle, as follows:
  - Starting with the *un-* prefix (beginning of word)—meaning "not"
  - Then moving to the *-able* suffix (end of word)—meaning "capable of"
  - And finally moving to the *avoid* base word (middle of word)—meaning "to prevent (something)."
- As students become more proficient with breaking down words, start including words with roots like *spect* instead of base words like *avoid.* Roots are usually more difficult for students to break down because they are not actual stand-alone English words. For example, when you apply the "break-it-down" game to the word *retrospect,* you get *retro* and *spect,* neither of which are words. *Retro* is a prefix meaning "before" and *spect* is a root meaning "look." Therefore, retrospect means to *look before,* or *look in the past.*

CONCLUSION

Zach has been in a vocabulary intervention for 9 weeks. His intervention included explicit instruction in (1) vocabulary words and their underlying concepts and (2) vocabulary strategies, including various four-square and concept of definition maps. Figure 6.10 shows Zach's solid vocabulary growth after this 9-week intervention.

Importantly, unlike word recognition and decoding interventions, many vocabulary strategies can be easily applied in middle-grades content-area classes, also. So, Zach's social studies, science, math, and ELA teachers were able to seamlessly integrate vocabulary graphic organizers, such as four-square and concept of definition maps, into their instruction *for all of their students.* They didn't feel like this was "an extra thing" they had to do. This not only supported Zach's vocabulary growth, but it also supported all their students' learning.

The North Star principles we introduced in Chapter 2 informed our intervention decisions and helped Zach make progress toward his goals. How did they play out across the interventions to build Zach's vocabulary? See Figure 6.11.

By the end of 9 weeks, Zach will:	This will be measured with:	Progress at 9 weeks:
• Be able to define and explain, in-depth 20 key domain-specific vocabulary terms and/or phrases in each content area (5 each chosen by the math, science, social studies, ELA teachers)	• A four-square concept map or other appropriate vocabulary map/graphic organizer to demonstrate knowledge of a content-area vocabulary term/concept (as chosen by Zach's content teachers)	• Zach was able to demonstrate his knowledge of 20 key domain-specific vocabulary terms using an appropriate vocabulary map on an end-of-unit quiz or test.
• Be able to use a vocabulary map (e.g., concept of definition map, four-square concept map) to learn a new word/concept in one of his content-area classes.	• See above	• Zach improved in his ability to use vocabulary maps while learning new vocabulary. While he is not yet independent, he is able to do so with limited support.

FIGURE 6.10. Zach's vocabulary goals and 9-week growth.

Principles	An example of how we used it:
1. What Do You Stand For? Articulate Your Literacy Beliefs	Based on the research on vocabulary, Zach's team followed the principles of effective vocabulary instruction, including activities that (1) actively engaged him and (2) encouraged him to personalize word meanings.
2. Don't Forget Your Map! Choose and Use an Intervention Model	Zach's team used the cognitive model to target Pathways #2 and #3.
3. Start with Assessments Get to Know Your Students	Importantly, Zach's team ruled out Pathway #1: automatic word recognition, based on assessment data.
4. Keep the Main Thing the Main Thing Design a Focused, Flexible, Doable Intervention Plan	Zach's team focused on two vocabulary objectives: (1) learning 20 domain-specific words, and (2) learning vocabulary maps he could use to independently learn words in the future.
5. Make the Invisible Visible Use the "I Do" to Be Explicit and Systematic	Each vocabulary lesson started with an explicit introduction, including why, and a think-aloud modeling. Vocabulary maps and graphic organizers served as explicit visual reminders of the underlying process.
6. Practice, Practice, Purposeful Practice Leverage the "We Do" and "You Do" for Long-Term Transfer and Independence	Zach had many opportunities to apply the vocabulary strategies he learned in his intervention across his four content area classes.
7. One Size Does Not Fit All Differentiate and Scaffold When They're Not "Getting It"	Zach was provided additional scaffolding and support as needed, including vocabulary banks.
8. Time Where Does It All Go and How Can I Get Some Back?	Zach's content teachers were able to save valuable planning and instructional time by focusing on a few vocabulary maps (four-square and concept of definition) that he could use in all his content classes.
9. Engagement Get Your Students to Buy In When They've Checked Out	Zach was motivated to complete the vocabulary work because much of it was done collaboratively in small groups.
10. Active, Not Passive Take a Critical Stance and Read with a Purpose	Zach was "in the driver's seat" for all his vocabulary work, creating the vocabulary maps, talking, writing, acting out words, and participating in the game-like reviews.

FIGURE 6.11. Zach's North Star principles.

APPENDIX: SAMPLE VOCABULARY LESSON

Concept of Definition Map

Figure 6.12 shows an example of how we might use Duffy's six components of explicit teaching (2014; see Chapter 2) in a vocabulary intervention lesson for Zach.

"I Do"— Directly and explicitly teach your concept
Make the Object Public:
By the end of the 9-week intervention, Zach will be able to use a *concept of definition map* to learn a new word/concept in one of his content area classes. The concept of definition map example we presented in Figure 6.7 (see p. 143) will serve as our anchor chart for this lesson.
Introduce the Lesson:
Teacher: Zach, today we're going to teach you a vocabulary strategy, called the *concept of definition map,* that will help you learn new vocabulary words and concepts in math, social studies, science, and ELA. Now, when you want to learn a vocabulary word, where can you look up its definition? That's right, in a dictionary or the glossary in your textbooks. Good definitions are a great start in learning a concept, but they're just a start.
State the Secret and Model Your Thinking:
Teacher: Zach, have you ever crammed on Thursday for a vocab quiz, gotten most of the words right on that Friday quiz, and then forgotten most of them by the following Monday? Well, we're going to teach you one of the "secrets" to remembering words and concepts for the long-haul. Our first tip is to go beyond the definition. One way we go beyond the definition is to use a *concept of definition map*—or COD map. I'm going to show you how to use a COD map to learn more about one of the key vocabulary words, *nonrenewable resources*. Now, you've already studied about *renewable resources,* right? What are some examples of renewable resources? That's right: solar power like the sun. What else? Right, wind energy's another renewable resource. Why are they both considered renewable resources? What does renewable mean? Right, it means they keep on coming, they can't be depleted. So I'm thinking to myself, NONrenewable resources might be the exact opposite, since NON means "not." So, what are some characteristics of nonrenewable resources that you've heard in class or read in your textbook? That's right, they can*not* be replaced by nature! Let's write that down in one of the cells on the COD map under "properties." What's another property of nonrenewable resources? Right again, it's going to be all used up at some point—what's the scientific word for that? *Unsustainable.* Yes, let's write that characteristic down, also.

(continued)

FIGURE 6.12. Sample lesson: Vocabulary.

"We Do"— Provide opportunities for scaffolded practice
After we've introduced the lesson and modeled how to use a COD map with Zach, it's time for the "We do" part of the lesson: scaffolded (or guided) practice. With vocabulary graphic organizers like a COD map, we usually ask students to try it out, in groups, with additional target vocabulary words as we provide feedback. Often, the deep thinking and discussion comes as students share their group-developed COD maps with the entire class. For example, suppose Zach and his group were sharing a COD map they completed on *geothermal energy:* **Teacher:** Zach, are there any characteristics of *geothermal energy* your group listed on the COD map that are similar to the characteristics that Jada's group listed for *hydropower?* What do folks think of their examples of geothermal energy? Grace, you said this reminds you of the hot springs you saw when you visited Yellowstone National Park. How many think Grace is right—that the hot springs are an examples of geothermal energy? Who doesn't? Why not?

FIGURE 6.12. *(continued)*

CHAPTER 7

Building Comprehension with Zach

In Chapter 6, we focused on what Zach's assessment results revealed about his *vocabulary* challenges. In this chapter, we will focus on what his assessment results reveal about his *comprehension* strengths and challenges, including his still-developing *text structure* and *comprehension strategy* knowledge. As we discussed in Chapter 6, Mr. Jackson collected assessment information on Zach and discussed the results with the intervention team. The more information they compiled about Zach, the more confident the team was in ruling out Pathway #1 (automatic word recognition and fluency) and focusing on:

- Pathway #2: Oral language comprehension, including vocabulary, background knowledge, and text structure
- Pathway #3: Strategic knowledge, including general and specific purposes for reading as well as knowledge of strategies for reading

DIAGNOSTIC FOLLOW-UP ASSESSMENTS

Let's return to the diagnostic assessment Mr. Jackson administered in Chapter 6. However, this time, we'll focus on the *comprehension* results. In that diagnostic follow-up assessment, Zach read a sixth-grade passage about pyramids using a think-aloud protocol (see Chapter 3) and answered comprehension questions. Mr. Jackson noted multiple instances where Zach experienced difficulty comprehending this passage. Next, Mr. Jackson *read aloud* a sixth-grade passage from the QRI-7 to Zach, titled "Clouds and Precipitation" (Leslie & Caldwell, 2021), to compare Zach's reading comprehension with his listening comprehension. Zach also experienced difficulty understanding this passage. As Mr. Jackson reflected on Zach's overall results, he identified a handful of specific factors impacting Zach's comprehension: *purpose for reading, inferring, text structure, self-monitoring,* and *strategy use.*

Overall Engagement, Purpose, and "Critical Stance" Toward Reading

Mr. Jackson reported that Zach seemed to fit the profile of a "word caller," a reader who thinks of reading as simply decoding the words on the page, but not as an active process of actually attempting to make sense of those words. Not only did Zach seem disengaged during reading, but Mr. Jackson noted that, "It was almost as if—after years of struggling to understand what he reads—Zach actually *expected* much of his reading to not make sense for him." Put simply, Zach was reading passively, without any real purpose or critical stance in mind. This lack of purpose became apparent during the think-aloud when Mr. Jackson asked Zach, "In this next section you're about to read, what do you want to find out about building pyramids? What questions do you have?" Zach replied, "I don't really have any questions. I guess I'll just see what it tells me."

Making Inferences

Zach answered a series of open-ended questions after reading both passages. He was able to successfully answer "right there" questions that had a straightforward answer explicitly stated in the passage. This was a strength for Zach. However, he struggled with questions when the answer was not "right there." These higher-level questions required Zach to "read between the lines," or make an *inference,* using text evidence to support his answer. For example, Mr. Jackson asked Zach why building pyramids was considered important work in ancient Egypt (as part of the open-ended, after-reading questions). Zach had difficulty making the inference needed to answer this question, which was based on a main point of the passage: The primary purpose of building the pyramid was to prepare the pharaoh—who was considered a god-king—for the afterlife.

Text Structure

Zach's limited text-structure knowledge was evident during the assessment, regardless of whether he read the passage himself or listened while Mr. Jackson read aloud. During the after-reading questions of the passage Zach read himself, Mr. Jackson had him look back in the text to find an answer to an open-ended question that he initially answered incorrectly. Zach was not able to efficiently find the place in the text where the relevant information was located. Instead, he started reading from the very beginning of the passage and kept reading until he found the relevant information—a very inefficient strategy suggesting he didn't have a good sense of the overall structure of the text.

After reading aloud the passage about precipitation to Zach, Mr. Jackson asked, "What happened to an ice crystal that resulted in a golf-ball sized hailstone?" The correct answer was that the ice crystal must have been (1) thrown up and down a lot in (2) a cloud that contained a large amount of water in order to get that big. This question required Zach to grasp that these two conditions *caused* the creation of big ice crystals. Zach's answer, "it was so big it had to fall out of the cloud," while making sense, did not get at the underlying cause–effect text structure that the correct answer required. Taken together, these assessments indicate that Zach did not have a strong sense of the different text structures in informational text (e.g., cause–effect, compare–contrast), resulting in his difficulty seeing the "big picture" in informational texts. This will hinder Zach's ability to successfully comprehend content information.

Self-Monitoring

Mr. Jackson noted a worrisome pattern during Zach's passage reading. Whenever Zach made a meaning-change error that did not make sense, he didn't stop and try to self-correct; rather, he simply continued to read on. Thinking back to an example we mentioned in Chapter 6, Zach substituted the word *organizing* for *organs* in the following sentence, "First, the Egyptians removed all *organizing* except the heart from the body," (Leslie & Caldwell, 2021, p. 280). Zach's inability to (1) identify when his reading did not make sense and (2) employ any "fix-up" strategies strongly indicated that he was not consistently reading for meaning.

Reading Comprehension Strategies to Increase Engagement and Boost Understanding

At preplanned stopping points in the think-aloud passage, Mr. Jackson asked Zach to pause and "tell me what you are thinking." Despite Mr. Jackson having previously modeled what to do at these think-aloud stopping points, Zach seemed at a loss for what to say. It appeared that Zach was not used to actively thinking or reflecting while reading.

With prompting from Mr. Jackson, Zach did eventually report some of his thoughts. However, his thinking indicated very little use of any strategies: He did not report any *questions* he had about the passage, did not *summarize* what he had read up to that point, nor did he connect anything in the passage to his *background content knowledge*. However, he did make one personal connection, mentioning how he and his brother used to build pyramids when they were younger. Mr. Jackson noted this instance of making a personal connection as a strength of Zach's to build on. As we saw in the previous chapter, Figure 6.2 (see p. 131) highlights the specific comprehension components in Pathways #2 and #3 that Zach needs support with.

ZACH'S TEAM'S QUESTIONS ABOUT COMPREHENSION

As Zach's team of teachers met with Mr. Jackson to discuss Zach's goals and develop their 9-week intervention plan, they had the following questions about his comprehension:

- What, exactly, is breaking down in Zach's "reading brain" that is affecting his comprehension?
- Why does Zach keep reading on, even when it doesn't make sense?
- What does the research say about effective comprehension instruction?
- How can we reset Zach's passive reading mindset so he can become an active, purposeful reader?

Comprehension Breakdown: What Is Going On in Zach's "Reading Brain"?

One of the clearest and most instructionally useful explanations of reading comprehension we know comes from the landmark RAND report: *Reading for Understanding: Toward an R&D Program in Reading Comprehension* (RRSG, 2002). RAND defines *comprehension* "as the process of simultaneously extracting and constructing meaning through interaction and involvement with written language. It consists of three elements: the *reader,* the *text,* and the *activity or purpose* for reading" (RRSG, 2002, p. xiii, emphasis added). Figure 7.1 shares the RAND report's heuristic for thinking about reading comprehension.

Let's break down this definition by starting with the three elements that impact comprehension:

- *The reader*—Each individual reader brings a particular set of literacy skills (e.g., strong sight-word vocabulary), a unique background knowledge (e.g., knowledge of U.S. history, how to play the guitar), and motivation and purposes for reading (e.g., self-efficacy, interest in certain topics). This is why different readers can read the same text and come away with different meanings: They are each bringing their unique background, experiences, and purposes to the table.

- *The text*—Each text contains different features that can impact a reader's comprehension, including the complexity of the ideas presented in the text, the underlying text structure, like cause–effect or narrative story structure, and the visible text presentation like headers or graphics.

- *The activity*—We read texts for different purposes and tasks, always within a specific social and societal context. Are you reading a textbook chapter to pass a Friday quiz for your history class, a short story for your book club's upcoming discussion at a local festive restaurant, or a technical manual to figure out how to put a lamp together? In each situation, you are reading a different text for a different purpose and in a different context.

All three elements—the reader, the text, and the activity—will impact your overall reading experience and comprehension. How might they impact a reader's comprehension and reading experience in a real-life situation? The best example from my (Kevin's) life is my two readings—25 years apart—of the classic American novel *The Grapes of Wrath* by John Steinbeck. I first read it in a high school English class. I didn't have the background knowledge or life experiences to connect with the Joad family as they traveled from Oklahoma to California during the Great Depression. I didn't understand the structure of the text (narrative chapters interspersed with "wide lens" general information chapters). We were given weekly Friday vocabulary and comprehension quizzes to test our comprehension, but rarely discussed the novel in class. Needless to say, it wasn't a personal favorite of mine.

Twenty-five years later, I voluntarily read *The Grapes of Wrath* as part of a book club. It was a completely different experience. There were no quizzes, just a deep and often rousing discussion at a local restaurant with my good friends over a tasty meal. At this point, I had 25 years of life experiences and felt I could connect on a much deeper level with the characters in the novel. The *text* was the same, but the *reader*, the *activity*, and the *context* had changed. *The Grapes of Wrath* is now on my personal top-10 novels list.

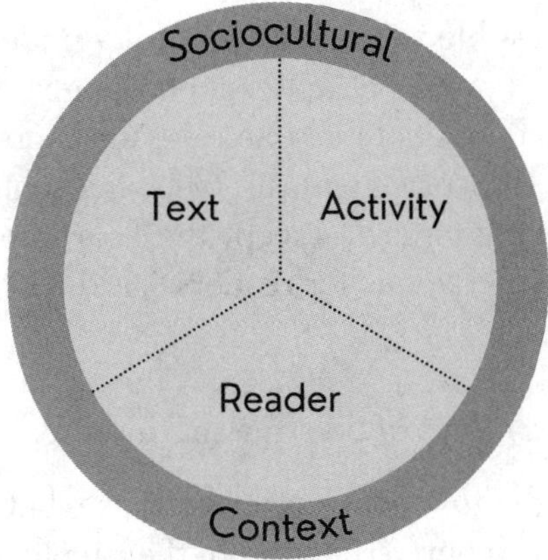

FIGURE 7.1. A heuristic for understanding reading comprehension. Reprinted with permission from RAND Reading Study Group (2002). Copyright 2002 by the RAND Corporation.

RAND's comprehension model and definition has a few important implications for those working with students experiencing comprehension struggles, like Zach:

- Meaning does *not* reside in the text. Meaning resides in the *interaction* between the text, the reader, and the context. All three are critical in comprehension instruction and, therefore, all three are possible points at which a reader's comprehension could breakdown. To boost comprehension, particularly for readers with comprehension challenges like Zach, we need instructional strategies that (1) support *readers*, by (2) scaffolding *texts*, and (3) creating supportive *contexts* with engaging *activities*.

- Some readers, like Zach, will have difficulty *extracting* information from the text. In Zach's case, his lack of familiarity with informational text structures (like cause and effect) is an obstacle to him extracting information—he doesn't know how the text is organized, so he can't find the information to extract it. And if he does find it, he has no sense of text structure to mentally organize it.

- As a reader *extracts* information from the text, they must simultaneously connect it with their *background knowledge* in order to *construct* meaning. A reader's comprehension can break down (1) if they don't have the needed background knowledge, or (2) if they have it, but have trouble accessing it. Therefore, Zach will benefit from instructional practices that build his background knowledge and/or help him access the knowledge he does have so he can connect it to new information in the text.

Why Does Zach Just Keep Reading On, Even When It Doesn't Make Sense?

There are a number of possible reasons why middle-grades readers may just continue to read on (1) when they do not understand the text or (2) when they make a meaning-change error that does not make sense. This happened when Zach substituted the word *organizing* for *organs* in the following sentence: "First, the Egyptians removed all *organizing* [organs] except the heart from the body" (Leslie & Caldwell, 2021, p. 280). The reasons for readers "reading on" when they shouldn't include:

- They may *not realize* the text does not make sense.

- They may realize the text does not make sense, but *don't know what to do about it* (i.e., they have no "fix-up" strategies in their toolbox).

- They may realize the text does not make sense, but *don't really care anymore*. This could be due to being so used to struggling, so used to reading texts and attempting tasks that are frustrating, that they don't see much reason to really engage anymore. Think of a time you've tried to develop a new habit, like eating healthier or working out. If, after a few months of effort, you didn't see sufficient results, there's a good chance you stopped trying.

- Finally, and perhaps at the heart of the issue for many readers, they are not reading with a purpose and thus have "no skin in the game." Developing a purpose-driven, critical stance toward reading will be job number one with Zach.

What Does the Research Say about Comprehension Instruction? How Can We Reset the Passive Mindset of Middle School Readers?

How can we reset Zach's overall reading stance from a *passive* to an *active* one? Unfortunately, Zach's indifferent attitude toward reading is a hallmark of too many older readers we work with. Many have been struggling with reading for so long, they almost expect the text to *not* make much sense. Many have given up on reading. Some don't see its purpose or use in their daily life. It's something they just have to "get through" while in school. So, what can we do to develop a reader who reads with a purpose and is actively engaged in trying to make sense of what they are reading? One who might actually be motivated to read, at least some texts and in some contexts?

To see things from Zach's perspective, let's consider a typical text-based reading assignment—an all-too typical reading experience—in a middle school content class:

- Read the text section.
- Answer the questions at the end.
- Turn in written answers to teacher for evaluation.
- Repeat.

Importantly, notice what is *not* occurring in this traditional scenario:

1. No clear *purpose* for reading established at the outset (other than to answer questions for evaluation)
2. No *activation* or *building of background knowledge* for the upcoming text
3. No *active engagement* or *higher-level thinking* fostered during reading
4. No *collaboration* or *discussion*, including *answering* and/or *generating higher-level questions*
5. No attempt to help the student see the "big picture" in the reading—how all the key concepts, vocabulary terms, and details fit into the overarching *text structure*
6. No explicit teaching of, or encouragement to use *comprehension strategies*, such as *inferring*, or use of *graphic organizers* to help grasp the *text structure*
7. No *motivating context* for reading, such as a follow-up debate

These seven missing elements can all be turned around into principles of effective comprehension instructions that are supported by decades of research (Duke, Pearson, Strachan, & Billman, 2011; NRP, 2000). So, to boost our middle-grades readers' comprehension, we need to (1) establish clear purposes for reading and (2) activate, or build, their background knowledge before they read a text. While reading, we need to (3) actively engage them in (4) higher-level, collaborative thinking and discussion, encouraging their application of (5) comprehension strategies and awareness of (6) text structure, as appropriate. Finally, this should all be done in a (7) motivating context. In the next section of our chapter, we discuss high-impact instructional practices that target these seven instructional elements. Importantly, you will notice that all of these instructional practices should not occur in isolation, but should be embedded in Zach's content learning, so he sees how he can use them outside of the "intervention room."

ZACH'S COMPREHENSION INTERVENTION PLAN

After some of their general questions about Zach's comprehension challenges were answered, Zach's team was ready to create a comprehension intervention plan to connect with his vocabulary work for the next 9 weeks (see Figure 7.2). Based on all of their assessment information and their knowledge about Zach, the team decided to target the following areas for the *comprehension* component of his intervention.

The Before, During, After Instructional Framework: Putting It All Together

How do you put each of the seven principles of effective comprehension instruction described above together into a single intervention lesson that makes sense? A lesson that's doable and applicable to a wide range of texts and instructional purposes? One you can use and reuse? While there are many possibilities, our core instructional framework for planning comprehension lessons is the before, during, after (BDA) framework (see Figure 7.3). The BDA framework identifies core instructional goals before, during, and after a reading (Vacca & Vacca, 2016).

Before Reading

Before reading, readers need to get their "reader stance" ready. They prepare for the *text* and the *task* at hand. They are starting to think about what they already know about the upcoming topic and ask questions that become their goal for reading that specific text. We can support this work by helping students:

- Activate, assess, and/or build background knowledge
- Set a purpose

By the end of 9 weeks, Zach will:

Develop a more engaged, critical stance toward reading, as evidenced by:

	This will be measured with:
• Inferring—Being able to use use the inferring strategy to answering higher-level, inferential questions using (1) background knowledge combined with (2) text evidence 75% of the time	• In response to higher-level questions, written answers on sticky notes and/or in writing response composition book • Oral answers during class discussion as recorded on teacher checklist according to following criteria of strategy use: 1. Inappropriate use of inferencing strategy 2. Appropriate use of inferencing strategy with teacher support 3. Independent use of inferencing strategy
• Question Generation—Self-generating at least 3 questions and/or sticky note ideas about a text during reading	• Sticky note questions/ideas

FIGURE 7.2. Zach's comprehension intervention plan and progress monitoring.

Before Reading	During Reading	After Reading
WHAT: Activate, Build, Organize, and/or Assess Background Knowledge HOW: • Brainstorm: Readers share what they think they know about a topic • Video clips, read-alouds, concrete experiences (science experiment, field trip) to build conceptual knowledge **WHAT: Set a Purpose for Reading** HOW: Make a hypothesis/prediction **WHAT: Motivate/Hook the Reader** HOW: Start with a story, a problem to solve, or a thought-provoking question	**WHAT: Actively Engage the Reader** HOW: Identify 2–5 stopping points for thinking and discussion **WHAT: Foster Higher-Level Thinking** HOW: • Teachers ask higher-level questions ("Why do you think that?") • Students answer with evidence from text • Sticky notes **WHAT: Monitor Readers' Comprehension** HOW: Teachers ask specific questions about important points or main ideas ("Do we know the story problem yet?")	**WHAT: Summarize, Synthesize, and/or Organize Key Concepts and Vocabulary** HOW: • Summarizing strategies • Sentence combining • Concept mapping **WHAT: Extend/Apply Learning** HOW: Make connections to previous learning and/or life

FIGURE 7.3. BDA instructional framework.

Activate, Assess, and/or Build Background Knowledge. Particularly for informational texts, it's critical that students activate their background knowledge about the topic in the upcoming text before they begin reading. For example, your students may actually have a good store of background knowledge about whales. However, this knowledge isn't very useful if it's still sitting "way back" in their long-term memory. Readers need to activate this background knowledge, retrieve it from their long-term memory, and bring it up to "the front of their brains." In this way, as they read new information about whales, the information they already know is right there, ready to be applied. Specifically, they'll be able to *connect* the *new knowledge* to their *existing knowledge*. This is critical, because it's when we make these meaningful, new-to-known connections that we can "make knowledge stick."

Many students who struggle with comprehension, like Zach, don't consistently activate their background knowledge so they can make these new-to-known connections. Failing to activate your background knowledge would be akin to having the necessary tools and materials for a carpentry job in the "storage section" at the back of your workshop (in your *long-term memory*), but not bringing those tools and materials up front to your work bench (your *working memory*)—so you can actually use them to make something.

Activating background knowledge could involve simply asking your students to do a quick-write for a few minutes and then sharing out with the class ("What do you think is the diet and habitat of a whale? Even if you're not sure, make a hypothesis before we read."). While you are activating your students' background knowledge, you can simultaneously *assess* it, determining if your students have enough of the assumed knowledge to make sense of the upcoming text. If you find they don't have the required knowledge, you'll need to help them build it. This could include preteaching key vocabulary terms and concepts, showing a video, or providing a concrete experience (like a science experiment) to frontload essential conceptual knowledge.

Set a Purpose. In addition to activating background knowledge before reading, you should invite your readers to set a clear purpose for reading. Think of how many times our students are asked to read something in school with no other purpose than just the vague directions "to answer the questions at the end." When we establish a specific, clear purpose *before* reading, we are more motivated and focused to build meaning *during* reading. Powerful purposes could include making predictions or hypotheses and then reading to confirm or modify them ("I think that whales eat smaller fish and kelp. I'm going to read this section on a whale's diet to see if my hypothesis was right."). Teachers could also offer interesting and motivating purposes, such as the following: "We're going to have a debate. I want this group to read this passage looking for reasons *not* to go to war. This group over here, you're going to read and look for reason to go to war. Then, we're going to have a debate."

During Reading

Have you ever drifted off while reading or listening to a book, realizing that you have no idea what happened in the last page or so? This is likely because you were not actively engaged during the reading (and might have been exhausted if reading right before bed!). To prevent this "mental drift," we can support our students during reading by:

- Actively engaging them
- Higher-level thinking

Actively Engage the Reader. Skilled readers are engaged during reading because they are mentally doing something while they're reading, whether it's asking questions of the text, pausing and reflecting, checking in on their purpose, or taking notes. You can engage readers during reading by planning a few stopping points, at which time the group discusses and debates what they have read. These stopping points should be predetermined at critical junctures of the reading (e.g., end of a subtopic to encourage readers to summarize their learning so far, or at a "cliffhanger" moment in a narrative story). Showing students how to use sticky notes to record their thinking is another excellent during-reading practice.

Monitor Comprehension and Foster Higher-Level Thinking. At each of your stopping points, ask questions that get students to summarize what happened or what they learned in the just-read section of text. If you find that your students' summaries are limited or not accurate, go back and reread a section to clarify. Also, ask questions that get your students to dig deeper in the text. Make sure these are higher-level questions requiring an inference. These questions often do not have a single correct answer. For example, you might ask: "What do you think about the author's writing style? Why do you say that? Should police have the right to search your school locker? Why or why not?" Following up with *why* questions gets students to (1) extend and clarify their thinking and (2) go back to the text to cite evidence for their viewpoint, all practices of skilled middle-grades readers. When crafting these questions, ask yourself, "Will this question deepen their learning?" If not, consider discarding it.

After Reading

If we really want conceptual knowledge to stick *after reading,* we need to do something *after reading.* For our middle-grades readers, this includes reviewing what they just learned, connecting it to known knowledge, and applying it to their own lives or other contexts. We can support our students after reading by asking them to:

- Wrap it up
- Extend and apply what they learned

Wrap It Up. After reading, provide opportunities for students to consolidate the key information and big ideas, to make them their own so the information "sticks" in long-term memory. This could include writing a brief *summary* or creating a *concept map* that shows the underlying *text structure*—how all the main ideas are tied together in a single "big picture." Even just a few minutes reviewing the key ideas in a text and bringing it all together can make a big difference later on.

Extend and Apply Learning. After reading, we can also ask our students to apply their learning to their own lives or different situations. "Now that we've read this section on our right to privacy, what's another area of your life where we should have the right to privacy? The internet? Our phones? How about while driving in our cars?" When we ask our students to apply their learning, not only are they further cementing a concept in their long-term memory, but we are also modeling how they can use their learning to "take-action" in their own lives and in the world around us.

All of the upcoming reading comprehension strategies and related instructional practices we will discuss in the remainder of this chapter and in Chapter 8 can fit somewhere into this BDA framework. As you read about them, consider where they might best fit in a lesson (before, during, after?) and what purpose they might best serve (activating background knowledge, fostering high-level thinking, actively engaging the reader?) with your students.

READING COMPREHENSION STRATEGIES: TEACHING OUR STUDENTS TO "LOOK UNDER THE HOOD"

A strategy can be thought of as a "plan in the head." We explicitly teach our middle-grades readers reading comprehension strategies, or "mental plans," so they have the necessary tools to make sense of difficult text. These strategies become particularly important when the text becomes challenging, when their comprehension begins to break down, or to serve a specific purpose or task (like an assignment to *summarize* a text section).

When our middle-grades readers begin to experience comprehension difficulties, it's as if the car they are driving is starting to run a little rough. We need to help them "look under the hood," identify what's breaking down, and provide them the necessary tools and skills to fix it. They won't be skilled with these tools, at first, so we need to explicitly teach them how to use them. So, remember to use the *gradual release model* when teaching each of the following research-based comprehension strategies we discuss in the rest of this section:

- Making inferences
- Questioning the author
- Self-monitoring and "fix-up" strategies
- Text structure: Using concept mapping to see the "big picture" in informational texts

Teaching Middle-Grades Readers to Make Inferences

Inferring and *summarizing* (which we discuss in Chapter 8) are two of the most important comprehension strategies we can teach middle-grades readers. According to Duffy, "all reading comprehension requires the reader to make an inference" (2014, p. 19). We heartily agree with Duffy: Inferring is at the heart of reading comprehension. So what, exactly, is an inference? An inference is a *meaningful connection* a reader makes between different pieces of information. There are three main categories of inferences (Hall & Barnes, 2016):

- Predictions
- Text-connecting inferences (within-text connections)
- Knowledge-based inferences (text-to-background knowledge connections)

Because many middle-grades readers we work with can already make adequate *predictions* in *narrative text*, and because predicting is a comprehension strategy focused on extensively in the primary grades, we usually focus on the second two types of inferences with our grades 4–8 students. However, we still work with our middle-grades readers on how to make predictions, or *hypotheses*, in *informational texts* ("I think they stuffed dead pharaohs with salt to dry them out so they wouldn't rot and they could preserve the mummified bodies forever. I'm going to read this next section to see if my hypothesis about salt is right or not."). Following are steps we use to teaching inferring as informed by Hall and Barnes (2016):

- *Start with higher-level focus questions.* Create higher-level "focus questions" that require students to make an inference. Often, these questions do not have a single correct answer. "Why do you think D.J., the main character in our story, went searching for the stolen money in the basement first, before looking in the attic?" While starting with focus questions may seem obvious, we don't always see this done when teaching inferring. Focus questions give students something to "push against" as they try out their thinking. Later on, as they become more independent, your students will increasingly make unprompted inferences in their own heads, without the need for external, teacher-created questions.

- *Identify text clues.* Model for students how to identify "text clues," including key words and phrases in the text. Writing on sticky notes and highlighting are engaging tools to get students to do this. "Zach, you highlighted *the damp, moldy shirt* that D.J. found as one of your text clues for why he went looking in the basement first. Why was that a clue for you? How do *damp, moldy shirts* and *basements,* our two key phrases, connect?

- *Connect text clues to your background knowledge.* Help students activate their background knowledge and connect it to the text clues to make an inference. "So, Zach, what do you know about basements from your own experiences that connects them with damp, moldy stuff? Oh, you've been in basements that are wet and moldy, because they are underground? Yes, that makes sense."

Zach's inference described in the bullets above is an example of a *knowledge-based inference,* because Zach had to (1) connect text clues (the damp, moldy shirt) to (2) his background knowledge about basements (they are damp and moldy) in order to (3) "read between the lines" and make an inference. See our sample inferring lesson at the end of this chapter for a detailed example of how to teach knowledge-based inferring. In this lesson, you'll see us use the following "inferring formula," which is an accessible way to think about and teach inferring to your middle-grades students:

Text Clues + Background Knowledge = Inference

Another common type of inference is the *text-connecting inference,* which involves a reader trying to connect two pieces of information *within the text,* such as a *noun or noun phrase* with the other words and phrases that it refers to. Take the following two sentences as an example: "Earthworms, fungi, insects, and bacteria all break down complex organic matter into simpler forms. *These decomposers* are essential to the health of an ecosystem." You can see how a reader with comprehension challenges, like Zach, might miss the fact that the noun phrase, *These decomposers,* is referring back to *worms, fungi, insects,* and *bacteria* in the preceding sentence. This is a common type of inference breakdown that also needs to be explicitly taught. As we discuss additional comprehension strategies and instructional practices to boost comprehension in the remainder of this chapter, you'll notice inferring at the heart of all of them.

Questioning the Author

Good readers constantly ask themselves questions as they read. "Does this make sense? What else do I know about this topic? Does this remind me of something else?" It's no surprise, then, that *teaching students to generate their own questions* while reading is one of the most powerful comprehension strategies known (Duke et al., 2011; NRP, 2000; RRSG, 2002).

Questioning the Author (QtA; Beck, McKeown, & Sandora, 2021) provides a structured and engaging way to guide students toward asking the types of questions that skilled, engaged readers ask as they wrestle with complex text. Importantly, QtA focuses on querying the author directly: in essence, getting at the person and thinking "behind" the text. Following is a procedure for implementing QtA:

- Select a section of text for students to read collaboratively in a small group.
- Identify a few stopping points for discussion. Depending on the length of text, two to five stopping points usually work well. Think of the most appropriate places for students to digest, reflect on, question, and discuss what they just read.
- Ask your students to create *their own questions* (or queries) that will guide *their discussion*. Importantly, you will initially need to model and think aloud as you demonstrate how skilled readers generate questions, which could include:
  - Initiating questions:
    - What is the author trying to say here?
    - What is the author's message?
  - Follow-up and critical author questions:
    - Does this make sense to you?
    - Did the author say that clearly? Why or why not? What's missing?
    - Did the author tell us why?
    - How do things look for this character now?

There are a number of reasons QtA can be so effective. First and foremost, it puts your students in the driver's seat by asking them to do the heavy lifting. *They* are the ones asking the questions, *they* are the ones going back to the text to justify their thinking, and *they* are the ones discussing and debating. Second, because of the very fact that they are asking the questions themselves, students are almost forced to take a critical stance toward reading. Encouraging our students to ask these types of questions helps to dispel the myth of the author as an invisible, faultless "being," rather than as a flesh-and-blood human behind the text whose authorial choices might not always be the best or clearest. For many students, this critical stance toward texts and authors is eye-opening. It can also be a lot of fun for a sixth grader to take an author to task and criticize their word choice, organization, or clarity! Finally, QtA encourages and facilitates rich discussion and collaborative work, much more so than traditional reading lessons. This not only leads to higher-level thinking, but it's also simply a lot more engaging.

Self-Monitoring and "Fix-Up" Strategies

As skilled readers, we constantly reflect on, monitor, and regulate our thinking processes. To do this, we must be actively aware of whether we understand what we are reading. Moreover, we must know how to deal with comprehension breakdowns as they come up. As with Zach, many middle-grades readers who struggle with comprehension are often unaware of these comprehension breakdowns. The RAND Study Group (2002) called this the "illusion of comprehension," meaning these students think if they can read or decode all of the words that they have accomplished their task and must have understood. This is where, as teachers, we need to teach students how to "look under the hood," so they can (1) see where, exactly, the comprehension process is breaking down for them and then (2) give them tools so they can fix it themselves.

Therefore, one of our most important goals for students like Zach is to help them realize when they experience a comprehension breakdown. Not only this, but we need to show them what to do when this happens—how to fix up these breakdowns. We start by talking to students about two types of "breakdowns": (1) we don't recognize *words* when reading and (2) we don't understand the *meaning* of a word, a sentence, or a paragraph (Almasi & Fullerton, 2012). If we don't know a *word,* then we can use our decoding strategies. It's the *meaning* breakdowns that are hard for students like Zach.

When meaning breaks down, we use the following fix-up moves:

- Reread
- Check the headings
- Read on
- Think about the text structure

We often demonstrate using *text structures* (see below) to help support fixing up a comprehension breakdown. For example, as we teach a text structure, we add them to our fix-up moves beside text structure. We teach students questions to ask, such as (1) Does this passage talk about a problem? (2) Does the problem have a solution? (3) Or is this text describing something or someone? (4) Do you see any key words to help (e.g., such as, including, as illustrated by)? When students know the text structure, then they can ask questions to monitor their understanding like *what is the problem?* and *what is the solution?* If they can't answer these questions, then they know they have a breakdown. They need to fix up. They can reread and check the headings. If that doesn't help, they may need to read on.

Text Structure: Using Concept Mapping to See the "Big Pictures" in Informational Text

When my family (Kevin) first opened a puzzle of the Golden Gate Bridge and poured out the hundreds of pieces onto our kitchen table, all we could see was an overwhelming number of odd-shaped, colored fragments that didn't appear to have any connection with each other. However, as we slowly put the puzzle together, piece by piece, the "big picture" began to emerge. We could gradually see the ocean, the fog rolling in, the bridge itself, and eventually San Francisco in the background.

For too many students, their understanding of science, social studies, math, and ELA is a lot like our initial view of the scattered puzzle pieces: a disconnected and overwhelming mix of vocabulary terms, formulas, and information to be memorized piecemeal. Wineburg (1991) found that high school students read history texts at a surface level just like this, simply trying to remember a dizzying array of unconnected names, dates, people, and events. This is in stark contrast to professional historians, who look for themes, patterns, and arguments to help them construct the "big picture" across the sweep of history. When you can see this big picture, not only does it help you to remember the small details, you can see how they all fit together, enabling you to actually use it and apply it in your own life.

Comprehension research shows that teaching students to use *concept mapping*—to graphically map information so they can see how ideas and concepts are related—significantly improves reading comprehension (Duke et al., 2011; NRP, 2000). Importantly, these concept maps often reflect the deeper, underlying *text structures*—the ways in which ideas and concepts are organized and related in a text. Following are three "big picture" concept maps that reflect three common text structures found in the middle grades:

- Compare–contrast
- In-depth exploration
- Cause–effect

As with all reader strategies, use the Gradual Release Model to teach your students how to use these graphic organizers and text structures, explicitly modeling each one and providing guided practice and feedback before expecting students to be able to use them independently.

Compare–Contrast

Comparing and contrasting things, whether it's which road to take home, which movie to watch, or which book to read, is a fundamental way we make sense of the world. We compare and contrast in content-area learning constantly: important historical figures such as *Sojourner Truth* and *Harriet Tubman* in social studies, important concepts such as *renewable energy* versus *nonrenewable energy* in science, or two books in the same genre, such as *Esperanza Rising* by Pam Munoz Ryan and *A Long Walk to Water* by Linda Sue Park (both works of historical fiction).

For middle-grades readers, we prefer the compare–contrast chart in Figure 7.4 to the traditional Venn diagram because of how explicitly structured it is (Flanigan

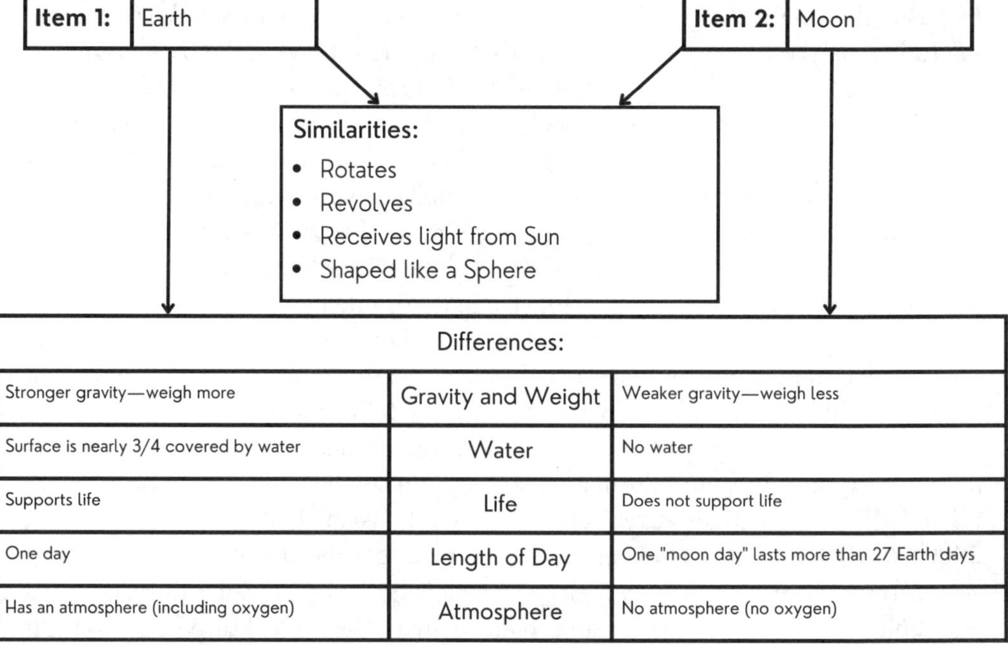

FIGURE 7.4. Compare–contrast chart of the Earth and moon.

et al., 2011). Notice the middle column in the figure, a compare–contrast chart of the Earth and Moon, which explicitly highlights the five features to contrast the Earth and Moon against: gravity and weight, water, life, length of day, and atmosphere. To help students make the transition from comparing and contrasting concepts *visually* in a concept map to comparing and contrasting them in *text,* we post a word bank of common, high-utility compare–contrast signal words such as *however, in contrast,* and *similarly* that signal compare–contrast relationships (see Figure 7.5). We ask our students to be aware of these signal words when reading and to use them when comparing and contrasting things in their own writing.

In-Depth Exploration (Description of a Hierarchical Relationship)

If you want to study one concept in depth, as opposed to comparing and contrasting it with another concept, the *in-depth exploration* concept map might be the right choice. Whether you are exploring (1) seals, including their diet, habitat, predators, and prey, (2) the different types of figurative language, or (3) the characteristics of a democracy, a visual that shows how these "big ideas" often consist of "smaller ideas" can pave the way to a deeper understanding for our students. Figure 7.6 is an example of an in-depth explanation concept map of the different types of figurative

Word Bank of Compare–Contrast Signal Vocabulary Terms

- although
- also
- however
- alike
- in contrast
- on the one/other hand
- but
- similarly
- in comparison
- yet
- likewise

FIGURE 7.5. Signal vocabulary bank of compare–contrast terms.

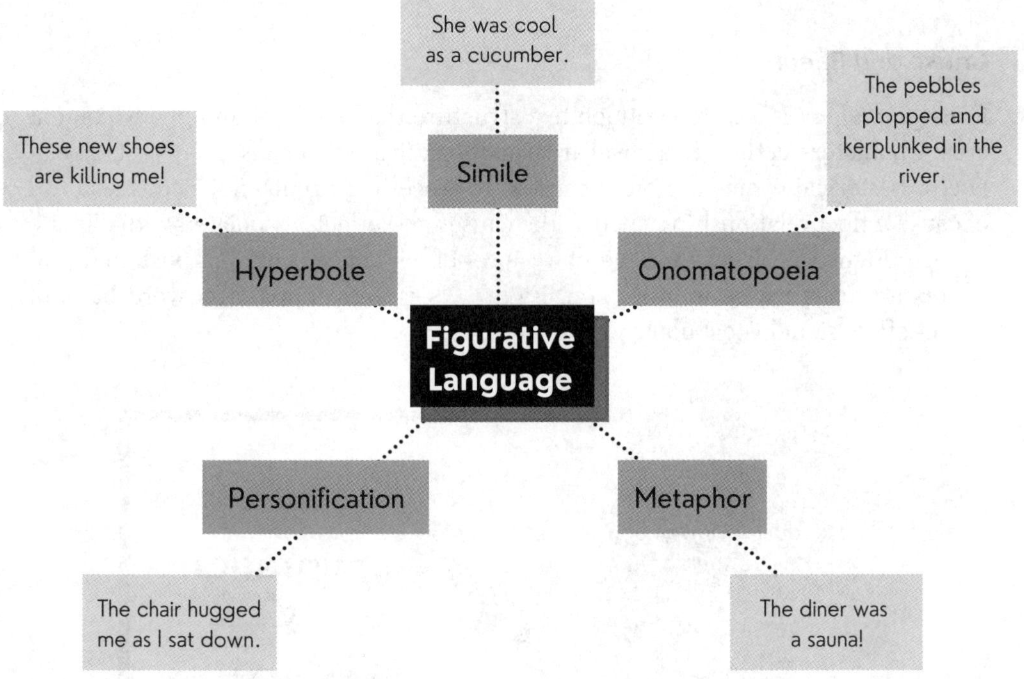

FIGURE 7.6. In-depth exploration map of figurative language.

Word Bank of In-depth Exploration Signal Vocabulary Terms

- for example
- is like
- including
- such as
- to illustrate
- characteristics of
- including
- additionally

FIGURE 7.7. In-depth exploration of signal words and phrases.

language. See Figure 7.7 for a word bank of in-depth exploration signal vocabulary words such as *to illustrate* and *including*.

Cause and Effect

Cause and effect is a third common text structure that can be found in any content area. Characters' actions in a novel are usually motivated, or caused, by past experiences. Historical events are often caused by preceding events. Science is also full of cause–effect relationships, such as the causes and effects associated with climate change. Figure 7.8 is an example of a cause–effect concept map of push and pull factors associated with immigration. Figure 7.9 is an example of a word bank of cause–effect signal vocabulary words.

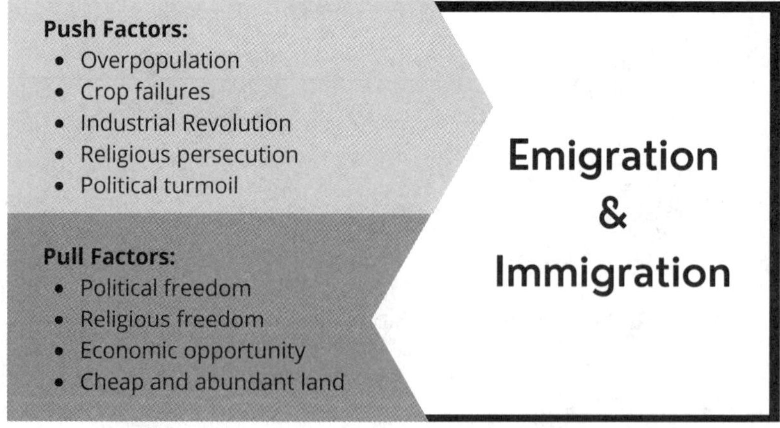

Push Factors:
• Overpopulation
• Crop failures
• Industrial Revolution
• Religious persecution
• Political turmoil
Pull Factors:
• Political freedom
• Religious freedom
• Economic opportunity
• Cheap and abundant land
Emigration & Immigration

FIGURE 7.8. Cause–effect map of emigration and immigration.

Word Bank of Cause–Effect Exploration Signal Vocabulary Terms

- If . . . then
- so that
- thus
- therefore
- as a result
- this led to
- due to
- because
- consequently

FIGURE 7.9. Cause–effect signal words and phrases.

MAKING MEANING IN AUTHENTIC READING CONTEXTS: DRIVING THE CAR

The ultimate goal of all of the reading comprehension strategies we discussed above—*inferring, questioning, self-monitoring, concept mapping*—is not to "do" strategies all day long, with no end goal in mind. This would be akin to spending considerable time looking under the hood of your car, tuning it up, but never actually driving it. So, in addition to explicit strategy instruction, we *also* need to provide our students authentic and engaging reading contexts in which students are reading for meaning, discussing, debating, grappling with interesting, complex, sometimes difficult ideas, and applying the strategies as needed to make sense of text. We need to drive the car *with* our students—yes, monitoring the repairs we just made to see if they are working—but with our eyes on the road and our final destination always uppermost in our mind.

Following are three instructional practices we use to create engaging, authentic, collaborative reading contexts in which students apply their background knowledge, use strategies as needed, and make meaning with text:

- Content-directed reading–thinking activity (informational texts)
- Directed reading–thinking activity (narrative texts)
- Using sticky notes to generate questions and analyze text (any text)

Content-Directed Reading–Thinking Activity

Developed by Russell Stauffer (1969, 1975) as a reaction to the passive reading instruction he saw occurring in too many classrooms, the content-directed reading–thinking activity (Content DR-TA) is a highly engaging instructional practice that provides a clear purpose for reading, activates students' background knowledge, and engages students during reading, all within a collaborative, discussion-based format. It's one of our go-to strategies we use when we want to reset the passive

Before Reading Prediction—How do you think the author will answer the focus question?	Focus Question	During/After Reading Was I right? What did I learn about..? Include page number.
	1. What are the main causes of climate change?	
	2. How is climate change affecting animals? People? Our farms and food?	
	3. What kind of pollution bothers you most? Why?	
	4. What can you do to make a difference with climate change?	

FIGURE 7.10. Content DR-TA example.

mindset of middle-grades readers with informational texts. (See Figure 7.10 for a sample Content DR-TA.) Following are instructional steps for the Content DR-TA.

Before Reading

- Identify a chunk of text that students will read. A textbook section or a chapter in a novel are usually appropriate-sized "chunks."

- Develop, or use/modify from the end of a text reading, approximately three to five "focus questions" and write them in the middle "focus question" column on the Content DR-TA template (see Figure 7.10). Importantly, arrange the focus questions in the same order that they will be answered in the text. These focus questions should represent the main ideas or key takeaways you want your students to know by the end of the reading. Consider making at least a few of them open-ended questions that require higher-level thinking (e.g., "What kind of pollution bothers you most? Why?").

- Briefly discuss the text title, topic, and focus questions. Ask students to take a few minutes and quick-write their hypothesis to the focus questions in the left-hand "Before Reading" column. If students say, "but I don't know," we simply reply,

"I know *you don't know*. That's why we're learning about this. I just want to know what *you think*." Providing just a few minutes to quick-write "primes the pump," gets every student engaged, and results in a much better ensuing class discussion, which is the next step.

- Ask students to share and discuss their hypotheses for each question with the class. Their hypotheses will set a powerful purpose for reading precisely because they will we want to see if they are right. Time and time again, we have found that middle-grades students may not initially care much about the topic, but they'll care about *their hypothesis* about the topic, because *they* made it. "Alexa, you think air pollution is the worst kind of pollution. Why? Give me a thumbs up if you agree with Alexa—that's about 10 people. Who disagrees with Alexa? Oh, okay Zach. You think it's water pollution? Why? Guys, let's start reading to see if you can find information that supports your opinion or causes you to change your mind."

- This prereading class discussion is where the fun and engagement really starts. Stir the discussion "pot" by asking students to explain their thinking. "Okay, Anaje, you think there should be an extra tax or a fine on anyone who pollutes—that's what you'd do to make a difference with climate change. Who agrees? Who doesn't? Ok, Kayleigh, why don't you agree with Anaje?"

- During this prereading discussion, in addition to *setting a purpose for reading*, you are *activating* and *building their background knowledge* about the topic as students share experiences, information, and ask questions.

During Reading

- We usually ask students to read in pairs for the during-reading section of a Content DR-TA lesson. One might read orally while the other follows, switching reading roles with every paragraph or so. As each pair comes to a point in the text that answers one of the focus questions, either confirming their initial hypothesis or causing them to modify it, they write their thinking in the right-hand "During/After Reading" column (Was I right? What did I learn about?).

- The engagement is often palpable as students find support for their hypothesis ("I knew air pollution was bad, but not this bad. It really affects pretty much everything around us.") or expressions of amazement if they missed something ("Wow—I didn't even think about how bad the effects of noise and light pollution were!"). Whether their initial hypotheses were "right," or they change or modify them or not is immaterial, they are engaged. Plus, it shows them that sometimes we read, learn something new, and have to rethink what we thought we knew—and extend our understanding of a topic, building our background knowledge.

After Reading

- Ask the pairs of readers to share out with the whole class what they learned, revisiting their focus questions one by one.
- There is a sense of competition and lively debate in the air as students share what they got right, what they missed, and, most importantly, what they learned.
- All of this rich discussion and deep thinking provides a solid launching point for writing in response to reading (see summarizing in Chapter 8).

The Directed Reading–Thinking Activity

In addition to the Content DR-TA, intended for informational texts, Russel Stauffer (1969, 1975) also developed a process for reading narrative texts, the directed reading–thinking activity (DR-TA). Conceptualizing reading as a thinking activity, Stauffer thought of reading as a cyclical process of (1) making predictions about the upcoming events or ideas in a story, (2) confirming or modifying these predictions after reading a section of text, and (3) making new hypotheses for the next upcoming section of text.

Following is an instructional routine and possible questions that a teacher could pose to a group of students at different stopping points in a story (Morris, 2014; Stauffer, 1975). Note how the questions are not the traditional low-level "gotcha questions" posed by a teacher to find out if you really read the novel instead of watching the movie ("What color were Abraham's shoes on page 293?"). Rather, they are thought-provoking questions adults might ask at a book club—questions we actually want to discuss. Following up with questions to facilitate collaboration and debate can help spark discussion (e.g., "Who agrees with Susan? Who disagrees? Why?" or "Whose thinking has changed after reading/listening to David's ideas? What made you change?").

- *Identify a text to read*—for middle-grades readers, a short story or chapter of a novel is a perfect sized "chunk."
- *Identify two to five stopping points placed at appropriate places*—with narrative texts, points of anticipation, such as "cliffhangers," are good choices.
- *Create possible questions to ask at these stopping points*—see Figure 7.11 for possible questions to ask *before, during,* and *after* reading.

Using Sticky Notes to Generate Questions and Analyze Text

When you ask your students to think about their reading, you can't really tell what's going on in their "reading brains." Are they actually thinking about the text? The question you just asked? Or are they thinking about what they're going to do after school with their friends? However, when we ask middle-grades readers to *write*

Before Reading	During Reading	After Reading
• What do you think this story's going to be about? • Why do you think that? • What do we know about the story or author from the cover, genre, or previous books read by the same author?	• What happened so far in the last section read? • Was your prediction right? Partially right? What made you change your mind? • Who are the main characters? What do we know about them? What's your evidence? • Would you like to be like any of these characters? Which one? Why/why not? • Do we know the story problem yet? Is there more than one problem? From whose perspective? • What is your text evidence to support that? Can you read it aloud so we can all follow along?	• What happened in this chapter/section? • Were you surprised? • How do you like this story so far? What do you like about it? Why? • Did you learn something to help you rethink your predictions? What did you learn and why do you think it's important? Where in the book did that happen? • Did the author have a message or lesson? If so, what do you think it was?

FIGURE 7.11. Possible questions to ask before, during, and after reading.

down their thinking, a couple of powerful things happen. First, because we can "see" them writing, we know who is doing something with the text and who may need a bit more support ("Zach, are you still thinking about the question, or could you use some help?"). In addition, when we write, we are immediately engaged.

This is where the humble, workday sticky note comes into play. The sticky note, for us, gives teachers one of the biggest bangs for its instructional buck, more so than any digital application, fancy literacy "game," or electronic device with all the usual bells and whistles. We use sticky notes all the time because of the simple fact that writing on a sticky note actively engages the reader in *doing something with the text.*

Sticky notes can be particularly powerful, even game changers, with our struggling readers who are used to reading passively. Following are a number of ways to use them:

- Use sticky notes for quick-writes *before* a discussion. When our students "prime their mental pump" first, our discussions are nearly always richer.

- Use sticky notes at stopping points *during* reading (as in the DR-TA example above). At each stopping point, readers jot down *answers, ideas,* or *predictions* to the questions posed by the teacher. Sticky notes also give those faster readers who finish a section before the others in the group a valuable task to do.

• Sticky notes can be equally powerful as places for readers to note their own thinking, their own questions, their aha moments, and any of their favorite words, lines, or scenes during reading. To provide readers a starting point and structure for what readers can note on their sticky notes, following are some prompts we post as "sentence starters" for our students (Beers & Probst, 2013):

- This made me think of . . .
- Yes, I already knew this.
- This is my favorite part/line/word because . . .
- I like . . .
- I wondered . . .
- This confuses me because . . .
- This surprised me because . . .
- I was surprised when . . .
- At first I thought . . . , but . . .

CONCLUSION

Zach has been in a comprehension intervention for 9 weeks (targeting Pathways #2 and #3). His intervention included explicit instruction in two strategies: (1) inferring, with a particular emphasis on using text evidence to justify his thinking, and (2) self-generating questions while reading, with the overarching goal of resetting Zach's passive reading stance to an active, critical, more engaged one. Figure 7.12 shows his 9-week comprehension goals and his progress toward those goals. After considering his strong progress, Zach's team has decided to continue with the same comprehension goals for 6 more weeks, focusing on moving his strategy use from a level 2 with teacher support, to a level 3—independent use of strategy.

The North Star principles we introduced in Chapter 2 informed our intervention decisions and helped Zach make progress toward his goals. How did they play out across the interventions to build his comprehension strategy use and guide him toward a more active, engaged stance toward reading? See Figure 7.13.

By the end of 9 weeks, Zach will: Develop a more engaged, critical stance toward reading, as evidenced by:	This will be measured with:	Progress at 9 weeks:
• Inferring—Being able to use use the inferring strategy to answering higher-level, inferential questions using (1) background knowledge combined with (2) text evidence 75% of the time	• In response to higher-level questions, written answers on sticky notes and/or in writing response composition book • Oral answers during class discussion as recorded on teacher checklist according to following criteria of strategy use: 1. Inappropriate use of inferencing strategy 2. Appropriate use of inferencing strategy with teacher support 3. Independent use of inferencing strategy	• On a 6th grade QRI passage and a social studies textbook passage administered at the end of the 9 week intervention, Zach was able to appropriately answer 80% of the inferential questions on sticky notes, using text evidence to justify his thinking. • Importantly, he moved from a level 1 to level 2. • Zach's teachers also report an increasing use of sticky notes while reading and ability to use text evidence to justify his answers.
• Question Generation—Self-generating at least 3 questions and/or sticky note ideas about a text during reading.	• Sticky note questions/ideas	• On these same passages, Zach was able to generate three questions/connections aloud to the teacher. He was able to do this at a level (3) independently, with no teacher support.

FIGURE 7.12. Zach's 9-week progress/growth.

Principles	An example of how we used it:
1. What Do You Stand For? Articulate Your Literacy Beliefs	Zach's team believes that good readers are active and take a critical stance toward reading (see principles 9 and 10 below).This is why they made it Zach's overarching goal—moving from passive to active.
2. Don't Forget Your Map! Choose and Use an Intervention Model	Zach's team used the cognitive model to target Pathways #2 and #3. They also used RAND's definition of comprehension (described in this chapter) to inform their understanding of Zach's needs: namely, that they need to focus on (1) the reader (Zach, including his background knowledge and strategy use) and (2) the context (creating an engaging and lively reading environment), not just (3) the text.
3. Start with Assessments Get to Know Your Students	Zach's team used the Maze to determine that there was a general comprehension issue and the ORF to rule out Pathway #1 (word recognition and fluency). They used follow-up diagnostic assessments administered by the reading specialist to pinpoint Pathways #2 and #3 (specifically text structure and comprehension strategy use).
4. Keep the Main Thing the Main Thing Design a Focused, Flexible, Doable Intervention Plan	From all the possible comprehension strategies, Zach's team focused on two they felt would give him the biggest bank for their instructional buck: (1) inferring and (2) generating questions. These were explicitly taught in the intervention setting and reinforced and applied across the content areas.
5. Make the Invisible Visible Use the "I Do" to Be Explicit and Systematic	Each inferring and questioning lesson started with an explicit introduction, including why, and a think-aloud modeling of how to implement the strategy—the "I Do" part of the lesson (see inferring sample lesson at end of this chapter).
6. Practice, Practice, Purposeful Practice Leverage the "We Do" and "You Do" for Long-Term Transfer and Independence	Each explicit strategy lesson introduction was followed up with multiple "We Do's." This section included Zach practicing and applying the strategy multiple times, with specific, precise feedback from the teachers. Finally, Zach was expected to start inferring and generating questions independently (e.g., with sticky notes while reading class textbook sections) while reading at least 30 minutes per day.
7. One Size Does Not Fit All Differentiate and Scaffold When They're Not "Getting It"	Zach was provided additional scaffolding and support as needed, including posting of inferring anchor charts, reminders to apply the strategies while reading from all content teachers, and periodic "refresher" application lessons in the intervention setting.
8. Time Where Does It All Go and How Can I Get Some Back?	Because Zach was immediately able to apply both the inferring and questioning strategies during reading that he was required to do in his content classes anyway, once the strategy introduction and initial teaching was done, there was not much additional time needed.
9. Engagement Get Your Students to Buy In When They've Checked Out	(1) As much as possible, Zach was given a choice in what he was going to read, even if a limited choice, (2) Zach was paired with a small group of students to collaboratively discuss their reading to increase engagement, and (3) Zach's 9-week goals were broken down to shorter term goals every 1-2 weeks (e.g., let's start with generating one question per reading this week) so he could see his progress more frequently. Choice, collaboration, and feedback on growth all improve engagement.
10. Active, Not Passive Take a Critical Stance and Read with a Purpose	Use of the Content DR-TA, higher-level questions, collaborative discussion, and reading with a purpose was a game changer for Zach. He was consistently asked what he thought and why, and his feet were "held to the fire" to justify his thinking. This all contributed to him starting to take a more active stance in his reading and ownership over his own learning.

FIGURE 7.13. Zach's North Star principles.

APPENDIX: SAMPLE COMPREHENSION LESSON

Inferring

Figure 7.14 offers an example of an inferring lesson we might use with Zach and his intervention group. We walk you through the "I Do" and "We Do" part of the lessons, including anchor charts and examples of teacher and student talk.

"I Do"— Directly and explicitly teach your concept
Make the Object Public: By the end of the lesson, the students will be able to make an inference based on a higher-level question using (1) text clues/evidence and/or (2) background knowledge to justify their thinking. Here's our anchor chart: 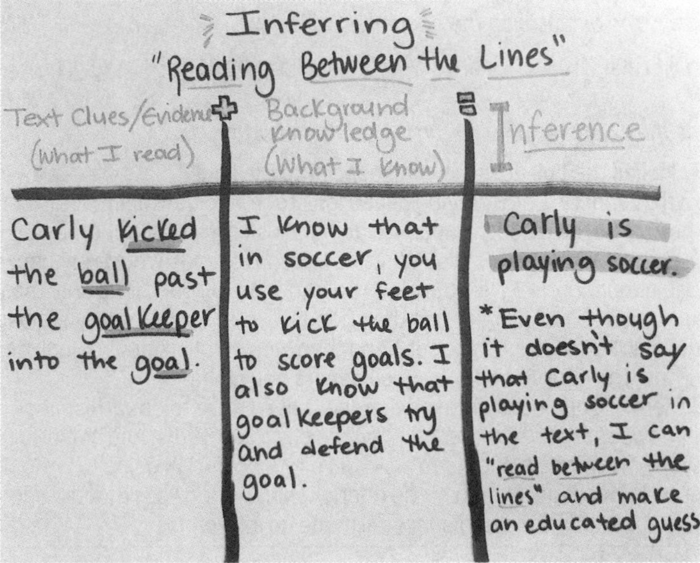 ***Introduce the Lesson:*** **Teacher:** I'm going outside. Look, I've got my umbrella and my raincoat on *[teacher puts on a raincoat]*. What's the weather like outside? **Students:** It's raining! **Teacher:** How do you know it's raining? I never actually said it was raining. Well, what you just did is make an educated guess about the weather based on what I was wearing—you made an inference! Inferences are educated guesses based on the clues we notice. The umbrella and raincoat were my clues.

(continued)

FIGURE 7.14. Sample lesson: Inferring.

We make inferences all the time in life: when watching movies, when we talk to our friends, and when we read. Whenever you read anything, the author can't write down every single little detail, or books would never end! The author has to assume that you know some things, because they can't explain everything to you. However, they do give you some clues in the text to help you out. When we find these "text clues" and connect them to what we already know, we can "read between the lines," or make an inference. Today's lesson is on how to make inferences.

State the Secret and Model Your Thinking:

Teacher: Now, there's a secret to making good inferences. Everyone look at our anchor chart as I explain it *[points to the inferring anchor chart]*. First, you use your text evidence, or text clues (what you've read) from the book. Let's all point at our books together to represent text clues. Then, you take what you already know—your background knowledge. Let's all point to our brains with our other hand to represent our background knowledge. When you put your text evidence together with your background knowledge *[teacher brings her hands together and claps]*, you've made an inference!

[Teacher points to the example on the anchor chart.]

Teacher: Okay, I'm going to model how to make an inference first. Then we'll practice some together.

[Teacher reads the example sentence on the anchor chart:]

Teacher: Carly **kicked** the **ball** past the **goalkeeper** into the **goal**.

So, what sport is Carly playing? Let's look for text clues. Hmm. Well, it says Carly **kicked** the **ball**. So, as a good reader, I'm going to ask myself about those text clues—in what sport do people kick balls? What do I already know—what's my background knowledge about sports? Well, they kick balls in football, but that's only the kicker who does that. Most football players use their hands. But, in soccer, everyone uses their feet to kick the ball. So maybe it's soccer? And then, yes, it talks about a goalkeeper and the ball going into the goal. Soccer has **goalkeepers** and **goals.**

So, there's four pieces of text evidence that all have to do with soccer: *[writes these on the anchor chart] kicked, ball, goalkeeper*, and *goals.* And since I already knew that they use their feet in soccer to kick and score goals, I'm going to write that in the background knowledge section of the anchor chart. When I put that all together, I'm pretty sure that Carly's playing soccer—I made an inference!

"We Do"—
Provide opportunities for scaffolded practice

Teacher: OK, now let's try making inferences together. Sometimes it's a little easier to do things with pictures before words. So, let's start with making an inference from a picture, and then we'll make an inference from some text. I'm going to show you a photo and I want you to try and tell me what you think is happening in the photos.

[Teacher shows a photo of a middle school lunch room. Most children are eating in groups at the various tables. However, one child in the foreground is eating with no one next to him. However, he has an older looking student sitting across from him. It looks like they are talking and laughing.]

(continued)

FIGURE 7.14. *(continued)*

Teacher: So, who can tell me what you think is going on in this picture? Remember, you need to tell me how you know, using <u>clues</u> from the picture.

Student: I think it's a lunch at a middle or high school. I'm pretty sure because the kids all look older than elementary kids, but they're definitely not adults.

Teacher: Okay, great use of clues, noticing how old they look. What else?

Student: I don't think that kid in the front has any friends. He's all by himself except for the older kid across from him.

Teacher: Okay, so who do you think this student is? Why don't you think anyone is friends with him? Who is this older student and why is he sitting across from him? Do you think they're friends?

Student: Well maybe no one is friends with him because he's new to the school? I know that's how I was when I first moved here. I was so embarrassed—I had to eat at the lunch table all by myself for the first few weeks until I met some friends.

Student: And maybe that older kid is like a counselor-in-training, or a high school football player (I mean, look how strong he looks), coming back to the middle school to help out. We had that at my old middle school—high school students who would come back sometimes and help the middle-schoolers who were having a hard time.

Teacher: So, do you think they're friends? Or is this the first time they've met? And how do you know?

Student: No, I think they've met before. I mean look at how they're laughing while eating pizza. It's like they've known each other and done this at least a few times before.

Teacher: I love how you all made so many inferences about the young boy and the older boy without being told anything—you had to use the clues in the picture along with your own experiences in school, your background knowledge *[points to anchor chart again]* to make in inference. We make educated guesses, or inferences, all the time when we read.

Now, let's move from <u>**pictures**</u> to making an inference with some <u>**text.**</u>

After we've done that, I want you to use these sticky notes and write down three inferences on them while reading your own books during independent reading time today. We'll share those sticky note/inferences tomorrow.

FIGURE 7.14. *(continued)*

CHAPTER 8

Building Writing with Zach to Support His Comprehension

In Chapters 6 and 7, we focused on what Zach's assessment results revealed about his *vocabulary* and *comprehension* challenges. We also discussed his intervention plan for those two literacy components. In this chapter, we focus on Zach's *writing,* particularly how writing can be used to support Zach's comprehension across classes, including his intervention. As we discussed in Chapters 6 and 7, based on all of Zach's screening assessments and follow-up diagnostic assessments, his intervention team ruled out Pathway #1 (see Figure 6.2 on p. 131) and focused his intervention on:

- Pathway #2 (*oral language comprehension,* including vocabulary, background knowledge, and text structure)
- Pathway #3 (*strategic knowledge,* including general and specific purposes for reading as well as knowledge of strategies for reading).

Mr. Jackson, armed with all of the assessment information and teacher input, identified intervention goals for Zach and his small intervention group. Now 9 weeks in, progress monitoring shows Zach's good progress toward his *vocabulary* and *comprehension* goals. He is successfully (1) using his writing response composition book for higher-level, *inferential* questions while reading, (2) marking spots in text with sticky notes for *text evidence,* and (3) responding during discussions with teacher support of the *inferencing strategy.* Seeing Zach's overall improved critical stance while reading during his intervention time is encouraging, but Mr. Jackson wanted to ensure this is generalizing into his content-area classes.

Mr. Jackson checked in with Zach's teachers and noted a pattern across their comments. Zach continues to have difficulty understanding complex texts and, importantly, *expressing his understanding in writing*—a critical skill for middle-grades students. For example, Zach's science class just finished learning about wetlands and estuaries. A recent assignment required students to write in response to this prompt: "Describe an example of a wetland and explain what an estuary is and its relationship to the wetland. Explain the factors that affect water quality in a watershed and how those factors can impact an ecosystem." The teacher provided a general outline and various resource materials to support the students' work.

Zach's paragraph (see Figure 8.1) demonstrated that he learned, and was able to articulate, some new information about wetlands and watersheds. This ability to learn some new information from informational text reading is a strength for Zach. However, older students need to do much more than this for success in the upper-grades curriculum. Zach's writing was not organized, nor did it directly address many of the requirements of the prompt, such as describing an example of a wetland. Based on this information, Mr. Jackson decided to administer some follow-up writing assessments to pinpoint Zach's specific areas of writing challenges.

DIAGNOSTIC FOLLOW-UP ASSESSMENTS

After talking with the content teachers, Mr. Jackson decided to assess Zach's (1) *note-taking* and (2) *summarizing skills*—two critical writing-based skills that Zach will be expected to use throughout middle school and beyond. Mr. Jackson began this

Marshes are wetlands a marsh can always be covered in water. Or just sometimes. They can be freshwater. Or saltwater. Marshes can help floods. Estuaries are where rivers come to oceans, they are like a wetland. Many things affect water quality like chemicals, they can be bad to water and put it in our drinking water.

FIGURE 8.1. Zach's science paragraph.

writing assessment by using a two-page, grade-level selection from a class textbook that Zach will be reading in an upcoming social studies class. This textbook section explains how geographic and economic factors influenced the westward movement of settlers. Mr. Jackson asked Zach to read the selection to himself and take notes while reading. After reading, Mr. Jackson had Zach explain his note-taking technique, asked Zach a series of open-ended questions focused on the cause–effect themes of the reading, and directed him to write a paragraph summarizing the main ideas of the selection.

It took Zach nearly 30 minutes to read the selection and take notes, with much of the time spent taking notes. Zach didn't appear to have a "go-to" procedure for taking notes. Mr. Jackson noticed that Zach's notes included some of the headers from the reading in an effort to organize his notes. However, his notes seemed to be mostly random details (as opposed to main ideas) and mostly complete sentences copied down verbatim from the textbook. When asked about his note-taking technique, Zach said, "I look for bold headers and then find sentences to copy that I think might be important. I usually try for one sentence for each paragraph, and if it's a long one, I might pick two."

Mr. Jackson followed Zach's reading and note-taking with open-ended questions about the selection. Zach didn't refer to his notes even though he was encouraged to do so, and his answers were variable, indicating he took away bits and pieces of information but not the main points. Mr. Jackson then asked Zach to write a *summary* based on the notes he just took. When he wrote his summary paragraph, Zach simply recopied the sentences from his notes, starting the paragraph with this topic sentence: "Lots of things made Americans want to move west." Zach made note that this was his *claim,* demonstrating some use of establishing a claim followed by *supporting key details*. Despite this strong start to his summary, the rest of Zach's summary read like a series of disconnected facts rather than the main ideas from the passage, which was not surprising given the fact that his notes contained many random details.

What Will Further Help Zach Learn from Reading? What Does the Research Say about Writing to Support Comprehension?

There is a strong relationship between reading and writing (e.g., see Graham & Hebert, 2011). This makes sense. When we teach a specific writing-related skill, its corresponding reading skill will improve and vice versa. For example, spelling instruction results in improved word reading skills. Teaching sentence construction can have a positive impact on reading fluency. Writing about what we read makes us think about what we've read and, therefore, increases our comprehension of that text. This said, reading alone won't make a student a better writer, and writing alone won't make a student a better reader. Taking advantage of their overlap means we need to devote instructional time and energy to both. Teaching students (1) to use *high-leverage writing activities*, and (2) explicitly teaching them *complex sentence structures* are two ways to boost their comprehension through writing.

High-Leverage Writing Activities

We can leverage writing to help students gather and organize knowledge, as well as explore, organize, and refine ideas as they actively engage with the texts they are reading. What are high-leverage writing activities? Hebert, Simpson, and Graham (2013) suggested five writing activities: answering questions, note-taking, summary writing, journal writing, and essay writing. Not only are these useful in extending learning, but they are also ways we commonly assess student learning. In this chapter, we focus on *note-taking* and *summary writing.*

Sentence Structure and Comprehension

Chapters 6 and 7 outlined the importance of vocabulary and active, purposeful reading to reading comprehension. Another contributor to reading comprehension is a reader's knowledge of *sentence structures,* particularly how words are related to each other both (1) *within* a sentence and (2) *across* sentences. The structure of sentences in written text is generally more complex than sentences in spoken language, and the textual demands in the middle grades increase with each grade. This requires syntactic awareness; up to this point, our awareness is tacit. Many of our students can verbally say a sentence with a dependent clause (e.g., Since she missed the bus, Tisha was late for school) or follow a conversation that includes pronoun references (e.g., Was Tisha on the bus this morning? No, she missed it.) without being able to consciously identify dependent clauses or pronoun references.

When we read, however, syntactic elements of sentences sometimes need to be explicitly addressed, especially with students who have reading difficulty. Syntax "directs the production and comprehension of sentences" (Soifer, 2019, p. 102). To comprehend, we must consider word order and how we connect words across a sentence. For example, shifting the subject and the object changes the meaning of the following sentence: "The student stopped the teacher" versus "The teacher stopped the student."

Clauses layer another comprehension challenge; consider this sentence: "When the teacher noticed *her* untied shoe, *she* stopped the student." Now we know why the teacher stopped the student. But do we? We have to figure out pronoun references. Was it the student's untied shoe or the teacher's untied shoe? Did the *teacher* stop the *student* to alert her to the untied shoe? This also brings in our assumptions. We might infer it's the student's untied shoe since children are more likely to have an untied shoe. If you are a student who has difficulty navigating these *cohesive ties* (words and phrases connecting words and ideas in sentences, such as connecting "the teacher stopped the student *because* she had an untied shoe"), your comprehension will necessarily suffer as text, and sentence, complexity increases.

When It Comes to Making Sense of What You Read, What Comes First? Thinking About What You've Read or Writing About It?

We're reminded of a question we heard Ray Jones ask years ago. "What do you think comes first? Writing or thinking?" We've followed up with this question: "Have you ever written something, and then realized what you wrote didn't capture what you really meant to say, causing you to adjust what you wrote?" This is a perfect example of how the very act of writing helped you make your thinking clearer. Put simply, writing and thinking are reciprocal; one doesn't come before the other.

Graham and Hebert (2011, p. 712) provided five ways that writing facilitates learning:

1. It fosters explicitness, as the writer must select which information in text is most important.
2. It is integrative, as it encourages the writer to organize ideas from text into a coherent whole, establishing explicit relationships among ideas.
3. It facilitates reflection, as the permanence of writing makes it easier to review, reexamine, connect, critique, and construct new understandings of text ideas.
4. It can foster a personal involvement with text, as it requires active decision making about what will be written and how it will be treated.
5. It involves transforming or manipulating the language of text so that writers put ideas into their own words, making them think about what the ideas mean.

In these ways, writing makes a student become "aware of their own thinking" (Hebert, Simpson, & Graham, 2013) as they create a visible, personalized record of connections, analysis, and manipulation of ideas.

What Does This All Mean for Zach's Intervention?

Zach's intervention should continue to focus on Pathways #2 and #3, focusing on his goals from Chapters 6 and 7. To further support Zach's reading comprehension, Mr. Jackson can incorporate writing activities (e.g., note-taking and written summaries) that include explicit introductions, models, and guided practice, as well as clear connections to their usefulness in Zach's content-area classes. This is especially important for the middle grades because students are increasingly expected to (1) learn through independent reading and (2) demonstrate their learning through writing.

Secondly, Mr. Jackson knows knowledge of both text structures *and* sentence structures are crucial to reading comprehension. The texts that middle-grades students encounter as they move through the grades become more complex with longer sentences that require a heavy lift to connect ideas. Not only this, but the academic structures of written language often don't mirror the language structures of our oral everyday conversation. Students learn how to navigate and make sense of these more complex structures through reading across content areas. So, students like Zach are facing two tough spots: (1) he's not reading enough to get the necessary exposure to these structures and (2) because he's not getting this practice, he gets lost and may give up when he reads texts with these complex structures.

ZACH'S INTERVENTION PLAN

Mr. Jackson spent time reflecting on Zach's note-taking, summary writing, and overall learning from the social studies text. He decided to focus on two additional, related goals for the next 9 weeks that leveraged writing to boost Zach's comprehension: (1) *summary writing* that clearly lays out the main idea and supporting details, including (2) *signal words* to emphasize conceptual relationships and text structures (see Figure 8.2). While Mr. Jackson is targeting summary writing for the next 9 weeks, this chapter will extend beyond this to include other ways to use writing in support of comprehension.

Mr. Jackson will use multiple samples of Zach's summary writing in order to fully determine mastery. Mr. Jackson will also break down these 9-week goals into smaller chunks to support Zach. For example, Zach might self-evaluate his ultimate summarizing goal (i.e., articulate his learning using the three-step summary writing process to produce written summaries that include main ideas and supporting key details, including appropriate signal words) using the following short-term goals: (1) identify main idea, (2) determine supporting details, (3) determine the relationship across details and how they contribute to the main idea, and (4) use signal words to reinforce the relationship.

By the end of 9 weeks, Zach will:	This will be measured with:
• Articulate his learning using the 3-step summary writing process to produce written summaries including main ideas and supporting key details	• Summary writing
• Accurately use signal words (i.e., connectives) in his written summaries to conceptually reflect the relationship (e.g., cause-and-effect)	• Summary writing with signal word banks

FIGURE 8.2. Goals and progress monitoring plan of action.

Intervention Lessons

In the next few sections, we show you activities Mr. Jackson plans to include in his intervention plans to reinforce writing to support comprehension. We cover (1) *note-taking,* (2) *summarizing,* and (3) *persuasive writing* to bolster Zach's comprehension through writing. To help Zach connect ideas in the complex texts found in the middle grades, Mr. Jackson plans to focus on using (4) *signal words* (or *connectives*) to connect ideas in his summary writing and to (5) *combine sentences.*

Note-Taking

We have been encouraged by recent research showing the positive impact of *note-taking* on reading (e.g., Chang & Ku, 2014). Note-taking helps students organize their thoughts and establish relationships across ideas. Moreover, it is active, encourages retention of information, and provides a permanent record to revisit information and reinforce learning. But have you ever gone back to notes you've written and gotten confused, perhaps because your notes are so sparse you can't make heads or tails of them?

It turns out more *is* better when it comes to note-taking. Having a more complete, detailed record of your thoughts helps you remember more and provides you with a better set of notes to revisit later to reinforce learning. You may be asking yourself how this might work with students who struggle to get their thoughts on paper and/or take exorbitant amounts of time with writing tasks. It helps to explicitly teach a specific note-taking strategy.

We've found success using a note-taking technique that's been around for decades—Cornell Notes. In short, Cornell Notes involves the following:

1. Identify and list key questions, main ideas, and/or critical vocabulary terms in the left column.
2. Write brief notes, answer questions, or define key terms in the right column.
3. Write a summary at the bottom (see three-step summarizing strategy on p. 197).

One big reason we've stuck with this technique is it reinforces our main idea/summarizing work. This technique is ubiquitous nowadays (and easily "google-able"), so we won't discuss Cornell Notes in detail. Instead, we share some adjustments we've used to help students use Cornell Notes: add visuals or graphics, pause for revision with scaffolding and collaboration, and use skeleton notes (see Figure 8.3). We've found combining a specific note-taking strategy like Cornell Notes with these adjustments improves students' note-taking and boosts their learning. It can also be empowering, especially when we help them leverage this skill for learning across their content classes.

Tweaks	How it works
Add Visuals or Graphics	We like incorporating visuals or graphics because they trigger students to process the information in a different way. Capturing what you are learning in a visual way boosts active learning because you are no longer passively getting down ideas. Instead, you are looking for relationships and visually depicting those relationships. In fact, one study showed adding drawings to notes to represent a concept or illustrate a relationship increased memory and learning (Wammes, Meade, & Fernandes, 2016). • One thing we establish quickly—this isn't about details or quality of drawings. This is about learning. We teach students a small number of ways to organize their thoughts visually, such as webbing or compare–contrast boxes and how to use key graphics like arrows to indicate relationships. • Think about your Cornell Notes sections. We use the top for the main topic (this is basically a superordinate header), and the bottom is reserved for our short summary. Down the left, we have a smaller column where we keep a list of main ideas as they relate to the larger column/space to the right for our key supporting details. This larger space for details is a prime space for incorporating visuals or graphics. And, while we encourage a graphic to highlight relationships across ideas in the summary section (e.g., a Venn diagram to emphasize similarities and differences of wetlands and estuaries), we always encourage a short, written summary as well. • We create a custom set of icons for key ideas that we know we'll use frequently, like a star for main ideas, a magnifying glass for supporting details, and a big, bold arrow for important vocabulary. Sometimes it helps to create sets specific to a content area. For example, in social studies, you might want a stick figure to indicate important people or a timeline for a sequence of key events. 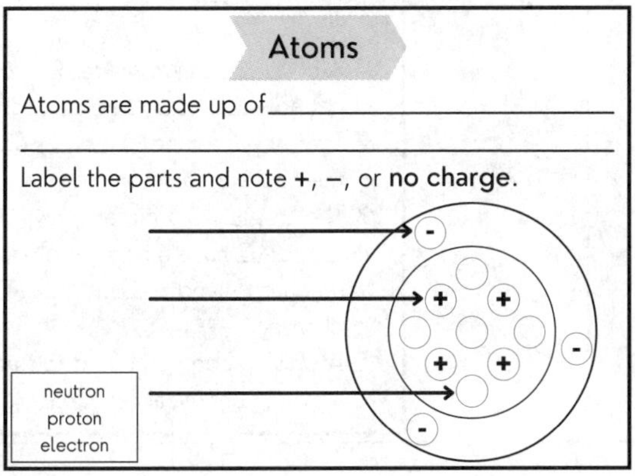 **Atoms** Atoms are made up of________________ ________________________ Label the parts and note +, –, or **no charge**. neutron proton electron

(continued)

FIGURE 8.3. Ways to increase note-taking success.

Tweaks	How it works
Pause for Revision with Scaffolding and Collaboration	We incorporate deliberate pauses during note-taking for two reasons. First, students retain more information and attend to main ideas/relationships when they are given the opportunity to revise or add to their thinking and rewrite notes. This kind of revision tends to be more beneficial when it happens *during* rather than *after.* Second, our North Star principle #6 guides us to always think about our practice, and we keep the 20/80 ratio on the forefront of our minds. But of course, this practice comes with immediate feedback. It's sometimes difficult to provide feedback in the moment of comprehension work, so intentional pausing helps with this. • As we pause, we also include time for collaboration. The importance of peer interaction during middles grades is well established. Specific to note-taking, Luo, Kiewra, and Samuelson (2016) found giving college students opportunities to collaborate during note-taking resulted in not only more complete notes but also higher scores on posttests—something we've also noticed in our work with middle-grades students. We incorporate partner and small-group work as we give a specific purpose for our pause and reflection.
Use Skeleton Notes	Skeleton notes is a type of scaffold where you, the teacher, provide some type of outline of the text, leaving key concepts out for students to fill in. Research has shown this to be highly effective across grades and through college as well as with students with learning difficulties (Haydon, Mancil, Kroeger, McLeskey, & Lin, 2011). The skeleton can be more or less detailed and can include text and/or graphics. • Here is an example of a very detailed skeleton where students need to read to find key terms to fill in the blanks.
	Atoms 1. All ________ are made of three smaller particles called ________, ________ and ________. 2. The ________ and ________ clump together at the center of an atom. 3. The ________ orbit far away. 4. ________ have a positive charge, ________ have no charge, and ________ have a negative charge. 5. Atoms can be combined to form ________ through chemical reactions.

(continued)

FIGURE 8.3. *(continued)*

<table>
<tr><th>Tweaks</th><th>How it works</th></tr>
<tr><td>Use Skeleton Notes
(continued)</td><td>• Here is an example of the same material with a less detailed skeleton.

Atoms
1. Atoms are made up of________________
____
2. Protons are located________________
and have a________ charge.
3. Neutrons are located________________
and have a________ charge.
4. Electrons are located________________
and have a________ charge.
5. Atoms are combined to form__________through
____

• Lastly, here's an example of a skeleton note set that includes a graphic. 

★ | main ideas
🔍 | supporting details
→ | important vocabulary
(person icon) | important people
↔ | sequence of key events

• Another option is to provide complete, well-written notes after students take their own notes. They can review yours and adjust their own notes as needed.</td></tr>
</table>

FIGURE 8.3. *(continued)*

To help Zach see the purpose in this work, Mr. Jackson brings in readings from Zach's content-area classes. This work includes selections from homework as well as prereading selections from upcoming lessons. Zach has been motivated by how his time with Mr. Jackson has helped him be, and feel, more prepared for his social studies class. Not only that, but Mr. Jackson has been able to support Zach in using his notes for written-response homework assignments in both science and social studies.

Summarizing

When you ask your students to write a summary, what do you get? Teachers tell us they sometimes get everything, sometimes get a random list of facts, and sometimes get an exact copy right from the textbook. So, why is summarizing so important for middle-grades students and how can we explicitly teach it to boost a student's comprehension?

Summarizing is a critical skill for at least three reasons. First, it requires the learner to distill the most important ideas (or main points) of something they've read or learned. It's not just "getting the gist"; rather, it is an understanding of the essential ideas of a concept or topic. Second, it is a common way we ask older students to demonstrate their learning. We often ask students to write a one-paragraph response summarizing key ideas, or a five-paragraph essay on a topic. Finally, we think of summarizing as the "gateway strategy" for much of the higher-level thinking involved in disciplinary learning in the upper grades. How can you hold a debate in science, analyze a short story in ELA, or write a persuasive essay in social studies if you are not able to summarize the source material—including identifying the main ideas—to begin with?

The good news is that there is a strong research base on summarizing. We know that explicitly teaching students to summarize improves their ability to (1) identify main ideas from a text and delete details and (2) integrate these main ideas to make generalizations (NRP, 2000). These are exactly the types of critical-thinking skills our middle-grades students need to make sense of the increasingly complex content in the upper-grades curriculum.

One of the biggest benefits of teaching summarizing to students with comprehension challenges is simply this: Teaching *summarizing improves students' overall comprehension and recall of text* (Pearson & Fielding, 1991). We think this is a big deal, particularly for students like Zach.

I (Kevin) worked with a high school student in our university reading center who was getting D's and F's on his weekly quizzes in biology, a required course that he had to pass for graduation. He was at a loss for what to do because these quizzes were based almost exclusively on the textbook, and he admitted in a heartfelt interview that he didn't have any "go-to" strategies to tackle difficult texts. We began with explicitly teaching him to summarize with his biology textbook. At first, his summaries were not very strong; however, his quiz grades immediately improved to B's and C's. Through this work, we made an important realization: The very act of attempting to summarize the text—even if the summaries themselves weren't particularly strong at first—actively engaged him in making sense of the information, improving his comprehension.

The act of summarizing is difficult, and students, especially those who struggle with reading, will need explicit instruction on how to do it. There is often a disconnect between what they think summarizing is versus what we want them to do when they summarize. Take a look at Figure 8.4 to think more about this tension.

Following is our "go-to" three-step strategy for teaching summarizing (Santa, Havens, & Valdes, 2004). The three steps are:

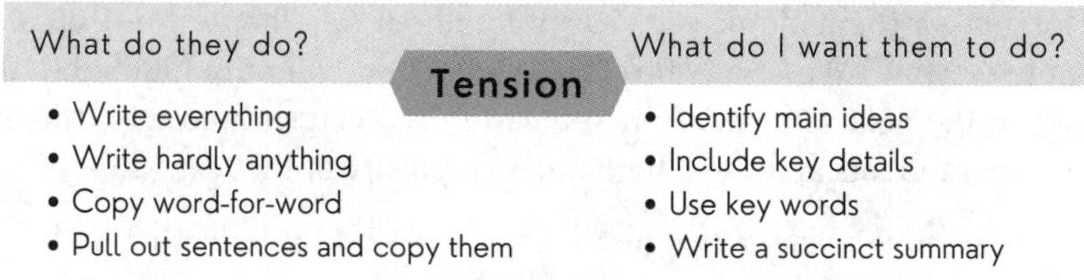

I've asked my students to write a summary...
What do they do?
Tension
What do I want them to do?
• Write everything
• Write hardly anything
• Copy word-for-word
• Pull out sentences and copy them
• Identify main ideas
• Include key details
• Use key words
• Write a succinct summary

FIGURE 8.4. Summarizing tension.

1. *Select the "treasure"*—identify key words, main ideas
2. *Reject the "trash"*—reject less important details
3. *Paraphrase*—Put it together in your own words using the key words and main ideas you selected in Step 1.

First, teach your students how to select the main ideas and key words in a selection. Model this by highlighting words or phrases, such as "Hmmm. I'm going to highlight the following phrase, *these 'pull factors' brought immigrants to the United States.* I think this is a main idea because . . ." Remind students to look for the following as text clues to important ideas: bolded words, repetition of phrases, transition words, headings, topic and concluding sentences, and even discussion questions. As you select key words and concepts, you'll also need to reject other pieces of information, explaining why you didn't highlight an extraneous detail.

Next, model for your students how to use the key words and phrases highlighted to write a concise summary. Some teachers like to write these key words and phrases separately on the board or have students write them on sticky notes and close their book (so they can't copy!). Providing word banks with transitions and signal words, like *first, next, however* (see Chapter 7 and later in this chapter), can be extremely helpful during this step. See Figure 8.13 at the end of this chapter for a sample lesson on summarizing. A few tips for you and your students when teaching summarizing:

- We remind our students that good summarizers *reread* sections of text. While rereading something to better understand it may seem like an obvious strategy, it's not to many middle-grades students.

- Use sticky notes or notepaper to write key words and phrases instead of a highlighter. Not only can you not highlight school textbooks, this prevents copying, because our students write their summaries from the sticky notes (not directly from the textbook, which is closed during Step 3).

- Give your students a limit to the number of words or phrases they can highlight. This makes them think very carefully about whether a word or phrase is "sticky-note worthy." We often start by saying, "You can only highlight 10 words or phrases in the next section, so choose carefully." Play around with this number based on your students and the length and complexity of the text.

- Start the first week or two just with Steps 1 and 2, selecting and rejecting. Ask students to discuss why they identified this word or phrase as a main idea or key concept but skipped that one. These discussions are critical in helping our students unpack the thinking involved in summarizing.

Persuasive Writing

We frequently use persuasive writing in our intervention work for four main reasons. First, it is an important skill for success in middle grades through high school. Many secondary teachers, especially in ELA and social studies, assign multiple persuasive writing assignments (Kiuhara, Graham, & Hawken, 2009). It is even a common task on high-stakes tests in most states. Second, persuasive writing tasks require students to (1) choose a side and defend their position by presenting claims, (2) provide evidence to support their claims, and (3) even offer up refutations to counter positions. Each of these builds, and sometimes changes, students' knowledge about a topic. Third, communicating and defending a position is an important skill in a democratic society. Fourth, we often turn this into a fun discourse while students take sides and try to persuade their friends to consider a different point of view.

We've used strategies for planning and drafting different types of writing from self-regulated strategy development (SRSD) in writing (Harris, Graham, Mason, & Friedlander, 2008). Students are taught two strategies that go together: STOP—a strategy to help them plan their writing—and DARE—a strategy to organize and execute their writing:

STOP steps:

- **S**uspend judgment
- **T**ake a side
- **O**rganize your ideas
- **P**lan more as you write

DARE steps:

- **D**evelop your topic sentence
- **A**dd supporting ideas
- **R**eject arguments for the other side
- **E**nd with a conclusion

The combination of STOP and DARE is particularly effective for persuasive essays in which students need to consider multiple sources. Students are prompted to think in advance about what they believe, what they want to say, and how they want to organize their ideas. Figure 8.5 provides a procedure for implementing STOP + DARE (Harris et al., 2008); Figure 8.6 offers a STOP + DARE anchor chart.

Using STOP + DARE

Develop Background Knowledge	• Discuss the STOP and DARE mnemonics—the steps and why each step is important. • Make note of transition words that can be useful in a persuasive essay. • Read persuasive essays to develop vocabulary (e.g., opinion, persuade), knowledge (e.g., parts of a persuasive essay), and concepts (e.g., how a writer substantiates a position). Use a graphic organizer to identify parts of persuasive essays, highlight transition words and discuss how they help the reader, and repeatedly review the steps. • Practice self-regulation strategies like goal setting and self-monitoring.
Discuss It	• Identify opportunities to use STOP + DARE in other classes. • Explore how procedures can be modified for other types of writing. • Evaluate success and discuss difficulty in applying STOP + DARE in other contexts. • Model how you set goals: include all five parts (i.e., topic sentence, at least three reasons, and a conclusion), use transition words, and ensure it makes sense and is convincing.
Model It	• Think aloud while modeling how to plan and write a persuasive essay using STOP + DARE anchor chart (see Figure 8.6) and a graphic organizer. • Invite students to help generate ideas and identify transition words. • Use self-questioning during modeling (e.g., What do I need to do here? What comes next? Does this make sense?). • Reinforce positive aspects (e.g., I like this word choice.) and demonstrate self-talk to overcome adversity (e.g., Keep going—I'm almost finished. This isn't easy, but I can stick with it.). • Model self-evaluation using goals.
Memorize It	• Continue recall practice of the steps and purpose of STOP + DARE.
Support It	• Review goals. • Collaboratively write essays together using STOP + DARE anchor chart and graphic organizer. Use self-questioning to check in on progress. • Encourage students to direct the process and support them as needed. • Self-evaluate essays using goals.
Independent Performance	• Shift to independent practice once students meet all goals without teacher prompting or support. • Provide opportunities for independently setting goals, completing graphic organizers, writing essays, and evaluating progress. • Think about application to other contexts.

FIGURE 8.5. Using STOP + DARE.

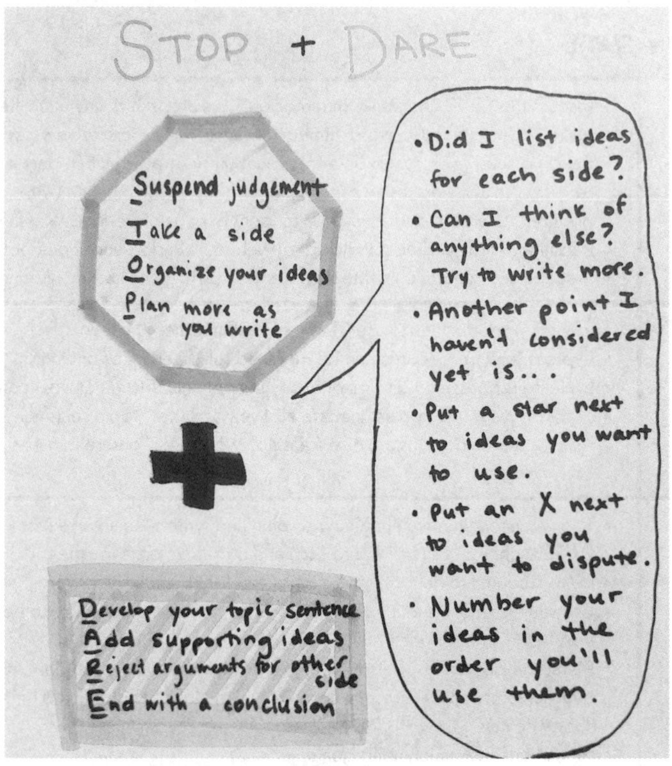

FIGURE 8.6. STOP + DARE anchor chart.

Signal Words to Connect Ideas

Sentences unveil the ideas of a text that add up to the main idea. They are the combination of words, phrases, and clauses that make up paragraphs and, ultimately, the texts we read. Within and across sentences we use connectives—the signal words from Chapter 7 that help us connect and integrate the information presented in the text. Consider this paragraph from Nic Stone's *Fast Pitch* (2021, p. 3):

> Their best batter is at the plate—Steph Mahoney. I know her name because of her rep as a home-run hitter. Not surprising once you see the latest Louisville Slugger LXT choke-gripped between her half-covered hands. Her batting gloves are fingerless, which I've never seen in our league. But considering that bat costs 350 buckaroos, it's clear good ol' Steph is serious about this sport.

The words, clauses, and phrases within and across these sentences help us understand what is happening here: Steph Mahoney is at bat, she has good equipment, and she's not only good but also dedicated. None of this is a surprise to the narrator. As a reader, I have to connect ideas such as *I know her name* to *her rep,* and *which I've never seen in our league* to *fingerless gloves,* and *but considering . . .* to *Steph is serious about this sport.* Sometimes there are specific words that signal me about the kind of connection I'm making, like *because.* That word lets me know the connection is causal—I know her name *because* she is known for being a good hitter.

We can pull these signal words (often referred to as connectives) into our summary and persuasive writing lessons as well. For example, when we are writing to persuade, we are often looking for words that *signal* we are illustrating our point or adding to it. We might also be interested in words that reinforce our points or words to signal that we are concluding our argument. We might practice using words like:

- Words to illustrate our points: *for example, such as, to show that, for instance*
- Words to add to them: *furthermore, as well as, also, in addition*
- Words to persuade or reinforce our points: *of course, clearly, surely, certainly, undoubtedly*
- Words to signal a conclusion: *in conclusion, finally, to sum up, on the whole, overall*

Signal words are *pivotal* words a reader must understand in order to infer the meaning of a text—the author's intent (Cain & Nash, 2011). For our purposes, we think about signal words as words or phrases that link ideas either clause to clause (e.g., *and, but, that*) or adjoining sentences (e.g., *however, although, on the other hand*). Mesmer (2017) calls these *sentence-linkers*—an apt term!

Let's consider these three sentences:

- I went to that movie *because* I love the director.
- *However,* the movie was sold out.
- *So,* I decided to grab an ice cream *and* go to the later show.

We can see how critical these are in understanding sentences. I went to that particular movie *because* I like other movies by the same director. *However* signals the reader what is happening in this second sentence is actually opposite of the first—I can't go to the movie. *So* lets the reader know what came next—the sold out movie caused me to grab an ice cream *and* go to a later showing of the movie.

We like to think about signal words in two ways: (1) how they link ideas in a sentence or link ideas across sentences and (2) how they can signal the structure of an expository text. Chapter 7 discusses how you can use connectives to signal text structure. In this chapter, we focus on how they function within and across sentences. See Figure 8.7 for a listing of frequent signal words (again, often called connectives) organized by function. We approach instructional practice with signal words in two ways:

1. Finding signal words in the texts we are reading so we can reflect on their function
2. Using signal words to combine sentences in our writing

One way to begin thinking about signal words is to start thinking about the function of words in sentences. Middle-grades students may still be unclear of the overall function of words in sentences, so we spend some time making sure that foundation is set. We use two routine activities to do this: (1) using structured questions to unpack a sentence and (2) sorting words from a selection into categories guided by our structured questions (Hennessy, 2020). See the example of each of

Function	Signal Words	Example Sentence
adding ideas joins clauses to add information	• and • in addition • as well as • furthermore • moreover • another	Preston plays golf, **and** Bella plays basketball.
alternative indicates choice	• or • either...or • otherwise	**Either** you feed our animals **or** get someone else to do it for you.
cause shows one thing causing another or provides a reason	• because • so • therefore • as a result • consequently	She has a smile on her face **because** she got a new puppy.
contrast connects opposite ideas or contrasts ideas	• but • although • however • though • on the other hand	It was snowing, **but** we still went to school on time.
condition points to what will happen based on something else	• if...then • unless • until • except	**Unless** it clears up, we'll have to cancel our picnic.
time points out when an event happened	• before • after • while • when • whenever • meanwhile • at the same time • finally • lastly • subsequently	**Before** I can go to the movies, I have to clean my room.

Sources: Mesmer, 2017 and various resources we've used over the years.

FIGURE 8.7. Common signal words in middle-grades texts.

these activities in Figure 8.8 using a paragraph from the sixth-grade social studies text.

Once our students are nimbler with words in sentences and their functions, we take an in-depth look at signal words. Some are easier than others (Mesmer, 2017), so we keep this in mind as we begin our study. Looking back at Figure 8.7, students tend to find *adding* and *time* signal words easiest, and we usually find they don't need to be explicitly taught. We focus our energies on *alternative*, *cause*, *contrast*, and *condition* signal words. Chapter 7 introduced signal words through the text structures of compare–contrast, in-depth exploration, and cause–effect, so you will (1) notice overlap and (2) see how lessons focused on signal words for comprehension and writing are complementary, with one bolstering the other.

We've found that sometimes middle-grades readers, like Zach, can define signal words, but they don't readily use them to support their comprehension when they read. For example, Zach might be able to say *however* means the opposite, but he doesn't always think about how it connects two ideas when he's reading. We follow a three-part routine for connectives: (1) teacher models thinking, (2) students analyze sentences, and (3) students extend with a short activity: either fill blanks for sentences with missing connectives or hunt for connectives (Mesmer, 2017). See Figure 8.9 for an example of how this routine might work for the word *however*.

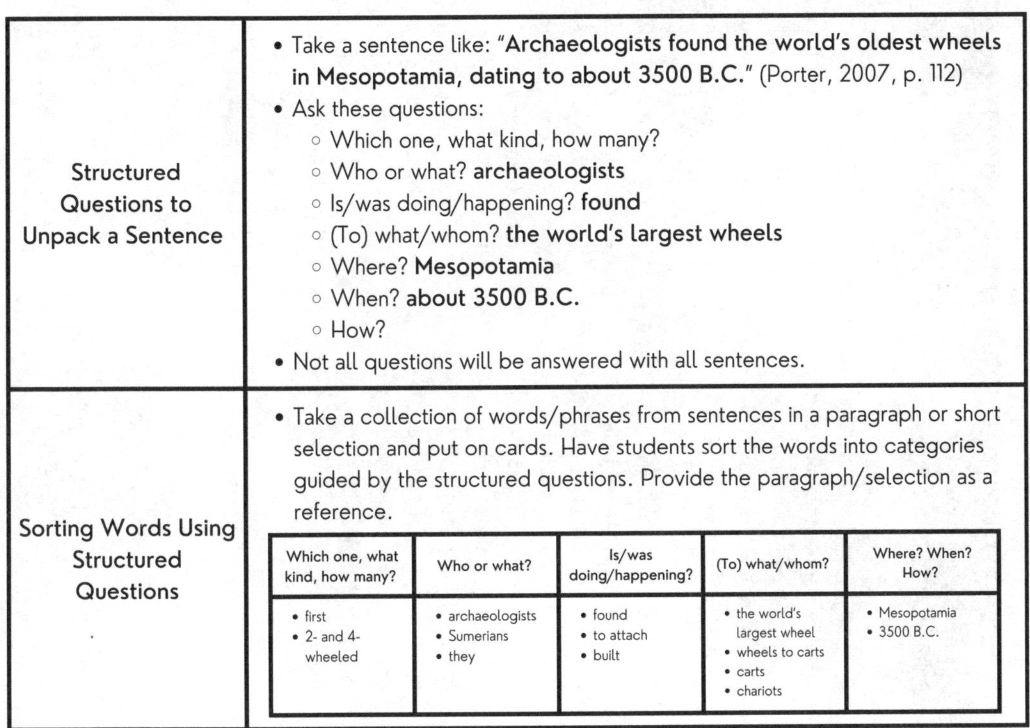

Structured Questions to Unpack a Sentence	• Take a sentence like: "**Archaeologists found the world's oldest wheels in Mesopotamia, dating to about 3500 B.C.**" (Porter, 2007, p. 112) • Ask these questions: ○ Which one, what kind, how many? ○ Who or what? **archaeologists** ○ Is/was doing/happening? **found** ○ (To) what/whom? **the world's largest wheels** ○ Where? **Mesopotamia** ○ When? **about 3500 B.C.** ○ How? • Not all questions will be answered with all sentences.
Sorting Words Using Structured Questions	• Take a collection of words/phrases from sentences in a paragraph or short selection and put on cards. Have students sort the words into categories guided by the structured questions. Provide the paragraph/selection as a reference.

Which one, what kind, how many?	Who or what?	Is/was doing/happening?	(To) what/whom?	Where? When? How?
• first • 2- and 4-wheeled	• archaeologists • Sumerians • they	• found • to attach • built	• the world's largest wheel • wheels to carts • carts • chariots	• Mesopotamia • 3500 B.C.

FIGURE 8.8. Structured questions, and sorting words using structured questions.

however

Model

- Display a sentence and read aloud: Kevin loves the Harry Potter movies. **However**, he prefers the books.
- Model: "The word **however** lets us know we are linking opposite or contrasting ideas. We know that even though Kevin loves the Harry Potter movies, he would rather read the books. It's not that he loves the books and hates the movies. Those are opposite ideas. In this sentence, however lets us know the contrasting feelings he has about the movies versus the books. He just prefers the books."

Analyze Sentences

- Create sentences for analysis like: "Joanne woke up with a stomachache. However, she went to work." Or pull sentences from books or content texts.
- Provide sentences for students to analyze in partnerships such as: "Some historians believe that ziggurats were built to represent mountains. However, others think they were built as bridges between the heavens and Earth" (adapted from Porter, 2007, p. 111).
- Have students:
  1. identify the connective
  2. identify the parts of the sentence being connected
  3. explain what the sentence means

Extension Activity

- Create sentences for fill-in-the-blank or pull sentences from books and take out the connective. Students work in partnerships.
- Make sure to bring in previously studied connectives. Here are two that might be used for ***however*** and ***because*** (a previously studied connective):
  - The weather is beautiful. ____________ , we didn't go outside.
  - We had a two-hour delay today, ______________ it snowed last night.

OR

- Provide texts for students to hunt for connectives. Students should record the connectives they find as well as the sentences they're in. Follow up by collecting the connectives and categorizing them as a group by adding ideas, alternative, cause, contrast, condition, or time. (See Figure 8.8)

FIGURE 8.9. Teaching signal words routine.

In Chapter 7, we talked about common words and phrases that signal expository text structures such as a compare–contrast text structure. We extend this comprehension work to writing summaries to extend our reading comprehension work to writing. Let's take the compare–contrast chart from Chapter 7 about the Earth and the moon (see p. 172). Once students have learned about the similarities and differences, then we can use that same *chart* to generate a compare–contrast *paragraph* about the Earth and moon. We provide a bank of compare–contrast signal words (such as *although, however, similarly, also*) but this time as connectives to use when they are writing to link their ideas. For example, students could connect a difference using *however*—"The Earth's surface is nearly ¾ covered by water; *however,* the moon has no water."

Sentence Combining

Sentence combining (Killgallon, 2000; Strong, 1986) is a strategy to improve writing (e.g., Limpo & Alves, 2013; Saddler & Graham, 2005) and allows students structured opportunities to use signal words. Sentence combining involves the deliberate practice of manipulating and rewriting simple sentences into a more syntactically complex form. It involves moving words or parts of the sentence around, deleting or changing words or parts, or adding to the sentence. For example, you might present a student with two simple sentences, like "my dog is sweet" and "my dog is little." The student's job is to combine these two sentences into a single, longer, more complex sentence, such as, "my little dog is sweet," by moving and deleting words. Or you could ask a student to combine sentences, adding a connective like *because* and *but.* Here you might ask a student to combine "I have a belly ache" and "I ate too much pizza" into "I have a belly ache *because* I ate too much pizza."

Sentence combining can be cued or not cued. Cuing the activity means you provide the simple sentences as well as the target signal word (e.g., *because*). We begin with *cued sentence combining* and progressively move to the less supportive *uncued combining* (see Figure 8.10). In the same way, we might move from asking students to combine two simple sentences and then move to combining three or four simple sentences. While focusing on combining ideas using signal words, we suggest focusing on one signal word category at a time. For example, you might use *cause* signal words (see Figure 8.7) using these possible steps:

- Introduce your students to two separate sentences. For example:
  - Elijah, Lucy, and Finnigan like to go on hikes.
  - Elijah, Lucy, and Finnigan go on hikes every weekend.
- Model combining the sentences using a cued support with the signal word *so:*
  - "When I think about how these two sentences are related, I'm thinking Elijah, Lucy, and Finnigan like to go on hikes so much that they go every

Cued Sentence Combining	Uncued Sentence Combining
Combine these two sentences and use *because:* • I hope I get a present. • Today is my birthday.	Combine these three sentences: • The day was sunny. • The girls play soccer. • It was the big game.
I hope I get a present because today is my birthday.	**The girls played soccer in the big game on a sunny day.** **On the sunny day, the girls played soccer in the big game.** **The day was sunny, and the girls played soccer in the big game.**
There's usually one option for the combined sentences.	There can be two or more options for how the sentences can be combined.

FIGURE 8.10. Cued and uncued sentence combining.

weekend. I'm going to start with how they like hikes. I'm going to write: Elijah, Lucy, and Finnigan like to go on hikes. Now, I'm going to use *so* to combine these ideas—the fact that they like hiking *causes* them to go every weekend. Elijah, Lucy, and Finnigan like to go on hikes, *so* they go on hikes every weekend."

- Provide guided practice using cued and then uncued activities.

As students learn to link ideas within and across sentences in their own writing, they become more aware of the ones they see when reading. The opposite is also true. As they become more aware of signal words in reading, they also become more likely to use them in their writing.

CONCLUSION

Zach has been in an intervention with a small group focused on Pathways #2 and #3. His intervention included explicit instruction and ample opportunities to practice with feedback as he learned (1) how to use writing, specifically summary writing, to support his comprehension and (2) how to look out for and use signal words to solidify his understanding. Let's check in on his progress toward his goals (Figure 8.11).

The North Star guiding principles in Chapter 2 informed the intervention decisions for Zach across both Pathways #2 and #3. How did these principles play out across intervention work designed to increase comprehension through writing? See Figure 8.12.

By the end of 9 weeks, Zach will:	This will be measured with:	Progress at 9 weeks:
• Articulate his learning using the 3-step summary writing process to produce written summaries including main ideas and supporting key details	• Summary writing	• Zach is writing summaries with main ideas and supporting key details using the 3-step process with greater proficiency with compare–contrast, cause–effect, and in-depth exploration structures.
• Accurately use signal words (i.e., connectives) in his written summaries to conceptually reflect the relationship (e.g., cause-and-effect)	• Summary writing with signal word banks	• Zach is using signal words in his written summaries with the support of a signal word bank.

FIGURE 8.11. Writing for comprehension goals and progress monitoring.

Principles	An example of how we used it:
1. What Do You Stand For? Articulate Your Literacy Beliefs	We used the cognitive model from Chapter 2 to pinpoint pathways and the developmental model to fine-tune our specific goals.
2. Don't Forget Your Map! Choose and Use an Intervention Model	Zach's team used the cognitive model to target Pathways #2 and #3. They also used research on how writing about your reading increases comprehension.
3. Start with Assessments Get to Know Your Students	Mr. Jackson used targeted diagnostic assessments, like note-taking and summarizing, to explore some of the difficulties his content teachers surfaced during a team meeting.
4. Keep the Main Thing the Main Thing Design a Focused, Flexible, Doable Intervention Plan	Zach's intervention layered summarizing as a way to support his comprehension, which also connected to his comprehension work through text structure and signal words.
5. Make the Invisible Visible Use the "I Do" to Be Explicit and Systematic	The summarizing lesson sample included an "I Do" section with explicit, systematic instruction including think-aloud modeling.
6. Practice, Practice, Purposeful Practice Leverage the "We Do" and "You Do" for Long-Term Transfer and Independence	Explicit instruction was followed up with multiple "We Do's." See summarizing lesson at the end of this chapter as well as lesson routines for signal words that also provide guided practice opportunities.
7. One Size Does Not Fit All Differentiate and Scaffold When They're Not "Getting It"	Anchor charts were used to support the concepts, reinforce during guided practice, and support independent application.
8. Time Where Does It All Go and How Can I Get Some Back?	Like inferring and questioning strategies, Zach was able to apply summarizing and signal words work to his daily reading and written responses in his content classes. This meant he was getting additional practice outside of the intervention.
9. Engagement Get Your Students to Buy In When They've Checked Out	Many of the lesson routines include collaborative practice (analyze sentences in signal word routines). Plus, he appreciated how his intervention work helped him in his social studies class.
10. Active, Not Passive Take a Critical Stance and Read with a Purpose	Throughout the activities in this chapter, Zach has to articulate his thinking (verbally or in writing) and explain his reasoning. Mr. Jackson also brought something to his attention that he hadn't noticed before—signal words, which encouraged more active reading.

FIGURE 8.12. Zach's North Star principles.

APPENDIX: SAMPLE WRITING LESSON

Summary Writing

The example in Figure 8.13 is a summary writing lesson we might use with Zach and his intervention group. We walk you through the "I Do" and "We Do" part of the lessons, including anchor charts and examples of teacher and student talk.

"I Do"— Directly and explicitly teach your concept
Make the Objective Public: By the end of the lesson, the students will be able to (1) select 10 key words, phrases, and/or main ideas in a section of text and be able to (2) justify why they chose them. (This lesson focuses on the first two steps in the three-step summarizing strategy below. We will teach Step 3, paraphrasing, after our students have mastered Steps 1 and 2 in this lesson.) Here's our anchor chart: 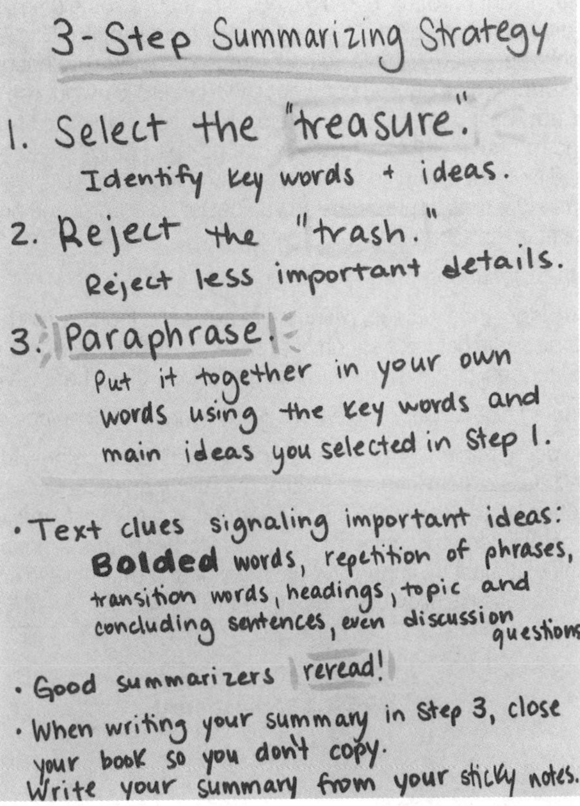

(continued)

FIGURE 8.13. Sample lesson: Summary writing.

Introduce the Lesson:

Teacher: Raise your hand if you've ever started to read a book or an article and become overwhelmed because there's just too much information? Have you ever wondered how you're supposed to remember everything?

Student: Yes! Sometimes I don't even know where to start. It's too much stuff to memorize.

Teacher: That's exactly right. We all feel that way when we read something hard. Well, one of the "secrets" to comprehending is that you don't always have to remember everything! In fact, if you can figure out what the main ideas are, in a sense, you only have to remember a few "big things" instead of tons of "small things." And those "small details" are actually easier to remember because they all fit inside the one of the few "big ideas."

State the Secret and Model Your Thinking:

Teacher: Now, there's a secret to making good summaries. Instead of trying to rush right into it and write the summary, there are three helpful steps you can follow. Most people skip the first two steps, and that's where they get into trouble with a capital T!

[Teacher points to the anchor chart.]

Teacher: First, as we read something, we have to select the "treasure." This means as we're reading we have to identify—either by highlighting or writing on sticky notes—the key words, most important phrases, and big ideas. And at the same time as we are selecting the treasure, everything we are NOT selecting, we are rejecting. This is the "trash." It's not really trash—these details have value, of course—but we are not going to focus on them just now. Once we've figured out what the treasure is—what the main ideas are—we take them, put them together, and write our summary, which is Step 3.

Today and for the next 2 weeks, we're just going to focus on Steps 1 and 2. So, let's get started as I model how to select and reject. Oh, and by the way, you only get to select 10 things—10 words or phrases—so you better be careful and not waste your 10 choices on unimportant details!

[Teacher points to the anchor chart.]

Teacher: To help me identify main ideas, I'm going to be on the lookout for the following clues in the text: words set in bold, repetition of phrases, transition words, headings, topic and concluding sentences, and even discussion questions. Okay, here we go!

[Teacher begins reading aloud a passage on the white board that everyone can see:]

Teacher: Hmmm. I'm going to highlight the sentence "Like all living beings, stars have life cycles." I think this is a main idea because of the following text clues. First, the name of this whole section is "Life Cycles of a Star." Second, the term "life cycle" is set in bold. Finally, they basically say this same thing at a few other points in passage—when they repeat something, it must be important! OK, highlighting that phrase counts as 1 idea. I've only got nine ideas I'm allowed to highlight left!

(continued)

FIGURE 8.13. *(continued)*

"We Do"— Provide opportunities for scaffolded practice
Teacher: OK, now let's try making summaries together with your small group. You're going to read the next section about the life cycle of stars. As you reread, highlight the key words and phrases that represent the main ideas. Remember to look out for those text clues to help you figure out if it's a main idea or not. And remember, you've only got 10!
[The students begin reading the selection in small groups as the teacher facilitates their discussion. She sees that Grace's group has highlighted the word mass *in their text.]*
Teacher: Grace, why did your group decide to highlight the word *mass?*
Student: Well, *mass* is set in bold, so it's got to be important right?
Teacher: That's a good text clue. Yes. Any other reason *mass* is an important word? What does mass have to do with the topic of the passage, the life cycle of a star? You can reread that part if you need to. Remember, good summarizers reread. *[The group begins to reread.]*
Student: Oh yeah, it says that a star's life cycle is determined by its mass. If the mass is larger, the life cycle is shorter—wow! We definitely need to highlight that!

FIGURE 8.13. *(continued)*

CHAPTER 9

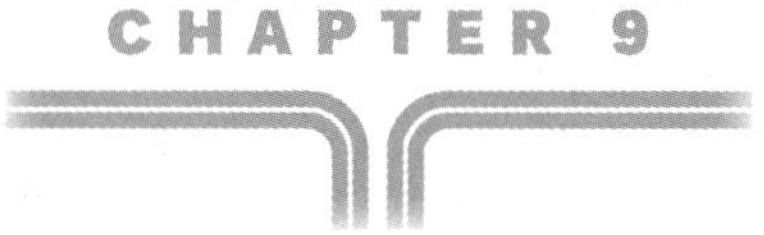

Building Engagement with Andres

Andres, our fifth grader introduced in Chapter 1, brings many strengths to the intervention setting. He shines in math and science and recently won a class award for his demonstration of the rock cycle using crayons. This demonstrates another of Andres's strengths—he is highly engaged with topics of interest and makes strong connections with content with scaffolds. His family is supportive of his work in school and frequently asks questions about how they can motivate him to read at home. Not only this but also Andres is bilingual with a rich cultural background—something he shares with his classmates on a daily basis. For example, he brought *parque* (Spanish for *park*) to the intervention group recently as he connected to *park* (during a study of various *r*-controlled vowels), which set off a brief discussion of Spanish cognates and spelling variations of /k/.

Andres has received literacy supports in school since kindergarten. While he didn't meet benchmark scores on his school's kindergarten literacy screening, he was also identified as a student needing language supports. Subsequently, he met with the school's ESL teacher to support his language development and provide follow-up practice with foundational skills from his core literacy instruction through second grade. In third grade, he started reading intervention as he exited his ESL support and remained identified for literacy support. While he has made significant progress in his literacy skills since third grade, his literacy screening in fifth grade (oral reading fluency passage and Maze task), showed he is still not yet on track to meet end-of-year grade-level benchmarks.

ANDRES'S READING CHALLENGES: INITIAL SCREENING RESULTS

Following are Andres's initial screening results and his team's thinking about his challenges:

- Maze: His Maze score fell below the benchmark, remaining at approximately the same level as in the previous year.
- ORF: He read the fifth-grade passage with 89% accuracy and 115 WCPM. While he met the *reading rate* benchmark, he did so at the expense of *accurate reading.*
- Ms. Hauser, one of the school's reading specialists and Andres's intervention teacher since fourth grade, checked in with his teachers and reported these main points regarding Andres:
  - Andres's engagement with tasks is variable; when he is interested and reading and writing responses aren't required, he can be highly engaged, particularly in math and science, at which he excels. Given sufficient scaffolds and extended practice, he can make meaningful connections with class topics.
  - He is challenged by fifth-grade-level materials and avoids reading and writing tasks. This can result in him sometimes "mentally dropping out" in class. Moreover, the topics in class have increased in complexity, and he sometimes doesn't have the needed background knowledge to support his learning. As a result, his engagement sometimes wanes even if his interest is piqued. When he feels overwhelmed, by either reading/writing or the content, he has a tendency to stop talking and engaging with his classmates.
  - His homeroom teacher offered up a specific example. As part of the fifth-grade curriculum, all students are graded using a common rubric for summary writing. Andres wrote quickly, produced a short response, and declined to add or revise when prompted. His summary showed he did not understand the main idea, and therefore, he didn't include relevant details. She followed up by saying that she was unsure if this sparse and scattered summary was due to issues with his understanding of what he just read, his skill at writing a summary, his motivation with the task, or a combination of any of these.
  - Ms. Hauser has noted a similar pattern of behaviors in the intervention setting, which seemed different compared to their work together when he was in fourth grade.

DIAGNOSTIC FOLLOW-UP ASSESSMENTS

Ms. Hauser decided to take a closer look at what is happening with Andres. She administered the graded word lists as part of the brief diagnostic assessment and made note of the significant difference between his automatic word recognition compared to his "untimed" word reading. In other words, when he hesitated on a word, skipped a word, or misread a word, she allowed him additional time to read the word. When words were presented in this "untimed" format, his scores increased at every grade level, indicating a strength in decoding and word reading.

She followed the graded word list reading with one oral passage reading at the fourth-grade level. Since she wanted to gauge his understanding of contextual reading and observe his reading behaviors in a lengthier text, she decided to use a think-aloud protocol (see Chapter 3). Before and after the reading tasks, she and Andres engaged in lively conversations about his sister's recent soccer game.

As he read the passage aloud, Andres seemed to move on through mistakes without noticing them and kept reading even if his errors didn't make sense. She rated his prosody as a 2, as he wasn't really reading in meaningful phrasal groupings and had no expressive interpretation. When Andres was prompted to "think aloud," Ms. Hauser noted that his responses were nonspecific and only tangentially related to the reading. Unsurprisingly, his answers to the comprehension questions seemed more about guessing than using text evidence.

Ms. Hauser had previously administered the survey portion of the Motivation to Read Profile—Revised (MRP-R; Malloy et al., 2013) to her fifth-grade intervention students and followed up the survey with MRP-R's conversational interview with Andres (see Chapter 3). The survey showed Andres did not generally identify as a reader, as he (1) demonstrated a variable self-concept and (2) placed limited value on reading. In the interview, Andres said it was easier for him to read words than it was to understand what he reads. When she asked what he needed to do to become a better reader, he responded, "Read more," and didn't elaborate when prompted by Ms. Hauser. Similarly, when she asked what she could do as his

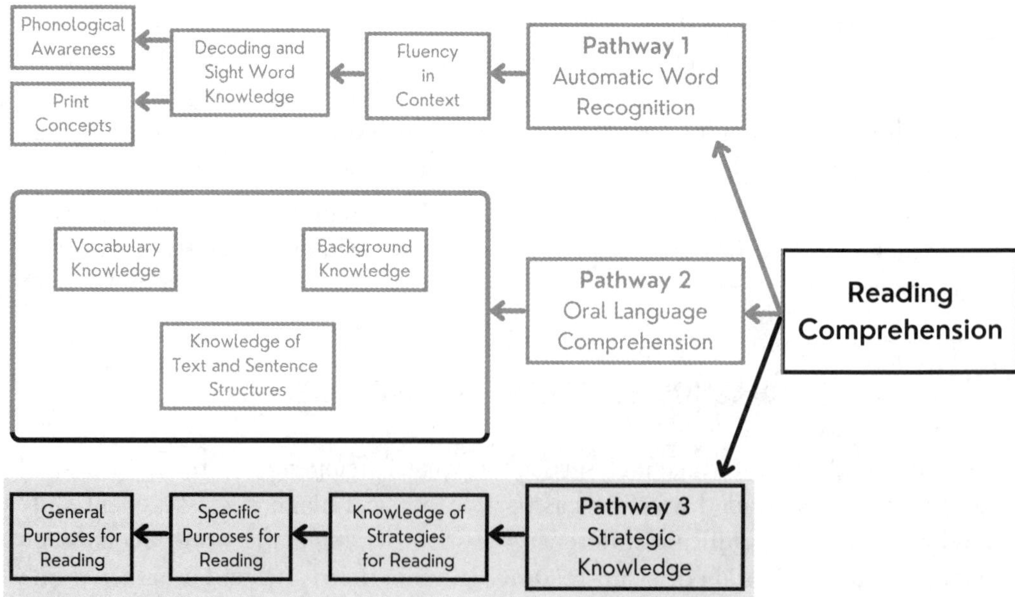

FIGURE 9.1. The cognitive model—focus on Pathway #3. Adapted with permission from Stahl, Flanigan, and McKenna (2020). Copyright 2020 by The Guilford Press.

teacher, he said, "Have us read more." He reported that he does read on a computer when it's a part of a game, but that he hasn't finished a book in a long time. While he acknowledged it's important to read well when you are in school, he was clear that he wouldn't be reading much when he grows up.

Given the information gleaned from the diagnostic follow-up assessments, Ms. Hauser felt foregrounding his motivation needs across his school day was necessary to engage him as a learner. As she put it, motivation is the "entry point" to his overall engagement. Figure 9.1 highlights building motivation through the general purposes for reading in Pathway #3.

ANDRES'S TEAM'S QUESTIONS ABOUT ENGAGEMENT

Ms. Hauser shared her thinking after the diagnostic follow-up with Andres's team, including his ELA/social studies and math/science teachers. As they contemplated this information and his overall performance this year across their rooms and content areas, they discussed the following questions:

- What do active readers do? And how can we support Andres to build a more active reading stance?
- Is there a difference between motivation and engagement? How do motivation and engagement factor into learning?
- How does motivation impact Andres's reading comprehension—our ultimate goal?

What Do Active Readers Do? And How Can We Support Andres to Build a More Active Reading Stance?

Take a minute and read the following paragraph from *Essential Cell Biology, Fourth Edition* (Alberts et al., 2014):

> When one atom forms covalent bonds with several others, these multiple bonds have definite orientations in space relative to one another, reflecting the orientations of the orbits of the shared electrons. Covalent bonds between multiple atoms are therefore characterized by specific bond angles, as well as by specific bond lengths and bond energies. The four covalent bonds that can form around a carbon atom, for example, are arranged as if pointing to the four corners of a regular tetrahedron. The precise orientation of the covalent bonds around carbon produces the three-dimensional geometry of organic molecules. (p. 45)

Was this easy for you to understand or perhaps a bit difficult (or a lot!)? What did you do to try to understand it? Did you reread? Did you use what you understood (e.g., terms like *atoms* and *electrons*) to try to think through the confusing parts? Did you make connections to things you already knew or are familiar with (e.g., periodic table)?

We are independent readers, so we pull out all the stops; we lean on our strategies to comprehend challenging texts like this selection on cellular biology. We do this automatically and are often unaware of it when it happens. It's only when we are faced with overly challenging text (like the one about atoms) that these strategic comprehension moves come to our attention.

It reminds me of my walks in my neighborhood. I (Tisha) live on a dead-end street, so when I go on walks, I hardly ever see cars. I usually get in a groove of walking and get lost in my thoughts. But then a car comes down the road. Suddenly, I become very aware of my surroundings. I begin to watch out for the car, move to the side, and pull in my dog's leash. I can hear my strategic thinking, "Get over and watch for your dog!" It's like that when I'm reading a challenging text. I think, "Wait a minute. I'm not sure about this. I better go back and reread that section."

In contrast, students like Andres are dependent readers. They are like walkers in my neighborhood who keep walking without looking when they cross the street as they move from point A to point B. Dependent readers have years of not understanding what they are reading, and many have developed a habit of relying on their teachers or giving up (like me, Tisha, when I read the paragraph about atoms). They often don't remember what they've read, either, because they are too bogged down in decoding unknown words, too overwhelmed by unfamiliar concepts, or both.

Any way you cut it, dependent readers are out of their comfort zone. They don't have an arsenal of strategies like skilled readers do to engage with texts, and therefore, they often become passive readers. They start thinking of reading as a task to accomplish without the expectation of understanding. Andres needs us to show him the strategies independent readers use subconsciously (Beers, 2003; see Figure 9.2). Chapter 6 shows you how we can make these *invisible* comprehension strategies *visible*. This chapter focuses on helping Andres become a more active reader through motivation and engagement.

Is There a Difference between Motivation and Engagement? How Do Motivation and Engagement Factor into Learning?

Motivation, engagement, and *self-efficacy* are three critical, interrelated concepts that play an outsized role in middle-grades readers' success. Guthrie (2001) defined *engagement* as "a merger of motivation and thoughtfulness" (p. 1). Reading motivation includes a student's goals as well as their *interest* in the topic, comfort with the process, and value of the outcome of a reading event (Guthrie, 2004). For example, Andres's family just got a puppy, so *he had a strong interest,* and he was *motivated* to read about different breeds as he learned more about his new dog. Another example is a recent reading assignment for social studies he just completed with

Independent Readers	Dependent Readers
• Figure out what's confusing and try to fix any misunderstandings • Set goals for reading • Use many strategies to comprehend a text • Have a dialogue with the text throughout the reading • Take what they read and add to new learning and gain insights • Maintain focus in longer texts	• Stop and give up • Appeal to the teacher for help • Read through confusions without going back to fix-up • Recite the words in their head only without new learning • Remember bits and pieces if anything at all • Lose focus in longer texts

FIGURE 9.2. Independent readers versus dependent readers.

Ms. Hauser; he was *motivated* to finish the assignment but *didn't have a strong interest*. Thinking about these two instances, we can see how motivation is tied to the reader, Andres, and the context, reading about his new dog versus completing an assignment.

Motivation and engagement are interrelated. Think about it this way. If I experience success as a reader, I am more engaged as a reader and am more motivated to read. But if I experience difficulty and setbacks, I am less motivated and, as a result, less engaged as a reader. In fact, it's estimated that an engaged student spends approximately 500% more time reading than a disengaged student does (Guthrie, 2004).

As students become more engaged, their *self-efficacy*, or their belief in their ability to complete a task successfully, also grows. It's not just about more, though. It's about success. Students who have experienced success see themselves as in control of their learning, which fosters motivation. They see themselves as readers and engage with reading tasks. This, of course, doesn't mean they necessarily have high interest in reading, but it does mean efficacious readers can engage with, and be motivated to complete, a reading task. In fact, they often see difficult reading tasks as a challenge and work toward accomplishing them (Schunk & Pajares, 2009).

We're reminded of a middle school student we worked with who wanted to improve his decoding and spelling skills. He was so motivated that he asked to do two lessons per week. To help him track his progress, a fellow teacher gave him a list of features to check off as he mastered each one. This simple "progress chart" was a game changer, as he saw himself mastering the material (most weeks, but not all), twice as fast. Checking off the progress chart gave him a concrete sense of ownership and control over his own learning. This is quite a powerful thing. Incredibly, he caught up to many of his peers by the end of the school year!

How Does Motivation Impact Andres's Reading Comprehension—Our Ultimate Goal?

Motivation is strongly correlated with reading comprehension and even learning more broadly. Not only does motivation impact overall learning, but it also leads to greater persistence and stamina, which in turn, impacts a student's interest and self-efficacy (Guthrie, 2004). Guthrie (2004) explained, "Engagement and achievement are reciprocal. Locked in a spiral, they grow together. . . . With increased amounts of reading, students' fluency and knowledge expand, increasing word recognition. Contributing to this spiral is a sense of identity and selfhood; improving readers see themselves as capable, which is gratifying. Beyond self-confidence, however, students on the upward spiral see themselves as readers who are learners and thinkers; these students internalize literacy as a part of who they are" (p. 6).

Importantly, some of Guthrie's concept-oriented reading instruction (CORI) efficacy studies show significant gains in reading achievement with robust effect sizes (e.g., Guthrie & Klauda, 2014; Wigfield, Mason-Singh, Ho, & Guthrie, 2014), translating to growth that made a difference. It's very rare to see this type of growth in reading research. It makes sense given that when students set goals, place value on reading, and believe in themselves, they more fully engage with their learning.

So, what exactly can we do to foster motivation? Duke and colleagues (2011) noted "we must be concerned with the will and thrill, not just the skill" (p. 61). Guthrie and Wigfield (2018) took this one step further: How do we develop sustained literacy engagement as opposed to episodic engagement in a one-off lesson? CORI outlines the following instructional practices to promote sustained literacy engagement. We unpack each of these instructional practices in the next section of this chapter:

- Start with concept goals linked to a conceptual theme
- Provide choice and control to students
- Use interesting texts of diverse genres
- Foster social collaboration

ANDRES'S INTERVENTION PLAN

After Andres's team talked through their questions, they made some decisions about what they would do collectively to help build his motivation. You'll notice in this case study chapter that we don't include progress-monitoring goals at the beginning or the end. This is because we believe engagement is not an intervention-specific literacy skill but rather a more holistic stance that should be addressed across the school day. So, his team discussed a layer of motivation across his school day and developed a plan across his content classes and his intervention.

- *Intervention*—Ms. Hauser will focus on reading stamina through explicit teaching, goal setting, and practice.
- *English language arts*—Mr. Allison will work closely with Ms. Hauser to support Andres's reading stamina growth and will add choice as well as more time for practice.
- *All teachers*—The entire team is committed to: (1) making reading purpose clear as well as (2) explicit teaching and scaffolding to build discussion skills to ensure engaging, organized, and equitable discussions.

Start with Concept Goals Linked to a Conceptual Theme

We don't read in a vacuum. We are always reading about something and for a purpose. Here we ask a simple question: What does the child view as the general purpose of reading? (Stahl, McKenna, & Flanigan, 2020). Independent, or proficient, readers often respond that it's to get the main idea, to learn about something new, or to understand what we read. Independent readers adjust their purpose based on the kind of reading they are doing.

On the other hand, dependent readers, like Andres, often respond that the goal is to read the words correctly or to complete the assigned reading. This understanding of the general purpose of reading does not encourage active, engaged reading for understanding. How do we help reset Andres's general purpose for reading? He won't see a *general purpose* for reading until he gets plenty of practice with the *specific purposes* of reading that we provide throughout the day. These experiences will help him begin to see the general purpose of reading in his own life.

All of Andres's teachers plan to make these goals and topics clear for him, and not just for him, but for their entire class. We've found framing the purpose as a question helps students shift their stance. For example, Ms. Hauser is working on summarizing informational text in the intervention group. The ability to summarize is their strategy goal. She decides to leverage a topic of interest—one of the students plays soccer and is recovering from a sports-related concussion, and the group is, understandably, incredibly interested in concussions because of their friend. She uses this student's specific questions about concussions (e.g., *What's the average recovery time? What are the long-term effects?*) to develop a purpose for reading, finds an article on concussions, and lets his questions set the group's conceptual purpose for reading. The group now has an authentic reason to learn to summarize.

Provide Choice and Control to Students

We are all more motivated and involved when we have "skin in the game," when we feel like we are invested and involved. Give your students some control and ownership in their own learning. Even limited choice can be a powerful motivator, such as providing a limited set of books or topics from which your students can choose to read or simply asking them which activity they want to do first, second, or third that day.

One major obstacle to feeling invested is a lack of reading stamina. If you know you don't have the stamina to read for the extended periods of time necessary to complete your daily assignments, you won't ever feel in control of your learning. Why? Because you are constantly playing catch-up with your schoolwork, and your peers with great reading stamina are "passing you by." This is why we often focus on building a student's reading stamina. As they read for longer and longer periods of time, they can literally count their growth in minutes, which is very motivating. As their "reading muscles" get stronger, they start to believe in their ability to sustain mental effort over extended periods of time. This increased reading competence and confidence results in a greater sense of control of their learning.

Andres's Reading Stamina Challenges

Ms. Hauser has noticed over the years that her intervention students have difficulty staying focused while reading, especially in longer texts. She's noted some common stamina patterns with students. Sometimes they are just nonstarters—they can't seem to get out of the gate. Other times they simply stop reading—they just can't sustain the effort past a handful of minutes (if that). She's noticed many instances of "fake reading," where they give the illusion of stamina, and other times where they persist but just can't remember what they've read. Depending on the day, Andres could fall into any of these categories.

Students like Andres are not usually in the habit of reading for lengthier periods of time. He'll need explicit instruction and scaffolded practice to do it. In fact, reading for long periods of time might even feel like a marathon for Andres. I (Tisha) remember training for a half-marathon years ago. I practiced over weeks as I built up my running stamina and had moments where I had to push through a challenge to make it to the next step. I had a moment where I almost gave up, but my dad explicitly taught me what to do when I needed to push myself (e.g., concentrate on my breathing) and helped me establish realistic short-term goals to incrementally increase my time. This is what Andres needs. He needs to develop more competence. How can you have control over something you don't have competence in? Building reading stamina is a concrete way to build competence and give students more control over their learning.

Ms. Hauser and Mr. Allison, Andres's fifth-grade ELA teacher, have decided to join efforts to help Andres build his reading stamina. As they discuss *teaching* stamina, they decide on three critical pieces of their plan: (1) explicitly teach what's involved to "read long," (2) establish goals, hold students to them, and monitor progress, and (3) build up reading stamina with consistent practice.

Explicitly Teach Reading Stamina

Explicit instruction in stamina begins with book choice. Our book options for students include a commitment to continuous upkeep of our classroom libraries. Harvey and Ward (2017) suggest customizing libraries for students by curating options matched to their interests and highlighting book options through displays, short read-alouds as a "hook," and book-talks. They also suggest "low effort-to-reward" books, likening reading to pedaling a bike from a dead stop, where it's hard to get going and you feel a bit off balance. "There is a lot of comprehension work to do at the outset. Whereas [independent] readers will readily expend effort and tolerate initial disorientation, confident that meaning will emerge, [dependent] readers benefit from immediate gratification as they make their way into an unfamiliar text" (p. 96). We also look for books with an eye toward text length and complexity. For some students, they need to *feel* what it's like to read with stamina again, or maybe for the first time. Here are some ideas for "low effort-to-reward" books (as with all literature for middle grades, use your discretion based on content matter):

- Shorter chapter books like *The Start-Up Squad* series by Brian Weisfeld and Nicole Kear can spur reading on with short chapters and overall shorter length.
- Chapter books with stand-alone chapters like Jason Reynold's *Look Both Ways* essentially work like a collection of short stories.
- Series are great options because once you've read one or two, you have the background knowledge on the characters and basic story architecture, making them predictable and, therefore, easier to comprehend. They can also create a buzz—we're reminded of Jerry Pallotta's *Who Would Win?* series sweeping through an entire fifth grade, Svetlana Chmakova's *Berrybrook Middle School* graphic novel series going from one sixth grader to the next, and Max Brallier's *The Last Kids on Earth* hybrid novel series that got quite a few middle schoolers reading during a university summer reading clinic.
- Hybrid novels with elements of traditional novels and graphic novels, like Terri Libenson's *Emmie and Friends* series, provide pictures to break up text and lead to a quicker page turn.
- Compendiums like Anna Claybourne's *100 Most . . .* series offer collections of bite-sized information for students to drop in and check out.
- Anthologies or bound sets like National Geographic's bound set of *Deadliest Animals Collection* provide short books in a set that looks like a longer chapter book.
- How-to books can spark interest and have clear text features with illustrations to support students; plus, they naturally set a purpose (e.g., how to draw Marvel characters).

- Nonfiction books provide readers with multiple entry points since the text is nonlinear; readers can jump in and out, paying attention to the parts they are most interested in, like reading about how an octopus changes colors in a chapter of Sy Montgomery's *The Octopus Scientists* or checking out an orchid mantis or a pinktoe tarantula in Jess Keating's *Pink Is for Blobfish.*

- Free verse novels give students access to a powerful narrative with respites of white space on the page, like Jacqueline Woodson's *Brown Girl Dreaming.*

- Graphic novels give readers access to complex storylines or content with relatively little text and illustration—these two things together are a perfect combo: (1) sparse text keeps the reader moving and (2) illustrations support inferring. Plus, there are so many options from stories of middle school life, like Shannon Hale's *Friends Forever* series (LeUyen Pham, illustrator) to different perspectives like Victoria Jamieson and Omar Mohamed's *When Stars Are Scattered* to nonfiction like Jim Ottaviani's *Astronauts: Women on the Final Frontier* (Maris Wicks, illustrator).

- Short texts like articles from Newsela are good options for students who are intimidated by length; a resource like Newsela has many options to meet a variety of interests, like their "everyday mysteries" series. (Have you ever wondered why we yawn? Check out the everyday mysteries!)

After text choice, the next step is to describe what goes into stamina for students. It's not as simple as "sit down and read for 20 minutes." We like to describe reading stamina by (1) time expectations, (2) reactions while reading, (3) resets when needed, and (4) goal setting/monitoring.

1. *Time indicator*—A long-term goal might be to read for around 20–30 minutes without looking away from the book. This number adjusts based on the students. For example, Andres isn't currently able to sustain his reading stamina past 10 minutes. So, 10 minutes might be an initial "what reading with stamina looks like" time indicator as you build toward that long-term goal of 20 minutes.

2. *Reaction indicator*—When you are interested in a book, you laugh at funny parts, grimace at the tough parts, and gasp when something unexpected happens. Sometimes these reactions are external like my (Tisha) facial expressions as I read with a student about the tongue-eating louse in Melissa Stewart's *Ick! Delightfully Disgusting Animal Dinners, Dwellings, and Defenses.* Other times they are internal. So, we don't expect to see them frequently, but Andres needs to know he should expect reactions while he reads.

3. *Reset indicator*—We all get distracted sometimes while we read and need to reset. Andres needs to understand two things: (1) getting distracted happens to all of us and (2) when it does happen, he needs to be aware of it so he can reset. Plus, it's okay to take a break. We all need them sometimes. So, if his ELA class has

a 15-minute independent reading time, and Andres knows this is a long stretch for him as a reader at this point, his teachers can support him by helping him independently take a break if he needs one. We've used sticky notes for this. For example, Mr. Allison, his ELA teacher, can put sticky notes every three or four pages (this might change depending on the book) for two reasons: (1) sticky notes break the reading up and give Andres short-term goals within this longer 15-minutes, and (2) they can act as places for him to reflect on if he needs a break.

4. *Goal indicator*—When we are working toward something, it's good to set goals. When Andres plays soccer, he might have a goal of scoring a goal every other game. Building reading stamina works the same way. Andres needs a goal to work toward.

Establish Goals, Hold Students to Them, and Monitor Progress

Help students identify their personal stamina goal. It could be the number of minutes of sustained reading without distraction, the number of pages in one sitting, or the number of books in a specified time period. Whatever it is, make sure it's realistic. No one likes a goal they can't reach (think about your last New Year's goal). We like to establish a baseline for a time goal and set short-term and long-term goals: (1) work with the student to see how many minutes they can generally read before getting off track, (2) add a minute or two for a 2-week goal as a short-term goal, and (3) work toward their long-term goal (e.g., 15 minutes). As we monitor, we make the progress visible with charts like line graphs.

For example, a fifth grader was once amazed by her baseline—she could initially only read for 3 minutes independently! I (Tisha) chuckled by the contrast of my dismay and her happiness. We set her short-term goal for 5 minutes (2 weeks) and her long-term goal for 15 minutes (end of the grading period). She used a line graph to track her minutes and see how her progress mapped onto her trend line. As you can see in Figure 9.3, her third plot was over her trend line, which motivated her to keep working—note her "Woot! Woot!"

Build Up Reading Stamina with Consistent Practice

Just like anything you are trying to improve, stamina takes practice. We can't expect all of our students to sit down and read for 15 minutes without building their reading stamina (even if they are in fifth grade like Andres). Our students also can't expect they'll be able to sit down and enjoy sustained reading for understanding straight out of the gate. It takes patience and a commitment to build it. If one of our students has stamina as an intervention goal, we commit to a percentage of our time every day to applied practice reading in texts, and once a week or once every other week, we have a stamina day where we practice reading for a sustained period of time (e.g., 15 minutes).

FIGURE 9.3. Stamina chart.

Use Interesting Texts of Diverse Genres

In addition to (1) reading with a purpose and (2) providing some choice and control to students, (3) thoughtfully using interesting and diverse texts also fosters student engagement. In conversation with Andres, Ms. Hauser found out that the last time Andres finished a book outside of the intervention group was, as he put it, maybe second grade. When she asked him why it had been so long, he replied that it takes too long, and he loses interest. She wondered about his reader stance of "read to finish" rather than "read to understand." Was this a result of not seeing the purpose of reading, limited stamina, or a disinterest in books that didn't reflect him and his interests? Or could it be a combination of all three? Could his motivation be reignited?

We want Andres to see himself as a contributing member of the academic conversation. We start with a simple question: What does Andres bring to our classroom as a member of our group, our school, his family, and our greater community? What are his *funds of identity*? Esteban-Guitart and Moll (2014) define *funds of identity* as one's "historically accumulated, culturally developed and socially distributed resources that are essential for a person's self-definition, self-expression, and self-understanding" (p. 31). One way we can acknowledge students' diverse funds of identity is with our text choices. As Bishop (1990) wrote, "Literature transforms human experience and reflects it back to us, and in that reflection, we see our own lives and experiences as part of the larger human experience. Reading, then, becomes a means of self-affirmation, and readers often seek their mirrors in books" (p. ix). A student once said to me (Tisha), "I've never seen a kid who looks like me on the cover of a book." We want Andres to see himself in books, too.

As we discussed in Chapter 1, Andres brings a tremendously rich funds of identity to the classroom. First, he is a fluent bilingual Spanish and English speaker who regularly translates for family members, including his parents, at school meetings, in the grocery store, and out in the community. He also has a great wealth of family stories and history that, when prompted, he enjoys sharing. Furthermore, when encouraged, he has a talent for connecting these personal experiences to his academic learning. Andres's funds of identity, represent a tremendous vehicle for engaging him in his learning and his reading. Our goal is for Andres to feel that he has a stake in and ownership over his reading progress.

Two ways to leverage his funds of identity to increase interest in reading, and ultimately reading volume, are through "next-up books" and "preview stacks" (Harvey & Ward, 2017). A next-up book requires knowledge about current children's and young adult literature. For example, Mr. Allison, Andres's ELA teacher, noticed Andres showed interest in the *Bad Guys* series by Aaron Blabey, so he thought Troy Cummings's *Notebook of Doom* series might be a good next-up book to suggest. A preview stack is a collection of books across genres and topics. Andres can freely provide Mr. Allison with his opinions of the book choices so Mr. Allison can better understand Andres's interests, and he can make progressively more targeted reading recommendations for Andres's independent reading time.

Foster Social Collaboration

Human beings are social animals. Not only are we social beings, but collaboration around texts bolsters student motivation. Unfortunately, too much reading and learning in school is done silently and individually. Swanson and colleagues (2016) found discussions occurred in less than 20% of middle and high school ELA and social studies classrooms. Walpole, Strong, and Riches (2018) found that discussions weren't even happening in all classrooms. Even more, the discussions observed were mostly probing only the students' surface-level knowledge in an effort to check for understanding. So how do you ensure a discussion is engaging, organized, and equitable while also an extension of the learning?

Andres's team of teachers talked about this aspect of motivation in terms of their entire class—not just Andres. They set a goal for themselves: help Andres (and many other students in their classes) become more engaged across his classes, especially during class discussions. They devised the following plan:

- *Set him up for success*—The team decided on these four considerations:

  1. Think about the size and the time. It's hard to participate in large-group discussions. Small groups of four to six students is ideal, or even talking partners.
  2. Get them ready. It's difficult to contribute to a conversation about a subject when you aren't prepared. Before any discussion (partners or small group), have all students do some comprehension work to ensure they have a basic understanding of the text/topic to participate.

3. Start out small and build up. Start with partnerships with a specific question and build up to an open-participation small-group discussion.
4. Take a step back. Explicitly teach students how to productively engage in a discussion that involves all group members.

- *Get him talking*—Here we use open-ended questions that encourage text connections and provide guided practice. Beers's "questions to ask students" are helpful to (1) support students as they think about texts and what they mean to them, (2) provide students with models of questions readers ask while reading, and (3) give us a set of at-the-ready questions we can use for different purposes across different texts.

  ▶ See *When Kids Can't Read: What Teachers Can Do* (Beers, 2003) for the complete set of these questions. Figure 9.4 provides some of our favorites. In fact, we post these on the walls for continued reference.

- *Wrap it up*—It's important to provide some sort of closure to a discussion. This can be as simple as providing your own summary of main topics you noted as you walked around and listened in to the various conversations. Or you could have your students individually or collectively provide something in writing as a record of their discussion. We like to connect to text structures when possible (see Chapter 7), so, for example, students might fill out a compare-and-contrast chart about the similarities and differences between the ways of life of early colonists and Native Americans.

CONCLUSION

While this chapter didn't connect directly to Andres's intervention, his teachers can reflect on his overall motivation in engagement across all of his classes. They can also reflect on how they are supporting Andres, using their literacy beliefs to ground their practice. In this way, they can reflect on the "instructional backbone" of their motivation push with Andres. See Figure 9.5 to see how their decisions about building Andres's motivation match up to the North Star principles.

Encourage a Personal Response	• Did anything in this text remind you of something in your own life? Or another book or movie? • Did you have a strong reaction to any part of the book? Which part and why? • What confused you or surprised you? • If you could talk to the author, what would you ask or say? • Do you think the title of this book works? Why or why not? What would you change it to?
Encourage Reflection About the Characters	• Do any of the characters remind you of yourself? Which ones? Why? • If you could talk to one of the characters, what would you ask or say? • What surprised you most about any of the characters? • If you could take on the qualities of any of the characters, what would those be? • If you were to eliminate a character from this book, who would you choose? Why? How would it change the book?
Encourage Reflection About the Theme	• What message did you take away from this book? Why? • If you talked to the author, what do you think they would say the theme is? Why? • Does the title and/or chapter titles help us think about the theme? Why or why not? • How did the changes the main character went through help you think about the book's theme? • Have you read another book or watched a movie with the same theme? What was it? How was it like this book?

See Beers (2003) pages 271–272.

FIGURE 9.4. Beers's questions to ask students. Based on Beers (2003).

Principles	An example of how we used it:
1. What Do You Stand For? Articulate Your Literacy Beliefs	Andres's team thought about and discussed how motivation impacts overall engagement and, ultimately, academic achievement. This prompted them to make a plan across classes to build Andres's motivation.
2. Don't Forget Your Map! Choose and Use an Intervention Model	The team used the cognitive model from Chapter 2 to pinpoint Pathway #3 as a specific overall need for Andres as a learner across all of his classes, including his intervention.
3. Start with Assessments Get to Know Your Students	Ms. Hauser used diagnostic assessments to better understand how he engages as a reader (think-aloud protocol) as well as his motivation to read (MRP-R).
4. Keep the Main Thing the Main Thing Design a Focused, Flexible, Doable Intervention Plan	Andres's teachers made a plan of action for themselves—ways they can support Andres. For example, all of his teachers made a plan for how they will consistently, across classes, support discussions.
5. Make the Invisible Visible Use the "I Do" to Be Explicit and Systematic	Ms. Hauser and Mr. Allison worked together to help make the act of reading stamina more visible for Andres.
6. Practice, Practice, Purposeful Practice Leverage the "We Do" and "You Do" for Long-Term Transfer and Independence	His teachers committed to ensuring time in class to support his motivation. For example, they all agreed to incorporate partner or small-group discussion at least two or three times a week.
7. One Size Does Not Fit All Differentiate and Scaffold When They're Not "Getting It"	Ms. Hauser and Mr. Allison considered Andres's funds of identity and his developmental needs to consider low effort-to-reward texts—to help Andres get a jump start to reading.
8. Time Where Does It All Go and How Can I Get Some Back?	Working collectively to build Andres's motivation helps with time—we are stronger together than we are alone.
9. Engagement Get Your Students to Buy In When They've Checked Out	Ms. Hauser plans to use personal stamina goals and a progress chart as one tool to motivate Andres, and Mr. Allison plans to use preview stacks to consider Andres's interests and better target book recommendations.
10. Active, Not Passive Take a Critical Stance and Read with a Purpose	The teachers' commitment to ensuring more productive and equitable discussions will help Andres become a more active learner across his school day.

FIGURE 9.5. Andres's North Star principles.

CHAPTER 10

Supporting Middle-Grades Students Across the Day

The first nine chapters of this book focused on literacy interventions with middle-grades readers like Andres, Zach, and Aliyah. While effective literacy interventions can make a significant impact with these readers, in terms of actual instructional time, they represent a relatively small portion of their day. Middle graders will spend the majority of their school day *not* in intervention settings, but in other classes, including their core content classes.

In their content classes, Andres, Zach, and Aliyah engage with many different teachers, and these content teachers can make a difference *outside* of the intervention settings. Darling-Hammond and Bransford (2007) assert that teachers are central to students' school experiences. With this in mind, what can content-area teachers do to support students with literacy challenges so these students can (1) learn the essential content while at the same time (2) continue to improve their literacy skills?

HOW CONTENT-AREA TEACHERS CAN SUPPORT STUDENTS WITH LITERACY CHALLENGES

This chapter focuses on instructional practices for content-area teachers that are doable, will support *all* of their students, and can be done with the content they are already teaching. In other words, we do not view these as "add-ons." We have organized this chapter around teachers' choices that center on three broad variables (Hiebert & Martin, 2009):

1. The *time* we spend
2. The *texts* we use
3. The *tasks* we choose

The Time We Spend

Research has established a positive correlation between time spent reading and reading achievement (e.g., Anderson et al., 1988; Cunningham & Stanovich, 1998). While the benefits of time spent reading are clear, studies have demonstrated that in many school settings, the reality is that students spend limited amounts of time actually reading during the school day (e.g., Brenner, Hiebert, & Tompkins, 2014; Swanson et al., 2016). Given the amount of content that must be covered, it may seem very difficult to provide extended periods of time for reading; however, even relatively small amounts of time spent reading can be beneficial. In fact, Fisher (2004) suggested shorter periods of 15–20 minutes twice a week are preferable to an occasional lengthy period.

It's not just about more time in text. While reading, students must also be engaged—not simply passing their eyes over the words—and read with enough stamina to take advantage of the time (see Chapter 9). Lupo, Strong, Lewis, Walpole, and McKenna (2018) noted a cyclical relationship: Time spent reading builds knowledge, knowledge on a topic makes reading easier, and ease of reading means we read more. If we think about it this way, it's about *the time students are involved in engaged, sustained reading to build knowledge that makes the real difference*. So, time is one critical variable, but it's not just about the *time*—even if it is engaged, sustained time. It's also about the *texts* we use and the *tasks* we choose.

The Texts We Use

How do we determine a text's level of complexity? We use readability measures, such as the Lexile framework for reading (MetaMetrics, 2022), to estimate how difficult a text might be based on word frequency (a proxy for vocabulary load) and sentence length (a proxy for language complexity). The idea is that the more complex the vocabulary and sentences are, the harder the text will be. While these estimates help provide ballpark information about the potential difficulty of a text, they don't tell the whole story. For example, a student may have background knowledge on a topic that would support their reading and understanding of a potentially challenging text. So, what else should we consider when we think about what makes a text hard? Consider the following qualitative features of texts when evaluating a text's complexity:

- *Structure*—Is the structure supportive? Is it clearly organized? How much of a lift will the student have to make meaning?
- *Language*—Are the sentence structures complex? Are there phrases and transitions (e.g., signal words) that require connections across ideas? Is academic vocabulary familiar to students?
- *Length*—How long is the text overall? How long are chapters or sections?

How much effort will the student need to put into making meaning and for how long?

- *Content*—Is the topic familiar to students? Is content vocabulary familiar to students?

There is another variable for us to consider when it comes to text complexity—*the reader.* When it comes to students who struggle with reading, we often prioritize reading level when choosing texts for them. Providing *easier texts* for students who find grade-level texts challenging is a common way we support students' fluency and comprehension. The thinking behind this decision is this: If a student can read a text more fluently, then they will be able to devote more attention to understanding what they are reading. However, if they are not able to read the text with an established fluency benchmark (i.e., accuracy and pace), then they will likely have little cognitive reserves left for comprehension. In addition to impacting *comprehension,* students who find themselves in a constant struggle with texts beyond their capabilities can experience decreased *motivation* to read (Guthrie, Wigfield, & You, 2012; McRae & Guthrie, 2009).

However, there is another school of thought regarding how to match students with literacy challenges to texts. Some believe that matching students' reading ability only to texts they can read fluently "ultimately denies students the very language, information, and modes of thought they need most to move up and on" (Adams, 2011, p. 6). Over time, restricting students to easier, more comfortable, texts might (1) impact comprehension growth because of limited access to, and practice with, complex vocabulary and language structures (e.g., Hiebert, 2017; Stanovich, 1986) and (2) lead to students "[taking] up and [taking] on levels as their reading identify" (Hoffman, 2017, p. 266). Lupo, Strong, and Smith (2019) suggested students practice reading in *challenging texts* with support to improve their reading comprehension. They went on to say that "teachers must provide a text diet rich with difficult texts to adolescents, including those who may struggle when reading them, to ensure equitable literacy instruction for all" (p. 552).

Different Texts for Different Purposes: A Two-Text Solution

Which texts should we choose? Easier texts for students who struggle to read the words, or more challenging texts so that students engage with advanced content and complex language structures? To illustrate this dilemma, let's consider Aliyah—our eighth-grade student with decoding and fluency challenges. On the one hand, Aliyah's difficulty decoding grade-level texts—which leads to slow, word-by-word reading—makes comprehension difficult when she reads texts herself. So, one approach might be to find texts she can read with adequate accuracy, rate, and prosody so that she can improve her fluency. On the other hand, if Aliyah *only* reads texts she can read relatively fluently, she won't have access to the grade-level content, concepts, and more sophisticated academic language only found in more challenging texts, such as her social studies and science textbooks.

We propose a *two-text solution* to work through this dilemma. Across a day and/or a week, Aliyah should be reading out of two types of texts for two different purposes:

- *Easier texts for practicing decoding and fluency.* For part of the day/week, perhaps 30 minutes per day, Aliyah should be reading out of texts she can read with adequate accuracy, rate, and prosody. Many of these texts will be at a lower level of difficulty than grade-level texts. She might do some of her fluency work (repeated readings from short sections from these texts—see Chapter 5) in these *easier* texts. While the instructional emphasis with these texts is building fluency, Aliyah should still discuss these texts for meaning—the ultimate goal of reading.

- *More challenging texts for boosting comprehension, academic vocabulary, and content knowledge.* Aliyah (and all students) should also be reading and working with more challenging texts, such as grade-level textbooks in science, middle-grades novels in ELA, and primary sources in social studies. This type of reading is critical for building the (1) content knowledge, (2) academic vocabulary, and (3) awareness of the complex language structures in written texts needed to succeed in the middle-grades curriculum. This chapter zeros in on this second instructional purpose: how teachers can support middle-grades students as they engage with these more *challenging texts.*

Supporting Students Reading Challenging Texts

Ensuring students engage with challenging texts is just the first step. What about students who are intimidated by challenging texts? A student's perception of text difficulty matters. In fact, the student's perception of difficulty can sometimes matter more than the text's estimated difficulty using a measure like a Lexile. Leveraging the knowledge students bring can help alleviate some of this fear. For example, you might engage your students in a conversation about the Earth and the moon before reading about the mechanics of day and night and the phases of the moon. Or you might watch a brief video to build background knowledge prior to reading. You might also support them with structures like Content DR-TA (Ogle, 1986; Stauffer, 1969, 1975; see Chapter 7) to help them go through an active process of reading informational texts. Following are four ways content teachers can support students as they read challenging texts: literary/informational pairings, text sets, textbook supports, and technology.

Literary/Informational Pairings. Juxtaposing literary and informational texts can build a natural connection for students and the concepts they are learning across content-area classes. The literary text grounds the content-area topic in a real-world context. This draws students into the story and helps them connect with a setting, a character, and a series of events or problems. The informational text adds a depth of understanding that can add to how the reader engages with the literary text. In fact, the National Science Teaching Association and the National Council for the Social Studies both recognize and support the use of fiction to teach content-area material across the curriculum. For example, a sixth-grade ELA team might choose Jacqueline Woodson's *Brown Girl Dreaming,* a novel in verse about Woodson's growing up as an African American in the '60s and '70s, coinciding with the social studies team reading and learning about the Civil Rights Movement with texts like CommonLit's *The 16th Street Baptist Church Bombing* by Jessica McBirney. Across both classes, the students can consider a common focus question, such as: How were members of different racial groups treated before and during the Civil Rights Movement?

Text Sets. Text sets are a second way middle-grades teachers can support students as they read challenging texts to change a potentially frustrating experience into a successful one. A text set is a collection of texts that are related by a topic or concept organized to build background knowledge. The idea behind a text set is we "organize . . . readings . . . so each text bootstraps the language and knowledge needed for the next. Gradually, students will be ready for texts of greater complexity" (Adams, 2011, p. 9). Text sets are created to develop knowledge about the topic and are intentionally sequenced with attention to increasing text challenge and building vocabulary and content knowledge (Lupo et al., 2018). In this way, the earlier texts in the set provide the knowledge and vocabulary students will need in the later, more challenging texts. The sequence of texts scaffolds the students in a way that makes texts that would generally cause students to struggle become more accessible. See Figure 10.1 for guidance on making your own text sets.

Textbook Supports. Students with literacy challenges often have significant struggles getting through textbook chapters and landing in a place where they have taken away key concepts. To help students—*all* students—achieve greater success engaging with textbooks, we use the before, during, after framework discussed in Chapter 7. Here's an example using a social studies text.

- *Before*—Build background knowledge, introduce related vocabulary, and set a purpose.
  - Preteach key vocabulary using activities from Chapter 6 (e.g., four-square concept map) and visually show how they are related. We've found this generally works well within the overall theme of the chapter. For example, a compare–contrast chart could help explore the reasons for and against American imperialism at the turn of the 19th century and include key vocabulary like *imperialism, expansionism,* and *Manifest Destiny.*
  - Set a purpose for the reading by previewing the chapter and establishing a focus question, such as: "What were the arguments for and against the

Identify the Topic	Select Texts (including a variety of text types)	Sequence Texts to Scaffold the Reader	Set Your Plan

• Connect with curriculum pacing guide or grade-level standard
• Create a focus question to guide the study
	• Consider texts that build knowledge and vocabulary related to the topic
	• Texts may be easier or more challenging based on readability measure or in relationship to the reader
	• Think outside the box: texts can be print as well as visuals (e.g., diagrams, photos), videos, etc.
		• Consider each text relative to the reading challenge based on:
		  • Readability
		  • Length
		  • Vocabulary
		  • Content
		• Remember: the sequence is about how one text helps students better understand the next one
		• Start with a text that gives an overview or is the easiest
			• Determine how students will interact with the texts (e.g., Will they work in groups? Will they use a tool like a graphic organizer?)
			• Map out the scaffolds necessary for students to successfully engage with each text (e.g., Will you preteach vocabulary?)
			• Decide how the students will demonstrate their learning

FIGURE 10.1. How to make your own text set.

push to expand the United States so that it stretched from the Atlantic to the Pacific Ocean?"

- *During*—Consider how students will engage with the chapter while reading.
  - Consider breaking up the chapter into meaningful, and manageable, chunks. Rather than assigning a chapter for the week, assign a section of the chapter one night, highlight key points in class, and then move to the next section.
  - Use a tool to engage with reading, such as a graphic organizer to emphasize text structure (e.g., a compare–contrast chart for and against American imperialism exploring economic, cultural, and political reasons discussed in the chapter) or sticky notes to indicate main ideas and key details (see Chapter 7).
- *After*—Determine how students will wrap up their learning.
  - Solidify understanding as you coalesce around main ideas and key details related to the focus question and related vocabulary.
  - Engage students in activities such as discussions (see next section, The Tasks We Choose) or summary writing (see Chapter 8). For example, students might use a compare–contrast summary paragraph using signal words like *similarly, however,* and *on the other hand.*

Leverage Technology. For students with an underlying decoding and fluency issue, ensure that all of their content texts are available via an audio-enhanced format and/or a print-to-speech application. This allows them access to the content they cannot easily process themselves. When listening to the text being read aloud, we strongly encourage our students to try to follow along with the textbook open, looking at maps, graphs, charts, headings, and so forth. For most students, following along is helpful, especially when you can adjust the speed. However, if trying to read along, word-by-word, with the narrator makes it harder to comprehend, we tell our students just to listen and look at the text during a stopping point.

Providing audio-enhanced texts can be a highly effective accommodation that helps deliver the grade-level content "through the ear" and can be a game changer for many students; however, remember that it is an *accommodation,* not an *intervention.* It will not address any underlying issues in other areas of literacy challenge. Students will not improve their reading skills without direct reading instruction and practice, and they often still require supports like building background knowledge and preteaching vocabulary *before* reading/listening.

The Tasks We Choose

As Hiebert and Martin (2009) put it, *tasks* are the "stuff" of learning and instruction. Tasks are the experiences that help students build background knowledge, use new vocabulary, and integrate skills and concepts. While tasks are always in support of the learning, a key to students' ultimate understanding is scaffolding their learning from surface to deep levels of knowledge (Webb, 2013). In this section, we'll outline tried and true, doable, instructional supports we recommend for content-area classroom teachers: vocabulary walls, root walls, quick-writes, and four-corners debates.

Vocabulary Walls

When you are in your classroom after school, talking with another teacher about one of your students, do you point to the chair they sit in during the day when you mention their name (even though it's currently empty)? Why do most of us do this? It's because of how our memory works. Our memories are supported by location, where we link something *new* that we are learning (a new concept, vocabulary term, or student's name) to something *known,* in this case the visual–spatial environment of the seats in our classroom. The ancient Greeks and Romans knew this and developed the "loci" (location) method of memory, in which they linked *ideas* they wanted to remember to *features* of a known physical location. For example, they might have visualized themselves walking down a familiar street, linking points in an upcoming speech they needed to memorize to a tree, a bench, and a fountain. Champions in memory contests today use similar methods, often called the *memory palace* technique.

If the vocabulary words and concepts we teach are important enough for students to remember, they are also important enough to be given a *physical location* in our classrooms. This is where *vocabulary walls* come into play (Templeton et al., 2015). When we post key vocabulary terms on our walls and keep them there, front and center, our students are more likely to be aware of them, remember them, and actually use them. We can't tell you how many times we've seen students searching for a word in their memories and then looking to the place on the classroom wall where that very word is posted to successfully retrieve and use the word. What's most amazing to us is that, *even after we've removed the vocabulary wall,* we've seen students still look to where the target word they are searching for *used to be* on the wall and "finding it" in their natural lexicon—supporting the power of location in our long-term memory!

Vocabulary walls can be simple, straightforward, and cost little planning or teaching time. Following are steps and tips for using vocabulary walls (Templeton et al., 2015):

- Choose words to post. These could include domain-specific terms from the current unit (e.g., *denouement, Manifest Destiny, tectonic plates, scatter plot*).
- Don't forget to post signal vocabulary words (see Chapter 7) such as *however, because,* and *therefore.* Students are more likely to use these words while talking and writing if they are also kept front and center all year. We like to organize these

signal vocabulary words by text structure (e.g., *however* signals a *compare–contrast* text structure).

- If you can't post the words on your wall due to lack of space or being an "itinerant" teacher, consider digital options such as a smartboard or on the class website.
- *Use* the words on the wall! Here are a number of different options:
  - Reward students when they use the words in conversation or writing. One enterprising teacher we worked with staged a class competition (period 1 vs. period 2, etc.). She kept a running tally of which class period used the words most frequently, and effectively, during class discussions.
  - Require students to use the vocabulary wall words in their quick-writes and summaries. For example, "Pick two words on the vocabulary wall and explain how they are related. Oh, Andres picked *deforestation* and *global warming* to link."
  - Ask students to write down the most important vocabulary wall word they learned about and why they think it's the most important.

Root Walls

A powerful variation of vocabulary walls are *root walls* (Templeton et al., 2015). Instead of (or in addition to) posting key vocabulary words, post high-utility roots and affixes. You can start by introducing your students to 20 common prefixes that account for 97% of all prefixed words found in school (see Figure 4.4 on p. 77 for this list). In addition to these prefixes, we recommend posting and introducing the following high-utility roots. Figure 10.2 lists (1) these common roots, (2) "anchor" words to help students remember the meaning of each root (e.g., *spectacles* help us "look," which is the meaning of the root, *spect*), and (3) some additional derived words that they will encounter across the content areas (e.g., *retrospect, prospector, spectrum*). This list is based on the work in *Words Their Way: Vocabulary for Middle and Secondary Students* (Templeton et al., 2015), which offers more extensive lists of affixes and roots organized by frequency, utility, and complexity.

Following are possible steps and considerations with root walls:

- Post these high-utility affixes and roots in all classrooms, since they will be found in social studies, science, math, and ELA vocabulary across the content areas.
- Introduce students to the roots one or two at a time. The introduction can be quick, involving the root, the anchor word to help your students remember the root's meaning, and some derived words.
- Teach your students how to break words down by affix and root with the "break it down" game (see Chapter 7).

Root	Meaning	Key Word	Derived Words
tele	"far"	Television—pictures you can see from "far" away	telescope, teleport, telegraph, telegram, telepathy
therm	"heat"	Thermometer—measures body "heat" or temperature	thermal, geothermal, thermos, thermonuclear, thermostat, thermodynamic
port	"carry"	Portable—able to be "carried"	import, export, report, support, transport, deport, portage, portmanteau, comportment
photo	"light"	Photograph—a picture "written" (graph) with "light"	photosynthesis, photocopy, photographer, photon, photogenic
tract	"pull"	Tractor—tractors can "pull" things	traction, extract, detract, retract, contract, distract, subtract, attract, intractable
spec/spic	"see"	Spectacles—spectacles help us "see"	spectator, inspector, inspect, speculate, introspection, retrospect, spectrum, spectacular, specimen, suspicion
dic/dict	"speak"	Diction—diction refers to proper "speaking"	dictate, dictator, dictionary, predict, verdict, benediction, contradict, dedicate, edict, indict, jurisdiction
rupt	"break"	Erupt—when a volcano erupts, it "breaks" the earth	disrupt, rupture, bankrupt, corrupt, interrupt, abrupt, disrupt
mal-	"evil, bad"	Maleficent—the evil queen in Sleeping Beauty	malicious, malware, malfunction, malnourished, malpractice, malignant, malign, maladjusted, malevolent

phobia	"fear"	Phobias are "fears"	claustrophobia, acrophobia, xenophobia, arachnophobia, technophobia
geo	"earth"	Geography—geography uses maps—literally "writing" (graph) the "earth"	geology, geode, geophysics, geothermal, geocentric, George (literally tiller of the "earth"—farmer)
bio	"life"	Biology is the study of "life"	biography, autobiography, biopsy, symbiotic, biodegradable, antibiotic, amphibious, biochemistry
graph	"write"	Paragraphs give us a structure to "write"	Autograph, graphics, biography, bibliography, choreographer, seismograph
-logy/-logist	"study of" or "one who studies"	Biology is the "study" of life	geology, mythology, psychology, sociology, theology, technology, zoology
syn-/sym-	"together, with"	Synthesis—putting things "together"	Synthetic, photosynthesis, molecular synthesis
-ism/-ist	"belief system/ worldview" or "one who believes in"	Socialist—one who believes in the philosophy of socialism	communist, Marxist, fascist, cubism, racism, sexism, classism, ageism, nationalism

FIGURE 10.2. High-utility affix and root list.

- Draw students' attention to words in your content area that contain these roots (e.g., *geothermal* = *geo* + *therm*—the *heat* within the *earth*). With a few roots under their belts, your students will start seeing them everywhere, sometimes before you do!
- Remind students that they can use their knowledge of roots to figure out the meaning of new, unfamiliar words on their own.

Quick-Writes: Focus Questions with Vocabulary Banks

As we discussed in Chapter 8, writing can be a powerful process for boosting thinking and comprehension. *Quick-writes,* in which students take a few minutes to brainstorm their thoughts to a prompt or question, are one of the most effective, low-cost (in terms of both planning and teaching time), high-impact strategies we know for older learners. Following are possible steps and considerations for a quick-write:

- Pose a question or a prompt (e.g., "What's the most impactful action you can take today to make a difference in global warming?").
- Allow students to write for a few minutes; 2–5 minutes seems to work best.
- If you have time, consider allowing students to share their thinking with a partner. This can happen before the quick-write or after based on your purpose and the level of support students need.
- Ask students to share their thinking about the question or prompt with the class. Our class discussions are almost always richer and more engaging if we've spent the few minutes up front allowing our students to "prime the pump" with a quick-write.
- Use quick-writes to activate background knowledge at the beginning of class as an *entrance slip,* in the middle of class to re-engage your students, and at the end as an *exit ticket* to consolidate information.

Do your students need a bit more structure and support with their quick-writes? Combining *focus questions with vocabulary banks* (Templeton et al., 2015) is a type of quick-write that content teachers we have worked with find particularly effective. It can be thought of as a more structured variation of the three-step summarizing strategy we introduced in Chapter 8. This is because when you provide your students the words in the vocabulary bank, you have essentially already done the first two steps of the three-step summarizing strategy for them (i.e., [1] *selecting* the key words and [2] *rejecting* the extraneous information). Following are the steps for a more structured quick-write (see Figure 10.3 for an example for a social studies unit on immigration to the United States):

Focus Question: During the mid-1800s to early 1900s, why did so many immigrants leave their native lands and immigrate to the United States?

Use at least 3 of the following vocabulary terms that we have discussed in your answer:

• push factors	• population boom
• pull factors	• jobs
• cheap and abundant land	• crop failures and famine
• political freedom	• religious persecution

Use at least 2 of the following signal words:

- for example
- as a result
- caused
- because

FIGURE 10.3. Focus question with vocabulary bank example.

- Choose or create a focus question (e.g., How is a human being like an ecosystem?).
- Provide a vocabulary bank of words students can or must (depending on your objectives) use in their answer (e.g., *biome, niche, community, adaptation*).
- Consider adding signal words to the vocabulary bank, such as *for example, as a result, caused.* Student answers are often more coherent as they become more proficient using these signal words to tie their ideas and thinking together.
- As with all quick-writes, allow students time to write (2–5 minutes or more) and, if you choose, to share with a partner before sharing out to class.
- Consider focus questions with vocabulary banks for homework and as excellent sources of assessment information on end-of-unit quizzes or tests.

Four-Corners Debates

Four-corners debates are a highly motivating way to get students to reflect on and take a position on a specific statement (Schulten, 2015). Students must use their knowledge of the content to take an informed position. This can be an effective activity at the *beginning* of a lesson or unit to initially engage students in the content. It can also be an effective wrap-up activity *after* a lesson or unit, requiring students to apply what they have learned. Following are possible steps:

- Discuss and establish the norms for a respectful, civil debate and thoughtful discussion in your classroom.
- Label the four corners of your room: (1) strongly agree, (2) agree, (3) disagree, and (4) strongly disagree. These can change based on your statement; for example, you might want to use (1) a lot, (2) somewhat, (3) a little bit, and (4) not at all.
- Introduce the students to a statement or statements that can be debated and that relate to the content being studied. For example, "In our democracy, the right to complete privacy is more important than our need for national security."
- Ask students to choose an answer and do a quick-write, justifying their position. Encourage or require them to use vocabulary terms from the vocabulary wall.
- Read the first statement aloud, allowing students to move to the corner in the room that is closest to their position. Students from each corner justify their position to the class, using content they learned as evidence. Remind them to use vocabulary terms from the vocabulary wall as appropriate. Students from other corners may ask questions and provide counter arguments.
- Remind students that they can switch corners if they modify or change their thinking during the debate.
- Consider a final written reflection on the position. Ask your students to consider what changed, modified, or strengthened their position. Inquire about additional evidence that made them uncertain and ask them to list any questions they still have. Or have students write to persuade someone to consider their position (see Chapter 8 on persuasive writing).

CONCLUSION

Keeping time, text, and task in mind can help content-area teachers across the middle grades support *all* students, including students with literacy challenges. The more *time* students spend with texts, the more comfortable they will become. This increased reading volume can, in turn, build content knowledge. The more intentional we are choosing *texts,* the more likely the time students spend in texts will lead to positive experiences with texts. The more we engage students with *tasks* that support these challenging texts, the more successful students will be while reading as well as grasping the content. When we support our middle-grades readers like Aliyah, Zach, and Andres both in and outside of their intervention classroom, we can significantly improve their literacy skills, their academic trajectory, and hopefully their futures.

APPENDIX

Differentiating during Interventions

Three Options for Organizing and Scheduling

How do you organize and schedule your intervention groups to be most effective? How might you schedule one group across a week? What if you have more than one group of students to work with during a single intervention block? How do you organize and schedule so you can differentiate and meet the needs of all students? In this appendix, we present three intervention options that will help answer these important questions and cover a variety of teaching contexts.

We understand that contexts are diverse, and intervention scheduling will look different depending on your context. For example, a daily pull-out intervention in an upper-elementary classroom will look different than a middle school intervention that might only meet three times per week during a dedicated intervention period. Feel free to modify the following three options, or even combine them, as you see fit.

THE DAILY A/B FLIPPED OPTION FOR TWO GROUPS

Our first option is a simple, straightforward schedule to consider when you have two different groups of students to work with during the same intervention block. This could mean (1) two groups with very different general needs (e.g., fluency vs. comprehension) or (2) two groups with the same general area of need but different sub-categories of need (e.g., both groups have word recognition needs, but one group is focusing on single-syllable vowel patterns and the other is working on multisyllabic words).

	Group A	Group B
9:00–9:15	Work with Teacher (I Do/We Do)	Independent or Paired Work (We Do/You Do)
9:15–9:30	Independent or Paired Work (We Do/You Do)	Work with Teacher (I Do/We Do)

- *Work with teacher* could include (1) explicit instruction with demonstration and modeling of a skill or strategy ("I Do") or (2) guided practice with timely teacher feedback ("We Do").
- *Independent or paired work*—work away from the teacher—is often best used to practice the just-taught skill or strategy in small groups, in pairs, or independently. This could include decoding practice with a set of word cards, contextual reading while practicing a just-taught comprehension strategy (like summarizing), or repeated reading for fluency work.
- *Paired work* can be particularly engaging and powerful if used effectively. This paired work could include guided practice with another student (e.g., two students practicing a fluency reading together), or it could involve one student performing a task while the student's partner provides feedback (e.g., one student performing a structured word sort of a certain spelling pattern while the peer times the first student and provides feedback on accuracy).

THE WEEKLY "WHOLE–SMALL–WHOLE" OPTION FOR A SINGLE GROUP

The *whole–small–whole schedule* is an effective schedule for planning work with one group on a targeted skill or strategy across a week.

- On day 1, the teacher spends the bulk of the allotted intervention time introducing, explaining, and modeling the target skill or strategy ("I Do" and perhaps some "We Do").
- On days 2–5, the teacher uses the whole-small-whole schedule. This includes:
  - *Whole group introduction/review*—a short 10-minute whole-class mini-lesson/review of the target/skill strategy introduced on day 1 ("I Do").
  - *Small-group/independent work*—the bulk of time, perhaps 30 minutes, is spent practicing the skill or strategy independently or in pairs while the teacher floats from group to group, monitoring and providing feedback.
  - *Whole-group wrap-up*—a short whole-class wrap-up (about 10 minutes) during which students share their work and/or share their main takeaways and remaining challenges/questions.

Monday	Tuesday–Friday
Spend bulk of day 1 in "I Do," introducing a new skill or strategy	whole-class introduction/review—10 minutes small-group/independent work—30 minutes whole-class wrap-up—10 minutes

THE FLEXIBLE "ON-THE-SPOT" DAILY OPTION

In some teaching contexts, and for some periods of time during the year, you will want an extremely flexible schedule you can create "on the spot," allowing you to modify each day, or even each period, to optimize differentiation. This is a schedule that *takes minimal planning time* and allows you to work with a small group of students while ensuring *the students who are not with you* are engaged in valuable practice that targets their intervention goals. With older, middle-grades readers, we've found that instead of literacy centers—a hallmark of many primary grade classrooms—a simple agenda or list of high-utility literacy activities written on the board at the beginning of class often works best.

We know teachers who refer to this student work list as *Today's Agenda, or "If you're not with me today, do the following. . . ."*

While there could be many options here, we've found the most effective reading intervention activities worth their salt boil down to one of the following four essential away-from-teacher activities:

1. Reading for fluency practice
2. Reading for comprehension practice
3. Writing to extend or build reading comprehension (e.g., summarizing a just-read text to support comprehension)
4. Word work for application to reading and writing (e.g., word sorts, practice decoding word cards, flip book practice, white-board spelling practice with a partner)

For example, let's say it's Tuesday, and you just decided that you need to work with a subset of your intervention group for a significant portion of the intervention block. Your observation and review of student work demonstrated some continued needs in summarizing informational text to support their comprehension. What should the rest of your class be doing? If the remaining students' primary area of need lies in Pathway #1, you might write on the board the following:

1. *Practice a writing sort on a whiteboard with your partner (give all 20 spelling words and then switch roles).—15 minutes*
2. *Fluency practice with a partner. Choose a page with your partner from the last chapter read of your small-group reading text. You will co-perform this page for the whole class during wrap-up.—15 minutes*
3. *If you have done numbers 1 and 2, and there is still time left in class, you can either (1) continue reading from your independent reading book or (2) play a word game chosen from the back shelf with a partner.*

A few points about this flexible "on-the-spot" daily schedule:

- A more structured variation of this option uses a learning contract in which students accrue points across a week for the assigned activities.
- Sometimes you may want to require a certain order of completion for your listed activities (e.g., word work before fluency work). Other times, you may give your students choice on the task order of completion.
- It's usually a good idea to have a final "sponge activity" that soaks up any extra class time if students finish all their work before class is over (see our number 3 above). Make this sponge activity engaging and/or provide a choice. Otherwise, students have less incentive to finish the required activities or transition to the sponge activity.
- It's usually helpful to (1) provide the number of minutes you want students to work on each task or (2) make clear what you mean by the completion of each activity (e.g., administer all 20 spelling words to your partner and check for accuracy before switching roles).

These are not the only options available to you, of course. However, we have found these to be our top three "go-to" options applicable to most common intervention settings. While thinking these options through, remember that the ultimate goal of any schedule you choose should be to "free you up" to spend the most time working directly with the students who need it, while also providing ample opportunities for those students who are not with you to practice the skills and strategies for eventual mastery.

References

Adams, M. J. (2011). Advancing our students' language and literacy: The challenge of complex texts. *American Educator, 34*(4), 3–11, 53.

Alberts, B., Bray, D., Hopkin, K., Johnson, A., Lewis, J., Raff, M., et al. (2014). *Essential cell biology* (4th ed.). Taylor and Francis.

Allington, R. L. (2012). *What really matters for struggling readers: Designing research-based programs*. Pearson.

Allington, R. L. (2013). What really matters when working with struggling readers. *The Reading Teacher, 66*(7), 520–530.

Almasi, J. F., & Hart, S. J. (2011). Best practices in comprehension instruction. In L. M. Morrow & L. B. Gambrell (Eds.), *Best practices in literacy instruction* (4th ed., pp. 250–275). Guilford Press.

Anderson, R. C., & Freebody, P. (1981). Vocabulary knowledge. In J. Guthrie (Ed.), *Comprehension and teaching: Research reviews* (pp. 77–117). International Reading Association.

Anderson, R. C., Wilson, P. T., & Fielding, L. G. (1988). Growth in reading and how children spend their time outside of school. *Reading Research Quarterly, 23*(3), 285–303.

Archer, A. L., Gleason, M., & Vachon, V. (2003). Decoding and fluency: Foundation skills for struggling older readers. *Learning Disability Quarterly, 26*(2), 89–101.

Archer, A. L., & Hughes, C. A. (2011). *Explicit instruction: Effective and efficient teaching.* Guilford Press.

Bear, D. R., Invernizzi, M., Templeton, S., & Johnston, F. (2020). *Words their way: Word study for phonics, vocabulary, and spelling instruction* (7th ed.). Pearson.

Beck, I. L., McKeown, M. G., & Kucan, L., (2013). *Bringing words to life: Robust vocabulary instruction* (2nd ed.). Guilford Press.

Beck, I. L., McKeown, M. G., & Sandora, C. A. (2021). *Robust comprehension instruction with questioning the author: 15 years smarter.* Guilford Press.

Beers, K. (2003). *When kids can't read: What teachers can do.* Heinemann.

Beers, K., & Probst, R. E. (2013). *Notice & note: Strategies for close reading.* Heinemann.

Bhattacharya, A., & Ehri, L. C. (2004). Graphosyllabic analysis helps adolescent struggling readers read and spell words. *Journal of Learning Disabilities, 37*(4), 331–348.

Biancarosa, C., & Snow, C. E. (2006). *Reading next—A vision for action and research in middle and high school literacy: A report to Carnegie Corporation of New York* (2nd ed.). Alliance for Excellent Education.

Bishop, R. S. (1990). Mirrors, windows, and sliding glass doors. *Perspectives, 6,* ix–xi.

Brenner, D., Hiebert, E. H., & Tompkins, R. (2014). *How much and what are third reading? Reading in core program classrooms.* Text Project. Available at *https://textproject.org/wp-content/uploads/papers/Brenner-Hiebert-Tompkins-2014-How-much-and-what-are-third-graders-reading.pdf.*

Buly, M. R., & Valencia, S. W. (2002). Below the bar: Profiles of students who fail state reading assessments. *Educational Evaluation and Policy Analysis, 24*(3), 219–239.

Cain, K., & Nash, H. M. (2011). The influence of connectives on young readers' processing and comprehension of text. *Journal of Educational Psychology, 103*(2), 429–441.

Capin, P., Cho, E., Miciak, J., Roberts, G., & Vaughn, S. (2021). Examining the reading and cognitive profiles of students with significant reading comprehension difficulties. *Learning Disability Quarterly, 44*(3), 183–196.

Catts, H. W., Hogan, T. P., & Adlof, S. M. (2005). Developmental changes in reading and reading disabilities. In H. W. Catts & A. G. Kahmi (Eds.), *The connections between language and reading disabilities* (pp. 25–40). Erlbaum.

Chang, W., & Ku, Y. (2014). The effects of note-taking skills instruction on elementary students' reading. *The Journal of Educational Research, 108*(4), 278–291.

Covey, S. R. (1990). *The seven habits of highly effective people: Powerful lessons in personal change.* Fireside/Simon & Schuster.

Crystal, D. (2002). *The English language: A guided tour of the language.* Penguin.

Cunningham, A. E., & Stanovich, K. E. (1998). What reading does for the mind. *American Educator, 22*(1 & 2), 8–15.

Curtis, M. (2004). Adolescents who struggle with word identification: Research to practice. In T. Jetton & J. Dole (Eds.), *Adolescent literacy research and practice* (pp. 119–134). Guilford Press.

Darling-Hammond, L., & Bransford, J. (2007). *Preparing teachers for a changing world: What teachers should learn and be able to do.* Wiley & Sons.

Dehaene, S. (2009). *Reading in the brain: The new science of how we read.* New York: Penguin Group.

Denton, C., Bryan, D., Wexler, J., Reed, D., & Vaughn, S. (2007). *Effective instruction for middle school students with reading difficulties: The reading teacher's sourcebook.* University of Texas System/Texas Education Agency.

Deshler, D. D., Palincsar, A. S., Biancarosa, G., & Nair, M. (2007). *Informed choices for struggling adolescent readers: A research-based guide to instructional programs and practices.* International Reading Association.

Diamond, L., & Thorsnes, B. J. (2018). *Assessing reading: Multiple measures* (2nd ed.). CORE.

Duffy, G. G. (2014). *Explaining reading: A resource for explicit teaching of the common core standards.* Guilford Press.

Duke, N. D., Pearson, P. D., Strachan, S. L., & Billman, A. K. (2011). Essential elements of fostering and teaching reading comprehension. In S. J. Samuels & A. Farstrup (Eds.), *What research has to say about reading instruction* (4th ed., pp. 51–93). International Reading Association.

Eeds, M., & Cockrum, W. A. (1985). Teaching word meanings by expanding schemata vs. dictionary work vs. reading in context. *Journal of Reading, 28*(6), 492–497.

Ehri, L. C. (1998). Grapheme–phoneme knowledge is essential for learning to read words in English. In J. L. Metsala & L. C. Ehri (Eds.), *Word recognition in beginning literacy* (pp. 3–40). Erlbaum.

Ehri, L. C. (2000). Learning to read and learning to spell: Two sides of a coin. *Topics in Language Disorders, 20*(3), 19–36.

Ericsson, K. A. (1996). The acquisition of expert performance: An introduction to some of the Issues. In K. S. Ericsson (Ed.), *The road to excellence: The acquisition of expert performance in the arts and sciences, sports, and games* (pp. 1–50). Erlbaum.

Esteban-Guitart, M., & Moll, L. (2014). Funds of identity: A new concept based on funds of knowledge approach. *Culture & Psychology, 20*(1), 31–48.

Filderman, M. J., Austin, C. R., & Toste, J. R. (2019). Data-based decision making for struggling readers in the secondary grades. *Intervention in School and Clinic, 55*(1), 3–12.

Fisher, D. (2004). Setting the "opportunity to read" standard: Resuscitating the SSR program in an urban high school. *Journal of Adolescent & Adult Literacy, 48*(2), 138–150.

Flanigan, K., & Greenwood, S. (2007). Effective content vocabulary instruction in the middle: Matching students, purposes, words, and strategies. *Journal of Adolescent and Adult Literacy, 51*(3), 226–238.

Flanigan, K., Hayes, L., Templeton, S., Bear, D. R., Invernizzi, M., & Johnston, F. (2011). *Words their way with struggling readers: Word study for reading, vocabulary, and spelling instruction grades 4–12.* Pearson.

Flanigan, K., Solic, K., & Gordon, L. (2022). The "P" word revisited: 8 principles for tackling common phonics questions and misconceptions about phonics instruction. *The Reading Teacher, 76*(1), 73–83.

Frayer, D., Frederick, W. C., & Klausmeier, H. J. (1969). *A schema for testing the level of cognitive mastery.* Wisconsin Center for Education Research.

Fry, E. (2000). *1000 instant words: The most common word for teaching reading, writing, and spelling.* Garden Grove, CA: Teacher Created Resources.

Ganske, K. (2014). *Word journeys: Assessment-guided phonics, spelling, and vocabulary instruction* (2nd ed.). Guilford Press.

Gough, P. B., & Tunmer, W. E. (1986). Decoding, reading, and reading disability. *Remedial and Special Education, 7*(1), 6–10.

Graham, S., & Hebert, M. (2011). Writing to read: A meta-analysis of the impact of writing and writing instruction on reading. *Harvard Educational Review, 81*(4), 710–744.

Graves, M. F. (2006). *The vocabulary book: Learning & instruction.* Teachers College Press.

Green, T. M. (2008). *The Greek and Latin roots of English* (4th ed.). Rowman & Littlefield Publishers.

Guthrie, J. T. (2001). Contexts for engagement and motivation in reading. *Reading Online, 4*, 8.

Guthrie, J. T. (2004). Teaching for literacy engagement. *Journal of Literacy Research, 36*(1), 1–30.

Guthrie, J. T., & Klauda, S. L. (2014). Effects of classroom practices on reading comprehension, engagement, and motivations for adolescents. *Reading Research Quarterly, 49*(4), 387–416.

Guthrie, J. T., & Wigfield, A. (2018). Literacy engagement and motivation: Rationale, research, teaching, and assessment. In E. Lapp & D. Fisher (Eds.), *Handbook of research on teaching the English language arts* (pp. 57–84). Routledge.

Guthrie, J. T., Wigfield, A., & You, W. (2012). Instructional contexts for engagement and achievement in reading. In S. Christenson, A. Reschly, & C. Wylie (Eds.), *Handbook of research on student engagement* (pp. 601–634). Springer.

Hall, C., & Barnes, M. A. (2016). Inference instruction to support reading comprehension for elementary students with learning disabilities. *Intervention in School and Clinic, 52*(5), 279–286.

Harris, K. R., Graham, S., Mason, L. H., & Friedlander, B. (2008). *Powerful writing strategies for all students.* Brookes Publishing.

Harvey, S., & Ward, A. (2017). *From striving to thriving: How to grow confident, capable readers.* Scholastic.

Hasbrouck, J., & Glaser, D. (2019). *Reading fluency: Understand, assess, teach.* Benchmark.

Haydon, T., Mancil, G. R., Kroeger, S. D., McLeskey, J., & Lin, W. J. (2011). A review of the effectiveness of guided notes for students who struggle learning academic content. *Preventing School Failure: Alternative Education for Children and Youth, 55*(4), 226–231.

Hebert, M., Simpson, A., & Graham, S. (2013). Comparing effects of different writing activities on reading comprehension: A meta-analysis. *Reading and Writing, 26*(1), 111–138.

Henk, W. A., Marinak, B. A., & Melnick, S. A. (2012). Measuring the reader self-perceptions of adolescents: Introducing the RSPS2. *Journal of Adolescent & Adult Literacy, 56*(4), 311–320.

Hennessy, N. A. (2020). *The reading comprehension blueprint: Helping students make meaning from text.* Brookes Publishing.

Hiebert, E. H. (2017). The texts of literacy instruction: Obstacles to or opportunities for educational equity? *Literacy Research: Theory, Method, and Practice, 66*(1), 117–134.

Hiebert, E. H., & Martin, L. A. (2009). Opportunities to read: A critical yet neglected construct in reading instruction. In E. H. Hiebert (Ed.), *Reading more, reading better* (pp. 3–29). Guilford Press.

Hoffman, J. V. (2017). What if "just right" is just wrong? The unintended consequences of leveling readers. *The Reading Teacher, 71*(3), 265–273.

Hoover, W. A., & Gough, P. B. (1990). The simple view of reading. *Reading and Writing, 2*(2), 127–160.

International Literacy Association. (2017). *Literacy assessment: What everyone needs to know* (Literacy leadership brief). Author.

Juel, C. (1988). Learning to read and write: A longitudinal study of 54 children from first through fourth grades. *Journal of Educational Psychology, 80*(4), 437–447.

Juel, C. (1994). *Learning to read and write in one elementary school.* Springer.

Kamil, M. L., Borman, G. D., Dole, J., Kral, C. C., Salinger, T., & Torgesen, J. (2008). *Improving adolescent literacy: Effective classroom and intervention practices: A practice guide* (NCEE #2008–4027). National Center for Education Evaluation and Regional Assistance, Institute of Education Sciences, U.S. Department of Education. Retrieved from *http://ies.ed.gov/ncee/wwc.*

Kearns, D. M., Lyon, C. P., & Kelley, S. L. (2021). Structured literacy interventions for reading long words. In L. Spear-Swerling (Ed.), *Structured literacy interventions: Teaching students with reading difficulties, grades K–6* (pp. 43–66). Guilford Press.

Kearns, D. M., Rogers, H. J., Al Ghanem, R., & Koriakin, T. (2016). Semantic and phonological ability to adjust recoding: A unique correlate of word reading skill? *Scientific Studies of Reading, 20*(6), 455–470.

Kearns, D. M., & Whaley, D. M. (2019). Helping students with dyslexia read long words: Using syllables and morphemes. *Teaching Exceptional Children, 51*(3), 212–225.

Killgallon, D. (2000). *Sentence composing for elementary school.* Heinemann.

Kilpatrick, D. A. (2015). *Essentials of assessing, preventing, and overcoming reading difficulties.* John Wiley & Sons.

Kiuhara, S. A., Graham, S., & Hawkin, L. S. (2009). Teaching writing to high school students: A national survey. *Journal of Education Psychology, 101*(1), 136–160.

Kuhn, M. R. (2005). Helping students become accurate, expressive readers: Fluency instruction for small groups. *The Reading Teacher, 58*(4), 338–344.

Kuhn, M. R., Schwanenflugel, P., Morris, R. D., Morrow, L. M., Woo, D., Meisinger, B., et al. (2006). Teaching children to become fluent and automatic readers. *Journal of Literacy Research, 38*(4), 357–388.

LaPray, M., & Ross, R. (1969). The graded word list: Quick gauge of reading ability. *Journal of Reading, 12*(4), 305–307.

Leach, J. M., Scarborough, H. S., & Rescorla, L. (2003). Late-emerging reading disabilities. *Journal of Educational Psychology, 95*(2), 211–224.

Leslie, L., & Caldwell, J. S. (2021). *Qualitative reading inventory* (7th ed.). Pearson.

Limpo, T., & Alves, R. A. (2013). Teaching planning or sentence-combining strategies: Effective SRSD interventions at different levels of written composition. *Contemporary Educational Psychology, 38*(4), 328–341.

Lovett, M. W. (2016). An overview of reading intervention research: Perspectives on past findings, present questions, and future needs. In C. M. Conner & P. McCardle (Eds.), *Advances in reading intervention: Research to practice research* (pp. 7–18). Brookes Publishing.

Lovett, M. W., Frijters, J. C., Wolf, M., Steinbach, K. A., Sevcik, R. A., & Morris, R. D. (2017). Early intervention for children at risk for reading disables: The impact of grade at intervention and individual differences on intervention outcomes. *Journal of Education Psychology, 109*(7), 889–914.

Lovett, M. W., Lacerenza, L., Borden, S. L., Frijters, J. C., Steinbach, K. A., & De Palma, M. (2000). Components of effective remediation for develop reading disabilities: Combining phonological and strategy-based instruction to improve outcomes. *Journal of Educational Psychology,* 9(2), 263–283.

Luo, L., Kiewra, K. A., & Samuelson, L. (2016). Revising lecture notes: How revision, pauses, and partners affect note taking and achievement. *Instructional Science, 44*(1), 45–67.

Lupo, S. M., Strong, J. Z., Lewis, W., Walpole, S., & McKenna, M. C. (2018). Building background knowledge through reading: Rethinking text sets. *Journal of Adolescent and Adult Literacy, 61*(4), 433–444.

Lupo, S. M., Strong, J. Z., & Smith, K. C. (2019). Struggle is not a bad word: Misconceptions and recommendations about readers struggling with difficult texts. *Journal of Adolescent & Adult Literacy, 62*(5), 551–560.

Malloy, J. A., Marinak, B. A., Gambrell, L. B., & Mazzoni, S. A. (2013). Assessing motivation to read: The motivation to read profile-revised. *The Reading Teacher,* 67(4), 273–282.

McBirney, J. (n.d.). *The 16th Street Baptist Church bombing.* CommonLit. Retrieved March 10, 2022, from *www.commonlit.org/en/texts/the-16th-street-baptist-church-bombing.*

McKenna, M. C., Conradi, K., Lawrence, C., Jang, B., & Meyer, J. P. (2012). Reading attitudes of middle school students: Results of a U.S. survey. *Reading Research Quarterly, 47*(3), 283–306.

McKenna, M. C., & Stahl, S. A. (2003). *Assessment for reading instruction.* Guilford Press.

McMaster, K. L., Jung, P., Brandes, D., Pinto, V., Fuchs, D., Kearns, D., et al. (2014). Customizing a research-based reading practice: Balancing the importance of implementation fidelity with professional judgment. *The Reading Teacher, 68*(3), 173–183.

McRae, A., & Guthrie, J. T. (2009). Promoting reasons for reading: Teacher practices that impact motivation. In E. H. Hiebert (Ed.), *Reading more, reading better* (pp. 55–76). Guilford Press.

Mesmer, H. A. E. (2017). *Teaching skills for complex texts: Deepening close reading in the classroom.* Teachers College Press.

MetaMetrics. (2022, March 09). Lexile framework for reading: Matching readers with texts. Available at *https://lexile.com.*

Moats. L. C. (2005). How spelling supports reading: And why it is more regular and predictable than you may think. *American Educator, 6*, 12–22, 42–43.

Moats, L. C. (2020). Structured language interventions for spelling. In L. Spear-Swerling (Ed.), *Structured literacy interventions: Teaching students with reading difficulties, grades K–6* (pp. 67–94). Guilford Press.

Mokhtari, K., Dimitrov, D. M., & Reichard, C. A. (2018). Revising the Metacognitive Awareness of Reading Strategies Inventory (MARSI) and testing for factorial invariance. *Studies in Second Language Learning and Teaching, 8*, 219–246.

Morris, D. (2005). *Howard Street tutoring manual: Teaching at-risk readers in the primary grades.* New York: Guilford Press.

Morris, D. (2014). *Diagnosis and correction of reading problems* (2nd ed.). Guilford Press.

Morris, D., Bloodgood, J. W., Perney, J., Frye, E., Kucan, L., Trathen, W., et al. (2011). Validating craft knowledge: An empirical examination of elementary-grade students' performance on an informal reading assessment. *The Elementary School Journal, 112*(2), 205–233.

Morsy, L., Kieffer, M., & Snow, C. (2010). *Measure for measure: A critical consumer's guide to reading comprehension assessments for adolescents.* Carnegie.

Nagy, W., & Anderson, R. C. (1984). How many words are there in printed school English? *Reading Research Quarterly, 19*(3), 304–330.

Nagy, W., & Townsend, D. (2012). Word as tools: Learning academic vocabulary as language acquisition. *Reading Research Quarterly, 47*(1), 91–108.

National Center for Education Statistics. (2019). *National assessment of educational progress: National achievement-level results.* Institute of Education Sciences, U.S. Department of Education.

National Center for Education Statistics. (2020). *National assessment of educational progress: Long-term trend assessment results in reading and mathematics.* Institute of Education Sciences, U.S. Department of Education.

National Reading Panel. (2000). *Report of the National Reading Panel—teaching children to read: An evidence-based assessment of the scientific research literature on reading and its implications for reading instruction*. National Institute of Child Health and Human Development.

Nelson, H. (2013). *Testing more, teaching less: What America's obsession with student testing costs in money and lost instructional time*. American Federation of Teachers.

O'Connor, R. E., Beach, K. D., Sanches, V. M., Bocian, K. M., & Flynn, L. J. (2015). Building BRIDGES: A design experiment to improve reading and United States history knowledge of poor readers in eighth grade. *Exceptional Children, 81*(4), 399–425.

Ogle, D. M. (1986). KWL: A teaching model that develops active reading of expository text. *The Reading Teacher, 39*(6), 564–570.

Padak, N., Newton, E., Rasinski, T., & Newton R. (2008). Getting to the root of words study: Teaching Latin and Greek word roots in elementary and middle grades. In A. E. Farstrup & S. J. Samuels (Eds.), *What research has to say about vocabulary instruction* (pp. 6–31). International Reading Association.

Pearson, P. D., & Fielding, L. (1991). Comprehension instruction. In R. Barr, M. L. Kamil, P. B. Mosenthal, & P. D. Pearson (Eds.), *Handbook of reading research* (Vol. 2, pp. 815–860). Routledge.

Pearson, P. D., & Gallagher, M. C. (1983). The instruction of reading comprehension. *Contemporary Educational Psychology, 8*(3), 317–344.

Perfetti, C. (1985). *Reading ability*. Oxford University Press.

Perfetti, C. (1992). The representation problem in reading acquisition. In P. Gough, L. Ehri, & R. Treiman (Eds.), *Reading acquisition* (pp. 145–174). Erlbaum.

Perfetti, C. A. (2003). The universal grammar of reading. *Scientific Studies of Reading, 7*(1), 3–24.

Porter, P. H. (2007). *Reflections: Ancient civilizations*. Harcourt School Publishers.

Quinn, D. M., & Kim, J. S. (2017). Scaffolding fidelity and adaptation in educational program implementation: Experimental evidence from a literacy intervention. *American Educational Research Journal, 54*(6), 1187–1220.

RAND Reading Study Group, & Snow, C. (2002). In *Reading for understanding: Toward an R&D program in reading comprehension*. RAND Corporation.

Rasinski, T. V. (1990). *The effects of cued phrase boundaries on reading performance: A review*. Kent State University. (ERIC Document Reproduction Service No. ED313689).

Rasinski, T. V. (1994). Developing syntactic sensitivity in reading through phrase-cued texts. *Intervention in School and Clinic, 29*(3), 165–168.

Rasinski, T. V. (2010). *The fluent reader: Oral and silent reading strategies for building fluency, word recognition, and comprehension* (2nd ed.). Scholastic.

Reutzel, D. R., & Hollingsworth, P. M. (1993). Effects of fluency training on second graders' reading comprehension. *Journal of Educational Research, 86*(6), 325–331.

Saddler, B., & Graham, S. (2005). The effects of peer-assisted sentence-combining instruction on the writing performance of more and less skilled young writers. *Journal of Educational Psychology, 97*(1), 43–54.

Salinger, T. (2011). *Addressing the "crisis" in adolescent literacy*. American Institute for Research.

Samuels, S. J. (1979). The method of repeated readings. *The Reading Teacher, 32*(4), 403–408.

Samuels, S. J. (2006). Toward a model of reading fluency. In S. J. Samuels & A. E. Farstrup

(Eds.), *What research has to say about fluency instruction* (pp. 24–46). International Reading Association.

Santa, C. M., Havens, L. T., & Valdes, B. J. (2004). *Project CRISS: Creating independence through student-owned strategies*. Kendall Hunt.

Schulten, K. (2015, December 10). Skills and strategies: The four-corners exercise to inspire writing and discussion. *The New York Times*. Retrieved March 10, 2022, from *https://learning.blogs.nytimes.com/2015/12/10/skills-and-strategies-the-four-corners-exercise-to-inspire-writing-and-discussion*.

Schunk, D. H., & Pajares, F. (2009). Self-efficacy theory. In K. R. Wentzel & A. Wigfield (Eds.), *Handbook of motivation at school* (pp. 35–54). Routledge.

Schwartz, R. M., & Raphael, T. E. (1985). Concept of definition: A key to improving students' vocabulary. *Reading Teacher, 39*(2), 198–205.

Seidenberg, M. S., & Borkenhagen, M. C. (2020). Reading science and educational practice: Some tenets for teachers. *The Reading League Journal, 1*(1), 7–11.

Shaywitz, B. A., & Shaywitz, S. E. (2020). The American experience: Towards a 21st century definition of dyslexia. *Oxford Review of Education, 46*(4), 454–471.

Shefelbine, J. (1990). A syllabic-unit approach to teaching decoding of polysyllabic words to fourth- and sixth-grade disabled readers. In J. Zutell & S. McCormick (Eds.), *Literacy theory and research: Analyses from multiple paradigms. Thirty-ninth yearbook of the National Reading conference* (pp. 223–229). National Reading Conference.

Slavin, R. E., Madden, N. A., & Datnow, A. (2007). Research in, research out: The role of research in the development and scale-up of Success for All. In D. K. Cohen, S. H. Fuhrman, & F. Mosher (Eds.), *The state of education policy research* (pp. 261–280). Erlbaum.

Snow, C. E., Griffin, P., & Burns, M. S. (2005). *Knowledge to support the teaching of reading: Preparing teachers for a changing world*. Jossey-Bass.

Soifer, L. H. (2019). Oral language development and its relationship to literacy. In J. R. Birsh & S. Carreker (Eds.), *Multisensory teaching of basic language skills* (4th ed., pp. 82–128). Brookes Publishing.

Stahl, K. A. D., & Bravo, M. A. (2010). Contemporary classroom vocabulary assessment for content areas. *The Reading Teacher, 63*(7), 566–578.

Stahl, K. A. D., Flanigan, K., & McKenna, M. C. (2020). *Assessment for reading instruction* (4th ed.). Guilford Press.

Stahl, S. A., & Hiebert, E. H. (2005). The "word factors": A problem for reading comprehension assessment. In S. G. Paris & S. A. Stahl (Eds.), *Current issues in reading comprehension and assessment* (pp. 161–186). Erlbaum.

Stahl, S. A., & Nagy, W. (2006). *Teaching word meanings*. Erlbaum.

Stanovich, K. E. (1986). Matthew effects in reading: Some consequences of individual differences in the acquisition of literacy. *Reading Research Quarterly, 22*(1–2), 360–407.

Stauffer, R. G. (1969). *Directing reading maturity as a cognitive process*. Harper & Row.

Stauffer, R. G. (1975). *Directing the reading–thinking process*. Harper & Row.

Strong, W. (1986). *Creative approaches to sentence combining*. National Council of Teachers of English.

Swanson, E., Wanzek, J., McCulley, L., Stillman-Spisak, S., Vaughn, S., Simmons, D., et al. (2016). Literacy and text reading in middle and high school social studies and English language arts classrooms. *Reading and Writing Quarterly, 32*(3), 199–222.

Templeton, S., Bear, D. R., Invernizzi, M., Johnston, F., Flanigan, K., Townsend, D. R., et al. (2015). *Words their way: Vocabulary for middle and secondary students* (2nd ed.). Pearson.

Tierney, R. J., & Readence, J. (2005). *Reading strategies and practices: A compendium* (6th ed.). Allyn & Bacon.

Toste, J. R., Williams, K. J., & Capin, P. (2017). Reading big words: Instructional practices to promote multisyllabic word reading fluency. *Intervention in School and Clinic, 52*(5), 270–278.

Tsesmeli, S. N., & Seymour, P. H. K. (2008). The effects of training of morphological structure on spelling derived words by dyslexic adolescents. *British Journal of Psychology, 100,* 565–592.

Vacca, R. T., & Vacca, J. L. (2016). *Content area reading: Literacy and learning across the Curriculum* (12th ed.). Pearson.

Valencia, S. W., & Buly, M. R. (2004). Behind test scores: What struggling readers really need. *The Reading Teacher, 57*(3), 520–531.

Vaughn, S., & Fletcher, J. M. (2021). Identifying and teaching students with significant reading problems. *American Educator, 44*(4), 4–12.

Walpole, S., McKenna, M. C., Philippakos, Z. A., & Strong, J. Z. (2020). *Differentiated literacy instruction in grades 4 & 5: Strategies and resources* (2nd ed.). Guilford Press.

Walpole, S., Strong, J. Z., & Riches, C. B. (2018). Best practices in professional learning for improving literacy instruction in schools. In L. B. Gambrell & L. B. Morrow (Eds.), *Best practices in literacy instruction* (6th ed., pp. 429–446). Guilford Press.

Wammes, J. D., Meade, M. E., & Fernandes, M. A. (2016). The drawing effect: Evidence for reliable and robust memory benefits in free recall. *The Quarterly Journal of Experimental Psychology, 69*(9), 1–25.

Webb, S. (2013). Depth of vocabulary knowledge. In C. Chappelle (Ed.), *Encyclopedia of applied linguistics* (pp. 1656–1663). Wiley-Blackwell.

White, T. G., Sowell, J., & Yanagihara, A. (1989). Teaching elementary students to use word-part clues. *The Reading Teacher, 42*(4), 302–308.

Wigfield, A., Mason-Singh, A., Ho, A. N., & Guthrie, J. T. (2014). Intervening to improve children's reading motivation and comprehension: Concept-oriented reading instruction. In S. A. Karabenick & T. C. Urdan (Eds.), *Motivational interventions: Advances in motivation and achievement* (Vol. 8, pp. 37–70). Emerald Group.

Wineburg, S. (1991). Historical problem solving: A study of the cognitive processes used in the evaluation of documentary and pictorial evidence. *Journal of Educational Psychology, 83,* 73–87.

Wolf, M. (2007). *Proust and the squid: The story and science of the reading brain.* Harper.

Wolf, M. (2018). *Reader, come home: The reading brain in a digital world.* Harper.

Zeno, S. M., Ivens, S. H., Millard, R. T., & Duvvuri, R. (1995). *The educator's word frequency guide.* Touchstone Applied Science Associates.

CHILDREN'S AND YOUNG ADULT LITERATURE CITED (**part of a series*)

*Blabey, A. (2015). *The bad guys.* Scholastic.

*Brallier, M. (2015). *The last kids on earth.* Viking.

*Chmakova, S. (2015). *Awkward: Berrybrook Middle School.* Yen Press.
*Claybourne, A. (2013). *100 most feared creatures.* Scholastic.
*Cummings, T. (2013). *The notebook of doom: Rise of the balloon goons.* Branches.
*Hale, S. (2017). *Real friends.* First Second Publishing.
Jamieson, V., & Mohamed, O. (2020). *When stars are scattered.* Dial Books for Young Readers.
*Keating, J. (2016). *Pink is for blobfish.* Dragonfly Books.
*Libenson, T. (2017). *Invisible Emmie.* Balzer + Bray.
*Marsh, L., & Stewart, M. (2019). *Deadliest animals collection.* National Geographic Kids.
*Montgomery, S. (2015). *The octopus scientists: Exploring the mind of a mollusk.* Clarion.
Ottaviani, J. (2020). *Astronauts: Women on the final frontier.* First Second Publishing.
*Pallotta, J. (2020). *Who would win? Shark rumble.* Scholastic.
Reynolds, J. (2019). *Look both ways: A tale told in ten blocks.* Atheneum/Caitlyn Dlouhy Books.
Stewart, M. (2020). *Ick! Delightfully disgusting animal dinners, dwellings, and defenses.* National Geographic Kids.
Stone, S. (2021). *Fast pitch.* Corwin Books for Young Readers.
*Weisfeld, B., & Kear, N. (2019). *The start-up squad.* Imprint.
Woodson, J. (2014). *Brown girl dreaming.* Puffin Books.

Index

K

L

M

Q

R

S

T

V